Christianity Worldwide: 1800 to 2000

SPCK International Study Guide 47

Christianity Worldwide
1800 to 2000

Edited by
Jehu J. Hanciles

First published in Great Britain in 2021

Society for Promoting Christian Knowledge
36 Causton Street
London SW1P 4ST
www.spck.org.uk

British Library Cataloguing-in-Publication Data
A catalogue record for this book is available from the British Library

ISBN 978–0–281–08612–2
eBook ISBN 978–0–281–08675–7

10 9 8 7 6 5 4 3 2 1

Typeset by Manila Typesetting Company
First printed in Great Britain by Severn, Gloucester

Produced on paper from sustainable sources

Contents

Illustrations

Contributors

Valerii Alikin is from Russia. He has a PhD in New Testament and early Christian literature from Leiden University, the Netherlands, and serves as rector and chair of the Theology and Church History Department at St Petersburg Christian University in Russia. He teaches various courses in Biblical Studies and Church History. His research focuses on understanding early Christian communities in their social and historical settings, as well as analysing expressions of individual religiosity in early Christianity.

Allan H. Anderson was born in London but raised in Zimbabwe, completing his higher education and first theological appointments in South Africa. He has enjoyed a long and distinguished academic career, holding posts in both South Africa and the UK, where he is now Emeritus Professor of Mission and Pentecostal Studies at the University of Birmingham. His extensive research and publications on Pentecostalism have made him one of the foremost scholars in this field.

Angus Crichton is from the United Kingdom and has spent the past 20 years learning about Christianity in Africa, particularly Uganda, where he taught in a theological college and developed a publishing initiative with Ugandan colleagues. He is a research associate at the Cambridge Centre for Christianity Worldwide and the Global Advocacy Manager at the Society for Promoting Christian Knowledge.

Pablo Deiros was born in Paraguay to Argentine parents and grew up in Argentina. He has consistently pursued the twin vocation of pastoring and serving in academia. This has led him to church posts in Buenos Aires and to a range of academic posts in Argentina and North America, in both Biblical Studies and Church History. He has recently retired from senior leadership positions at the International Baptist Theological Seminary, Buenos Aires.

Issa Diab is Lebanese and an ordained pastor in the Presbyterian Church, and holds four PhDs – in theology, ancient history, Islamic thought and biblical philology – and an HDR (accreditation to supervise research). He is a professor of Semitic and Interfaith Studies at Saint Joseph University, Beirut, and teaches at the Near East School of Theology, Beirut. He is a

Global Translation Advisor at the United Bible Societies. He has written several books and research articles.

Jehu J. Hanciles is from Sierra Leone. He is the D. W. Ruth Brooks Professor of World Christianity and director of the World Christianity Program at Candler School of Theology (Emory University) in Atlanta, Georgia. He is author of *Euthanasia of a Mission: African church autonomy in a colonial context* (2002) and *Beyond Christendom: Globalization, African migration and the transformation of the West* (2008), and editor of *The Twentieth Century: Traditions in a global context*, volume 4 of *The Oxford History of Protestant Dissenting Traditions* (2019). He has also published numerous articles and book chapters. His current research interests centre on migration and religious encounter, and his new book is titled *Migration and the Making of Global Christianity* (2021).

Julie C. Ma is from Korea and serves as Professor of Missiology and Intercultural Studies, Oral Roberts University, Tulsa, Oklahoma. Previously she served as a Korean missionary in the Philippines (1981–2006) and as Research Tutor of Missiology at Oxford Centre for Mission Studies, Oxford, UK. Her publications include *When the Spirit Meets the Spirits: Pentecostal ministry among the Kankana-ey tribe in the Philippines* (2000). She served as a general council member and executive committee member of Edinburgh 2010.

Hugh Morrison is from New Zealand where he has pursued a professional and academic career in education and the religious history of New Zealand. He is currently an associate professor at the University of Otago where he teaches on the social science curriculum, the history of children and young people, and education history. His research is on the interface between New Zealand and the UK, particularly through the missionary movement, and on the religious identities of children and young people.

Mark Noll is from the United States and is a historian specializing in the history of Christianity in his home country. He holds the position of Honorary Research Professor of History at Regent College, Vancouver, having previously been Francis A. McAnaney Professor of History at the University of Notre Dame, Indiana. His extensive research and publications have made him one of the foremost experts on the history of Christianity in North America and worldwide.

George Oommen is an ordained presbyter of the Church of South India. He received his doctorate at the University of Sydney, Australia. He is a former Chairperson and Professor of History of Christianity and Dean of Graduate Studies at the United Theological College, Bangalore, India, where he taught

Indian and Asian Christianity. His publications and research focus on Dalits and Christianity, and Protestant Christianity in India.

Louise Pirouet joined the staff of the newly inaugurated Department of Religious Studies at Uganda's Makerere University in 1963. She led an innovative project to collect church history records from across East Africa, which fuelled her own groundbreaking PhD on the role of African evangelists in the expansion of Christianity in Uganda, subsequently published as *Black Evangelists* (1978). She lectured at Makerere and Nairobi universities before returning to the UK to lecture in Religious Studies at Homerton College Cambridge from 1978 to 1989. She was also a passionate advocate for the rights of refugees, both in East Africa and in the UK. She passed away in 2012.

Chansamone Saiyasak is from Thailand. He serves as President of Mekong Evangelical Mission, President of the Asian Society of Missiology and President of Mekong Bible Seminary in Thailand. He is also on the faculty of Olivet Theological College in the United States. His research focuses on Christianity and leadership in a Buddhist context.

The SPCK International Study Guides: purpose and access

Purpose

The International Study Guides (ISGs) are clear and accessible resources for the Christian Church. The series contains biblical commentaries and volumes on pastoral care, church history and theology. The guides give voice to the experience and thought of Christians around the world today, particularly from the new heartlands in the Global South. They are ecumenical in their orientation and emphasize practical outworking as well as contemporary scholarly reflection on the Christian faith.

The series was originally conceived and is still commissioned for those training for Christian ministries and pursuing this training in English although it is not their first language. However, all Christians who can access these volumes will find them of great benefit, particularly the newer volumes in the series (ISG 38 onwards). For these volumes, chapters have been commissioned from authors from different countries and church backgrounds around the world. Therefore readers hear multiple voices from different perspectives addressing a single biblical book, a period of church history or a theological theme. This is rare in a world where too often a single voice predominates. There is a rich tapestry of world Christian reflection to enjoy within these covers.

Access

For readers in the Global South, the ISGs are made available by SPCK through generous rights agreements with regional publishers and individual theological institutions. Please contact SPCK if you want to explore this for any ISG title, including this one. Below is a list of the newer titles in the series that bring together contributors from around the world. For readers in the Global North, the ISGs are available from SPCK's own website and other book-retailing websites.

Angus Crichton
Series Editor, International Study Guides

Introduction

Jehu J. Hanciles

The previous edition of this volume was published in 1989 with the title *Christianity Worldwide: AD 1800 onwards*. It was the fourth in the ISG Church History series, preceded by *The First Advance: Church History 1 (AD 29–500); Setback and Recovery: Church History 2 (AD 500–1500);* and *New Movements: Church History 3 (AD 1500–1800)*. The 1989 study was a valuable resource that presented the story of the global spread of Christianity from 1800 to roughly 1980. More than 30 years since it was published, much has happened or become more obvious within world history and worldwide Christianity. Among other things, the fall of the Berlin Wall, an occurrence considered to mark the end of the Cold War, took place in 1989; Liberation Theology, so much in the ascendant, has lost much of its force; religious conflict (notably between Christians and Muslims or Hindus) has intensified in places such as India and Nigeria; the decline of Christianity in the West is arguably more evident; global economic inequalities are more menacing; and the phenomenal swelling of international migration (particularly South–North flows) has become an inescapable fact of our times.

While much of the basic historical material is the same, the contributors in this volume have presented a more up-to-date account of the complex historical developments that explain the present shape of global Christianity. One significant advantage this volume has over the previous is that there is now a wider pool of non-Western scholars to draw from. Thus, the majority of chapters have been written by scholars who are indigenous (local) to the region they are writing about. However, since these scholars come from a particular country in the region, aspects of the story still reflect an 'outsider' understanding. But proximity to place means at the very least that their scholarship is informed by particular insights and affinities that bridge both cultural and intellectual distance. This 'local' representation, so to speak, is perhaps the most important quality of the present study.

Having the previous volume at hand was a tremendous advantage. But to say that what is provided here is a 'revised' edition is only partially true. Only in one or two cases have previous versions of chapters been fundamentally revised, and even then the material is often reinterpreted and much new data added. As a case in point, I have revised, filled important gaps in, or added substantial material to, the two chapters on Africa (my own continent of origin). But, for the most part, the contributors to this volume have chosen to write afresh, adopt a new approach in treating the subject matter or

1

incorporate fresh perspectives from recent scholarship. Moreover, a whole new chapter on Pentecostalism and Charismatic movements (a major omission from the earlier volume) has been added. The regional framework adopted in the 1989 edition is preserved in the interest of simplicity and comprehensiveness. But the year 2000 must be treated as a notional cut-off date, since contextual peculiarities and the approach adopted by individual contributors will help determine the end point of each regional account.

The life and vitality of Christian movements in each context is significantly shaped by specific socio-political, cultural and economic factors (even a particular ecclesiastical heritage) that account for divergences of experience and outlook. In this regard, this study captures a multiplicity of perspectives, realities and approaches in keeping with complex developments within global Christianity in the past 200 years. At the same time, the nature, experience and expression of Christianity in various parts of the non-Western world share a number of common threads and general trends – many linked to the experience of colonization and the interaction between the Christian message and indigenous culture. Contributors had the freedom to frame their accounts in a way that breathes life and substance into the historical record and stimulates the understanding of readers. But in order to preserve a certain balance and symmetry among the various regional contributions, some specific issues received attention by all (though some more so than others, depending on the region). Among these are:

- the socio-economic, political and cultural material that constitutes the environment in which the Church emerges, develops and survives;
- the contribution of indigenous/local agents, as well as that of foreign missionaries, to the spread of the gospel and the growth of Christianity;
- the nature and significance of indigenous initiatives or movements (including Pentecostal–Charismatic forms);
- the varieties of Christian movements active in each context: Protestant, Roman Catholic and Orthodox;
- the nature of Christian engagement with other religions (where applicable);
- connectivity to global realities and the worldwide Christian faith.

Western missions and local agents

The strong link between Western missions and colonial expansion granted the former unprecedented access to non-Western societies. It also contributed to the considerable influence Western missionaries exercised in the areas where they established mission schools and churches. That said, many of these men and women went overseas out of a true sense of Christian calling and, especially in the early nineteenth century, often brought the message of the gospel to distant lands at tremendous personal cost. In the final analysis, the pivotal role of the Western (European and North American) missionary movement in the global spread of Christianity over the past four to five centuries is undeniable.

The problem, however, is that this contribution is generally emphasized at the expense of extensive indigenous agency and initiatives (the term 'indigenous agency/agents' is used throughout this volume in comparison to external missionaries, with the former referring to the role of local converts in spreading Christianity). Ironically, this means that the most important legacy of the Western missionary movement is usually overlooked. To the churches in non-Western societies, Western missionaries often became powerful models of self-sacrifice, heroism and Christian humanitarianism. And, by their very existence, foreign missions exemplify cross-cultural missionary action as a central function of the Church. At the same time, to make exaggerated claims about the impact and contribution of Western missions is to overlook the critical and indispensable role of indigenous agency in the establishment and growth of Christianity in the non-Western world.

While foreign missionary activity often began the spread of the faith in non-Western contexts, it was hardly ever the main driving force. For one thing, foreign missions operating in these societies were not as dominant as is often imagined. In Latin America, where the Roman Catholic Church enjoyed a complete monopoly over religious life, the chronic and severe shortage of priests meant that large proportions of the indigenous or non-European population remained unevangelized or neglected. The voluntary missionary society model served Protestant foreign missions well; but, for all their evangelistic zeal, foreign agents were limited in their impact by the need to master a variety of vernacular languages, and by susceptibility to disease and death. The fact of the matter is that the vast majority of African, Asian and Latin American Christians heard the message of the gospel not from a foreign missionary but from compatriots or indigenous agents – typically nameless catechists. This volume has been edited so that all named individuals are given their birth and death dates when they first appear in the book. If these are unknown, the approximate dates when the individual was active are given, preceded by the abbreviation '*fl.*', meaning 'flourished'. This recognizes the contribution of all actors, be they Bulgarian Pentecostals, Italian popes or Korean 'Bible women'.

Some of these indigenous agents mainly imitated European forms and practice. But many became religious innovators who worked hard to translate the message of the gospel in vernacular terms and adapt foreign practice to local reality. Consequently, mass movements of conversion or revival reflect the ministry and initiatives of indigenous Christians. Indeed, it is noteworthy that non-Western Christianities have experienced their most vigorous growth *after* colonialism and *after* the heyday of Western missionary enterprise.

✳ The *re*-globalization of Christianity

In its simplest sense, the term 'globalization' describes processes of change that have implications for the whole world and account for increased inter-dependence and interconnectedness among its inhabitants, regardless of dis-tance. Thus, whatever claims to be 'global' must simultaneously have direct 'local' impact on, or application to, different and distant parts of the world. From this perspective, processes of globalization do not all flow in one par-ticular direction and their impacts are not always predictable. It is also impor-tant to remember that the various dimensions (economic, political, cultural and so on) are intertwined. The phenomenon is not new; rather, the pro-cesses associated with it have grown in velocity and visibility with each pass-ing century, arguably since the beginning of human existence. Undoubtedly, the most tremendous acceleration has occurred in the last half a century or so, thanks to new technologies of communication and travel.

While economic dimensions receive the most attention, it is possible to argue that cultural forms are the most pervasive because they include the spread of ideas, beliefs and practices (especially religious kinds), as well as large-scale people movement. In fact, religious expansion and human migrations are not only inseparable; they are also among the most pow-erful instruments of globalization. In this regard, the worldwide spread of Christianity in the past 300 years (certainly in the past two centuries) repre-sents one of the most extraordinary forms of globalization.

By 1800, principally as a result of European colonial expansion and Roman Catholic missionary initiatives, the worldwide spread of the faith was under way through cross-cultural encounters with peoples in Asia, Africa, Latin America and the Caribbean. For complex reasons, including the devastating religious conflicts unleashed by the Protestant Reformation and the lack of contact with non-Christian peoples, Protestant foreign mission efforts lagged behind those of Roman Catholics by at least a century and a half. Energized by post-Reformation revival movements – first the Pietist movement in Germany and then the eighteenth-century Evangelical Revival in Britain (and America) – the Western Protestant missionary movement surged in numbers and momentum precisely when Roman Catholic mis-sions began to experience temporary but steep decline. But the tremendous gains made outside Europe by Roman Catholicism gave it a head start in global spread and influence that it has not lost (see Fig. 1), even though the shape of global Christianity has changed radically in the past 100 years.

According to estimates, Christians accounted for some 23 per cent of the world population in 1800. By 1900, due mainly to the establishment and growth of new Christian communities throughout the non-Western world, the number of Christians in the world increased by about 172 per cent (or more than doubled) and represented 35 per cent of the world population. Christianity's worldwide growth in the twentieth century was even more

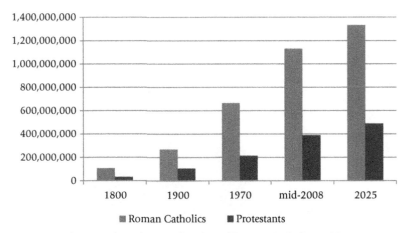

Figure 1 The growth in the membership of Roman Catholic and Protestant churches worldwide since 1800

Source: David B. Barrett et al., 'Missiometrics 2008: reality checks for Christian world communions', *International Bulletin of Missionary Research*, vol. 32, no. 1 (January 2008), pp. 27–30

spectacular. It grew by 259 per cent to over two billion. The number of Christians as a percentage of the world population remains around 34 per cent only because the world's total population grew at the same rate (see Fig. 2 overleaf).

In any case, Christianity's rate of expansion over the past 100 years exceeds any other period in its 2,000-year history. Significantly, much of this recent growth has taken place in areas of the world where there were no Christian communities just over a century ago. By 2000, a greater variety of cultures and societies had yielded adherents to the Christian faith than in any other period previously. Not only that, but the vast majority of this extraordinary growth took place in the non-Western world. The same period witnessed a dramatic decline of Christian faith and presence in Western countries, partly due to increasing secularization. By the end of the twentieth century, Africa and Latin America had emerged as the new heartlands of the global Christian faith.

Integral to the story is the extraordinary upsurge of Pentecostal–Charismatic movements (see Chapter 11). The 1906 Azusa Street Revival (in the USA) may have provided a particularly prominent demonstration of the work of the Holy Spirit, but it did not mark the starting point of the global Pentecostal movement, as is often believed. Global Pentecostalism had multiple starting points on different continents. Indeed, Christian believers in the non-Western world emphasized spiritual power and Charismatic dimensions of the faith from the earliest contacts with the gospel. This is one reason why Pentecostal forms of worship are often strongly present in these

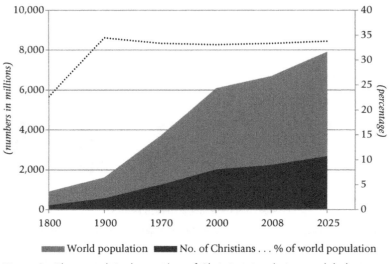

Figure 2 The growth in the number of Christians in relation to global population since 1800

Source: Barrett et al., 'Missiometrics 2008', pp. 27–30

regions, even within churches belonging to traditional mainline denominations. In any case, the Pentecostal movements and ministries throughout the world, in their variety of indigenous forms, represent the most dynamic segments of Christian existence.

New developments in global missionary outreach

The recent transformations within global Christianity, combined with a new era of global migratory flows, have also given rise to unprecedented non-Western missionary activity. As indicated above, indigenous Christians in the non-Western world have always been key agents of the transmission of the gospel within their own countries or communities. Except as a by-product of displacement or migrant relocation, international missionary initiatives were rare. From the 1970s, the massive increase across the globe in the number of international migrants, the majority of whom come from non-Western or developing countries, has changed that. These voluminous migrations from parts of the world that are also Christian heartlands have created a considerable growth in immigrant churches within major cities in the West. Many of these mainly serve immigrant communities, but their commitment to missionary outreach cannot be doubted.

The sending of missionaries to international destinations by mission agencies established in countries such as South Korea and Brazil has also increased dramatically in the past three to four decades. From roughly 500 in the 1980s, the number of Korean missionaries serving overseas had grown to over 14,000 by 2006. By then, also, some 10,000 missionaries from hundreds of mission organizations in Latin America were on international assignment. Inadequate training, limited resources and dependence on out-dated models can present major challenges to these groups. But at the start of the twenty-first century, initiatives from the non-Western world represent the major, and increasingly dominant, segment of the global Christian missionary movement.

All this is not to suggest that Western missionary initiatives are no longer important. In fact, they remain the most visible and the best funded, though the predominance of 'short-term' mission trips raises questions about long-term impact. Importantly, many Western missionary agencies are also employing increasing numbers of indigenous or national workers who can serve their own communities more effectively than foreign agents. In effect, like the worldwide Church itself, the Christian missionary movement now comprises a multitude of agents and initiatives from around the world, with no privileged centre.

Taken together, these new developments – recent transformations within global Christianity, the great variety of initiatives that characterize new missionary movements, and the variety of experiences (including persecution and sustained encounter with other major faiths) that mark the world's Christian communities at the start of the twenty-first century – call for fresh analyses. They also invite a re-examination of the Christian story in which voices from around the world are meaningfully represented. This volume is compiled with this objective in mind.

1

Western Europe and North America

Mark Noll

In 1800 about 90 per cent of the world's Christians lived in Europe. But European Christianity, including the European settlements of North America, was not in good shape. The difficulty could be described as two different assaults on Christendom, or the traditional intermingling of church and state, church and education, church and law. In Europe the threat came from new sources of power competing with Christianity, in North America from the absence of structures for any kind of power.

The churches in Europe were reeling from a double blow: first, in the centre of Europe, leaders of the French Revolution of 1789 had ruthlessly attacked France's hereditary Catholic institutions; to them, Catholicism was only the corrupt religious reflection of France's corrupt and outdated absolute monarchy. Second, the armies of Napoleon, which had emerged from the tumult of the French Revolution, were conquering more and more European territory. By dismantling traditions of cooperation between church and state that extended deep into the past, Napoleon was undermining Europe's historic reliance on its Catholic and Protestant churches. He also pointed the continent to the nation-state itself as the institution best suited to guarantee security and public order.

In North America, there was a different kind of crisis. In a continent of vast physical space, a few million colonists of European descent were struggling to set up Christian institutions and support structures, but without the usual apparatus of European Christendom. The new United States, which became a nation in 1776, soon thereafter moved decisively to separate church and state. The reason was that too many churches were represented among the European settlers, which made it impossible for governments to support a single church. To European Christians, this move seemed extremely dangerous; it went against more than a thousand years of European practice. In a word, throughout Europe and North America, Christendom – the old social–political order that had supported the local practice of Christian faith for many hundreds of years – seemed on the verge of collapse.

Along with social–political challenges, new intellectual challenges also confronted European Christians. The intellectual movement known as the

Europe

Enlightenment had gathered strength throughout the eighteenth century. Some of its leading exponents depicted 'the light' of learning as a contrast to mental darkness created by the churches. Leading intellectual figures, including some contributors to the great French *Encyclopédie*, even advocated atheism. Most Europeans did not go that far, but an increasing number of intellectuals were questioning traditional belief in the Bible. They were dispensing with traditional statements of Christian belief. And some directly challenged the authority that church leaders had traditionally exercised over daily life.

In the century that began in 1800 even broader challenges would come from economic, cultural and social changes. Unlike the intellectual challenges, which were mostly restricted to elites, the latter changes would transform the lives of ordinary Europeans and North Americans.

The churches laboured under special difficulties at the start of the nineteenth century. Differences between Roman Catholics and Protestants, which dated back to the Reformation of the sixteenth century, were as strong as ever. These differences meant that antagonisms between believers

9

North America

in different streams of Christianity loomed larger than the challenges of the new secularism. Some Protestants were enduring the heavy hand of state interference. In 1817 the King of Prussia, Frederick William III (1770–1840), forced the Lutheran churches and the Reformed (or Calvinist) churches of his realm into a forced union. Among Catholics, the Jesuit order remained suppressed; it had been the Catholics' most effective missionary and educational order, but it was dissolved in 1773 when enemies of the Jesuits convinced the pope that this order had become too much involved in European politics. Throughout all of Europe the wars propelled by Napoleon's armies involved much suffering and many difficulties for members of almost all churches.

At the same time, signs of spiritual life were by no means absent. Renewal movements from European Pietism and British Evangelicalism were continuing to expand. The Methodists, who had been inspired and organized by John Wesley (1703–91) and Charles Wesley (1707–88), continued effective ministry in the cities and countryside of both Britain and North America. In Norway, Hans Nielsen Hauge (1771–1824) was only one of the leaders who successfully promoted Pietism's stress on personal faith and active discipleship. In their darkest days under pressure from Napoleon, Roman Catholics were inspired by the courage of Pope Pius VII (1742–1823). And at least some believers were carrying on the work of faithful intellectuals from the previous century. Among the most memorable of these stalwarts had been a Church of England bishop (George Berkeley 1685–1753), a pastor on the American frontier (Jonathan Edwards 1703–58) and a French Catholic priest (Nicolas Malebranche 1638–1715). Their work held out the hope that the intellectual challenges of the future could be met with the same dedication to God's glory that these ones had shown.

✳ The age of Napoleon (c. 1800) to the rise of Pentecostalism (c. 1900)

Already by 1800 day-to-day Christian life was encountering increasingly strong challenges from the rapid growth of industry and the even faster rise of great cities. The Christian churches were historically strongest in small towns and the countryside where face-to-face relationships defined the rhythms of largely agricultural societies. Women, in their roles as wives, mothers and grandmothers, were especially important in sustaining families in regular Christian practices. When citizens moved into the cities and found either improved economic prospects or harsh poverty, older habits suffered. The ability of more people to buy more manufactured goods opened the way to a fuller life, but also allowed fixation on consumption to push aside prayer, church attendance, family worship and private devotion. For the vastly increased numbers of the new urban poor, poverty, disease, and the break-up of families were even more harmful. In the USA, opportunities for getting ahead often upset steady Christian adherence; all throughout the nineteenth century, European visitors marvelled at the energy of Americans but also wondered what constant pursuit of the dollar would do to Christian faith.

Increasingly, throughout the nineteenth century, the growth of nation-states meant that services once provided by the churches were now being taken on by governments. Growing concentrations of state power also paved the way for increasingly destructive periods of international warfare. In sum, what historians have called 'secularism' grew ever stronger as the century unfolded. Such secularism might mean active rejection of Christianity. More dangerously, it meant simply paying less and less attention to God.

Yet even as secularism advanced, dedicated believers addressed the new problems of European society. In Britain, urban reformers came from the same circles that campaigned against the slave trade. One of several Quakers actively engaged in reform was Elizabeth Fry (1780–1845), who pioneered efforts to make prisons more humane. Anthony Ashley Cooper (1801–85), the seventh Earl of Shaftesbury, campaigned on behalf of the mentally ill, workers in mines and factories, and children who lacked educational opportunities. William Booth (1829–1912) and Catherine Booth (1829–90), founders of the Salvation Army, offered a wide variety of social services to the urban poor of London – and then other cities – even as they proclaimed an evangelical message of new life in Christ.

In Germany, a Catholic bishop of Mainz, Wilhelm Ketteler (1811–77), became a strong supporter of labour. Also in Germany Johann Blumhardt (1805–80) of Bad Boll proclaimed the slogan 'Jesus is Victor' as the key to revival, physical healing and labour reform. His son, Christoph Blumhardt (1842–1919), continued with these programmes even as he moved to propose a distinctly Christian form of socialism as the antidote to the exploitation of workers.

In the United States, Frances Willard (1839–98) led the Women's Christian Temperance Union; its goal was to reduce alcohol abuse and thereby help the women and children who were so often the casualties of drunkenness. Also in the USA a general movement called the Social Gospel followed teachers such as the German-American Walter Rauschenbusch (1861–1918) in seeking to reform city life.

The most influential Christian attempt to deal with Europe's urban crises came from the Vatican. In 1891 Pope Leo XIII (1810–1903) published the encyclical *Rerum novarum*, which charted a course between laissez-faire capitalism and socialism. It advocated for working people, but in the context of stable communities and specific local conditions.

Christian responses to the economic and social crises of the nineteenth century were never comprehensive or entirely effective, but they existed in many varieties, and they did make a difference.

Personal piety was also strengthened in many ways throughout this same century. Among Roman Catholics, Pope Gregory XVI (r. 1831–46) and Pope Pius IX (r. 1846–78) spurred a devotional revival that featured new attention to the Virgin Mary. They also urged Catholics to orient ritual life around the parish church and to heed the guidance of parish priests. This revival worked with special effect in places such as Ireland and Poland that were subject to harsh rule by imperial powers.

Protestant piety was structured by increasing attention to Scripture, a project in which the British and Foreign Bible Society played a leading role. Its agents were responsible for the first effective Protestant outreach in far-flung places, including the Russian Empire and strongly Catholic Latin America. Periodic revivals drove home the need for conversion and dedicated Christian living in many places: Holland and Switzerland in the 1830s, the United States and English Canada periodically through the century, Northern Ireland and the USA in the late 1850s. Leading revivalists of the era often set the tone for preaching, established expectations for conversions and helped popularize new hymns. Especially important as such leaders were the Americans Charles G. Finney (1792–1875), active in the century's middle decades, and Dwight L. Moody (1837–99), active in the last third of the century.

The nineteenth century was also a great age of Protestant hymnody, with hymns serving to unite singers from many denominations as they effectively drove home important Christian teaching. Many of the most renowned hymn writers of the era were women, including Anglican Charlotte Elliott (1789–1871): 'Just as I am without one plea'; Swedish Lutheran Lina Sandell (1832–1903): 'Children of the heavenly Father'; and American Fanny Crosby (1820–1915): 'Rescue the perishing' and 'To God be the glory'.

Intellectual challenges came from many sides during this era. Most obvious were the efforts to overthrow central teachings of the faith. A few scholars described the New Testament as a discordant mixture of teaching – some from Paul, some from Peter – that was only smoothed over late in the second century. Others pictured Jesus as a simple Galilean rabbi who never claimed to be divine. Against such radical views, more traditional believers made a spirited response. Most effective in biblical scholarship were the so-called 'Cambridge Triumvirate' – F. J. A. Hort (1828–92), J. B. Lightfoot (1828–89) and B. F. Westcott (1825–1901). This trio of Anglican scholars used careful research to defend more conservative views of the writing and transmission of the New Testament. In general, students of the Scriptures were increasingly divided between those who read the Bible as just another text from the ancient world, and those who continued to believe it was the inspired word of God. The considerable number of scholars who tried to use modern methods to better understand the God-given Scriptures sometimes found themselves scorned by other academics for their naivety and mistrusted by their fellow Christians for their impiety.

Against the century's chorus of sub-Christian and anti-Christian philosophical voices (for example, G. W. F. Hegel (1770–1831), Karl Marx (1818–83) and Friedrich Nietzsche (1844–1900)), one of the most effective responses came from the Danish writer and philosopher Søren Kierkegaard (1813–55). While answering non-Christian challenges, Kierkegaard also urged churches to teach Christian authenticity instead of serving as mere props for social custom. Later in the century, the Dutch theologian, publisher and politician Abraham Kuyper (1837–1920) likewise called secular philosophy into question. His form of Christian activism was based on perceiving the differences in the various spheres of existence that God had created.

Challenges in science were focused on Charles Darwin's *Origin of Species* (1859) and its presentation of evolutionary biology. Darwin's description of gradual change in organisms, occurring over immense aeons and caused by the accumulation of minute variations, posed difficulties for traditional interpretations of the Bible. Believers were divided on how to respond. Some chose to defend early Genesis as a literal account of how God made

13

the world. Others adjusted their interpretation of Scripture while defending God's direction of the evolutionary process. By the end of the nineteenth century, the official position of the Catholic Church was also the view of some conservative Protestants, such as the learned Benjamin B. Warfield (1851–1921) of Princeton Theological Seminary. This stance held that God had created the world and the human soul by direct acts and also providentially supervised all other physical phenomena; but it left scientific research to investigate these phenomena. This picture seemed too conservative for some believers and too liberal for others.

From the standpoint of the twenty-first century, the two most important nineteenth-century developments in organized Christianity were the conservative retrenchment of the Roman Catholic Church and the innovations in organization under way in North America. For Catholics the forces of liberalism and nationalism posed a direct threat to ideals of papal supremacy. Pope Pius IX (1792–1878), who in 1846 had begun his tenure with liberal sympathies, was turned into a staunch conservative by the dramatic revolutions of 1848 that attacked all forms of European tradition. In response, Pius IX condemned liberal or democratic notions such as the separation of church and state as a threat to the Catholic claim for leadership in European society. The Vatican Council convened by the pope in 1870 carried conservative reaction further by defining a strong doctrine of papal infallibility. Yet even as the Council met in Rome, the armies that created the modern Italian nation-state stripped away the pope's control over the Papal States, which he had held since early in the Middle Ages. The result was that that pope's claim to infallibility coincided with a dramatic reduction in the pope's temporal authority, a situation that the papacy would protest for more than 50 years. Pius IX's successor, Leo XIII (1810–1903), made an important move by restoring Thomas Aquinas as the Catholic Church's leading theological authority. This restitution led almost immediately to fresh Catholic efforts in philosophy, as well as pioneering social theory.

In North America, a very different transformation was under way. While churches in Canada remained relatively close to their European heritage, in the United States the ethos of democracy combined with the separation of church and state to create a new religious dynamic. Throughout the first two thirds of the century, American churches expanded rapidly, but did so almost entirely through their own exertions. Led by Methodists and Baptists, US Protestants organized themselves with voluntary principles that stressed local initiative, local direction, local recruitment and local funding. Techniques that seemed hopelessly democratic to Europeans were working to form churches. But they also led the way in founding schools, civilizing the frontier and promoting social reform. The US experience of voluntary, non-established church life represented a successful adjustment to a social order where traditional Christian establishments no longer existed.

What did not succeed as well were democratic approaches to conflict. In the American North, many believers grew convinced that the Bible condemned slavery. Many in the South, where slavery had become a way of life, turned to the Scriptures to show that Abraham, Moses, Paul and even Jesus had accepted slavery. American defenders of slavery usually forgot that slaves in the Bible were almost always white people enslaved by other whites. But they nonetheless made a strong case for their biblical interpretation. The evil consequence for the churches was the American Civil War (1861–5), which divided the nation's believers into hostile warring camps. After the war, which ended slavery, African-American churches grew like wildfire. But among the white churches, earlier energy was blunted. The power of the government, along with a boom in US industry, soon became the guiding forces in society.

Amid such difficulties, Europeans, with support from North America, undertook a great surge of missionary activity that eventually helped to transform the worldwide Church. Where Catholic cross-cultural efforts had earlier dominated missions, the nineteenth century witnessed increased Protestant efforts from the European continent, Britain, Canada and the United States. Some of that missionary activity represented just a religious side to the expansion of European colonial power. But much of it pointed beyond colonization to the indigenization of Christianity in new cultures. Especially important were leaders who saw their role as preparing new churches to become full participants in worldwide Christian fellowship. Henry Venn (1796–1873) of Britain's Anglican Church Missionary Society encouraged local leaders, such as Samuel Ajayi Crowther (c.1807–91) of Nigeria who became the first African Anglican bishop under Venn's direction. Rufus Anderson (1796–1880) of the American Board of Commissioners for Foreign Missions joined Venn in urging mission agencies to work at making new churches self-supporting, self-governing and self-propagating. John Nevius (1829–93), an American Presbyterian missionary in China, was not particularly successful in implementing such principles there. By contrast, in Korea he found a ready welcome for these ideas among missionaries, pastors and lay workers (both male and female). Throughout the century and beyond, women always made up a majority of those in missionary ranks.

From the rise of Pentecostalism (c.1900) to the Second Vatican Council (1962)

Transformation was also the order of the day at the start of the twentieth century when revival focused on the Holy Spirit led to new emphases on spiritual and physical healing. It also lay behind movements that stressed 'consecration', 'holiness' and 'total surrender' in the Spirit. Pentecostalism, a sharply focused manifestation of this new emphasis on the Spirit, emerged most visibly in a revival during 1906 in Los Angeles. Led by an African-American holiness preacher, William Seymour (1870–1922), the revival at the Azusa Street chapel placed special emphasis on speaking in tongues as prime evidence of Spirit baptism. Soon delegations were coming from many parts of North America, and then from Europe and beyond, to experience what was called 'the latter rain' of Spirit endowment. In 1900 there were only a handful of Christian believers in the world who sought the gifts of the Holy Spirit recorded in the New Testament; by the end of the twentieth century, perhaps 500 million Charismatic and Pentecostal believers were active around the world.

Pentecostal and Charismatic currents would come to influence much of later Christian history. But at the start of the new century, traditional missionary efforts were in the forefront. In 1910 a landmark missionary conference was held in Edinburgh, Scotland, which represented the climax of the great Protestant missionary movements of the previous century. The conference assembled missionaries and delegates from the European continent, Britain and North America, as well as a handful of believers from outside the Western world (there were no Africans in attendance). This Edinburgh conference marked the handover from Britain to America in leadership of Protestant missions. Especially after the First World War, recruits, money and church models from North America would increasingly take the place of what had once been Britain's leading role.

The Edinburgh conference took up a range of topics having to do with missionary preaching and the gospel, the recruitment of missionaries, relations with non-Christian religions and the goal of Christian unity. An important legacy of Edinburgh was the ecumenical International Missionary Council, which also played a background role in the eventual formation of the World Council of Churches in 1948. The networks that planned the Edinburgh conference also included a number of individuals who would work together in support of the League of Nations and the League's pursuit of world peace. In retrospect the conference marked a transition from Christianity defined instinctively as a Western faith to a situation where the Christianities of North America and Europe would exist alongside the expanding Christianities of the southern hemisphere.

One of the major events that undercut the self-confidence of the Christian West and that spurred the indigenization of Christianity elsewhere was the First World War (1914–18). The immense destruction unleashed by this conflict was cataclysmic. Millions of young men died to rearrange the European balance of power, only to leave unresolved disputes that would shortly lead to the even more destructive violence of the Second World War (1939–45). For any who still considered Europe the centre of 'Christian civilization', the First World War spelled disillusionment. For the families of the dead, wounded and traumatized, it was a severe test of faith. In the wake of the war, much of Europe and North America turned more rapidly away from God to pursue pleasure; in the United States this manifested as 'the roaring twenties', in Berlin as the promotion of blatant public decadence. In Switzerland, Karl Barth (1886–1968) was a young pastor who concluded that the First World War showed the folly of theological liberalism, with its seeming confidence in the inevitable improvement of the human race. Barth's *Commentary on Romans*, first published in 1917, proclaimed anew the sovereignty of God, the all-sufficiency of Christ and the folly of trusting in mere human effort. It marked the public appearance of the twentieth century's most important theologian and the inspiration of what would come to be known as 'neo-orthodoxy'.

Among Catholics a similar search for theological roots inspired the work of Jacques Maritain (1882–1973) in France; with several like-minded colleagues, Maritain brought the theology of Thomas Aquinas into dialogue with the urgent problems of the post-war world (hence, the theology was called 'neo-Thomism'). A network of institutions known as 'Catholic Action' also took root in many parts of Europe and Canada with the goal of bringing to life historic Catholic doctrine in day-to-day situations. It influenced numerous figures, including the young Karol Wojtyla (1920–2005) in Poland, who later became Pope John Paul II.

The Second World War produced death and destruction on an unimaginable scale. The murderous assault of Nazi Germany on European Jews posed the special problem of theodicy for Christian theologians as well as Jewish thinkers: how could a loving God allow such devastating slaughter to take place? Convincing answers were hard to come by, even as the faithful witness of believers under great pressure testified to the enduring power of the gospel. In Germany, the young Lutheran pastor Dietrich Bonhoeffer (1906–45) boldly attacked 'cheap grace' and called nominal believers back to the integrity of Christ – before he was executed by the Nazis in the last days of the European war. Courageous Christian witness also came from German Catholic individuals, including Sophie Scholl (1921–43) and Hans Scholl (1918–43) in Munich who were inspired by their faith to question Hitler's policies – for which they too were executed. Later, it was significant that Germany's post-war recovery was led by Konrad Adenauer (1876–1967), leader of the Christian Democratic Party. Adenauer had taken refuge in a monastery during the war and emerged in its wake to employ Catholic principles of social solidarity to help rebuild his shattered country.

For traditional Protestants, the cumulative effect of twentieth-century traumas was exhaustion. Increasingly, the vision and energy for Europe and North America came from the more sectarian movements that stressed personal encounter with Jesus. In the USA, Billy Graham (1918–2018) emerged after the Second World War as the most effective public preacher of personal salvation. His prominence, in turn, spoke for a general revival among believers who came to be called 'new evangelicals'. In the UK, John Stott (1921–2011), rector of All Souls Church in London, enjoyed a similar status as a leader of resurgent Evangelicalism. Graham and Stott were both significant, moreover, for how they deliberately built ties between Christian institutions in the West and newer Christian movements in the non-Western world.

For Roman Catholics, the key event early in the century came in 1929 when the Church of Rome signed a concordat with the Italian government. From 1871 and the unification of Italy, successive popes had protested the loss of the Papal States by treating themselves as 'prisoners of the Vatican'. With the concordat, the papacy accepted the one square mile of the Vatican as its territory, popes began to travel in Italy and normal relations began with Italy's government. For the more general history of Christianity, the event was highly significant. The Catholic Church was by far the world's largest Christian organization. But so long as the popes hankered after their old power on the Italian peninsula, the whole church remained overinvested in the machinations of Italian politics. After the great distress of the Second World War, the new arrangement secured in 1929 made it possible for the world's largest Christian tradition to function more for the world than it had ever done before.

However, the traumas of the 1930s and 1940s did pose great difficulties for the Roman Church. In 1933 Pope Pius XI (1857–1939) signed a concordat with Adolf Hitler (1889–1945), which in his judgement was the best way to stabilize the German Catholic Church under the Nazis. But in 1937, after Hitler's destructive policies against Jews and other opponents became clearer, Pius XI issued an encyclical, *Mit brennender Sorge* (With Burning Concern), that criticized the Nazis' lust for power. Much controversy has followed the career of the next pope, Pius XII (1876–1958), especially over whether he did enough to protect Jews and others whom the Nazis targeted for destruction. The debate over Pius XII's actions is serious, but it should not blind observers to the general movement of the Roman Catholic Church. Pius XII's successor was an elderly Vatican diplomat who took the name John XXIII (1881–1963). In his first years of service (1958–63), he called the Second Vatican Council into being, an event that dramatically changed the shape of Christianity in Europe and the rest of the world.

From the Second Vatican Council (1962) to the installation of Pope Benedict XVI (2005)

The Second Vatican Council, which met from 1962 to 1965, was the most important institutional event in the recent history of Christianity. Its significance for world Christianity has been matched only by the upsurge of Pentecostal and Charismatic forms of the faith that have spread around the world. The Second Vatican Council represented the effort by Pope John XXIII to refit the Catholic Church for the modern world, while at the same time maintaining its continuity with the past. Liberal and radical interpreters of the Council saw it as a complete reshaping of the church for social reform; conservative critics saw it as a cave-in to theological and political modernism. A better reading is to gauge the Council's consequences. They included much better ecumenical communications with Orthodox Christians, many Protestants, Jews and Muslims; much more focus on Scripture alongside Catholic traditions; much more attention to the laity as contributing to 'the people of God'; much less European-centred traditionalism. After the Council, the Catholic Church became both more cohesive (with greater authority flowing from the Vatican) and more diffuse (with greater variety of belief and practice among local Catholic communities).

Another great transformation occurred at the end of the 1980s when the Soviet Union collapsed. Modern communism had been the most systematic opponent of Christianity in the modern world. In every case where state communism triumphed, the churches suffered. Poland, with a strong Catholic consciousness built into its national identity, preserved the most active Christianity. But signs of Christian life also survived elsewhere amid the rubble (to paraphrase the great Russian writer Aleksandr Solzhenitsyn (1918–2008), himself an Orthodox believer). In Europe, Christian movements played unusually prominent parts in the great changeover from communism. Most important was the Polish pope, Karol Wojtyla, who in 1978 became the first non-Italian in nearly 500 years to head the Catholic Church. As Pope John Paul II, he lent spiritual support to Poland's Solidarity movement, which stoutly resisted and then overcame institutional communist power. Elsewhere, Protestant churches were in the lead. Romania's communist dictatorship cracked when it was unable to silence a Reformed pastor, Lazlo Tokes (b. 1952), in the city of Timisoara. In East Germany, hundreds, then thousands and finally tens of thousands gathered peacefully for prayer meetings in Lutheran churches. These meetings played a key role in the peaceful dismantling of the Berlin Wall in November 1989.

The churches did not necessarily regain strength as the communists lost control, but peaceful Christian witness from Protestants and Catholics alike testified once again to the power of Christian conviction to transform the social order. In the mid 1930s, when he was told of the Vatican's disapproval of certain Soviet actions, the Soviet dictator Joseph Stalin (1878–1953) sneered, 'How many [military] divisions does the pope have?' A generation later, Protestants joined Catholics in replying that spiritual strength remained in some instances more powerful than military might.

Yet despite the signal visibility of churches in altering the political face of Europe, the process of de-Christianization went on. A provocative thesis by the British sociologist Callum Brown (*The Death of Christian Britain: Understanding secularisation 1800–2000* (London: Routledge, 2001)) has offered one plausible explanation. In his reading, Christianity remained central to European society so long as it provided the most important vocabulary for defining existence and so long as it retained the loyalty of women, who had always transmitted Christianity to the rising generation. The earlier frame of reference was illustrated during the Nazi era when Allied leaders such as Winston Churchill (1874–1965), though not an active believer himself, called Europe's conflict a struggle for 'Christian civilization'. Similarly,

19

alongside much falling away from the churches, Europeans generally maintained church-sanctioned practices of marriage and child-rearing into the 1940s. In Brown's account, the Christian frame of reference gave way in the 1950s. Prosperity, new forms of entertainment, the pervasive presence of television and a redefinition of personhood in terms of self-fulfilment – all reflected a new approach to life in general. When large numbers of women began to view themselves as autonomous actors in modern society, de-Christianization became even more pronounced.

Whether Callum Brown's theory is correct, he and other observers were certainly right in noting seismic changes in European religious life after the 1950s. Church attendance declined steeply everywhere, with Scandinavia and other historically Protestant regions showing the steepest drop-offs. Renewal movements certainly did exist, with Charismatic influences reviving some of the churches. In addition, the immigration of new populations also brought signs of Christian life. Many commentators have noted the religious changes in Europe arising from the increasing number of Muslims. Fewer have noticed how significant the new Christian immigration has become: from churches serving African immigrants in France, to large churches filled with Caribbean and African newcomers in the UK, and many contributions from the Majority World to Catholic parishes throughout Europe. In world Christian terms, the most significant recent development has been that the regions once considered 'mission lands' have become important sources of hope for formerly 'Christian Europe'.

In the United States, the civil rights movement of the 1950s and 1960s brought sharply focused Christianity back into the public square. The leading civil rights spokesman, Martin Luther King Jr (1929–68), skilfully combined pacifism influenced by India's Mahatma Gandhi (1869–1948) with a traditional African-American Christianity. King's most effective supporters were African-American church people who embraced a more basic version of Bible-based faith. Together, leaders and followers pushed the United States to extend basic civil rights to its African-American communities, which had long suffered systematic discrimination.

The Christian community that was most obvious in following African Americans into public activity was made up of conservative white Evangelicals. Although most white Evangelicals eventually accepted civil rights for black Americans, many objected to the expanded role of the US government in enforcing civil rights. They objected even more when court rulings and federal legislation banned prayer and Bible reading in public schools, legalized abortion on demand and relaxed restrictions on homosexual practices. The result was a 'New Christian Right'. This political movement linked conservative white Protestants to the Republican Party and played a significant part in electing US presidents Ronald Reagan (1980 and 1984) and George W. Bush (2000 and 2004). The political activity of white Evangelicals became controversial at home and abroad when it was linked to American prosecution of the Iraq War that began in 2003. The lessons for world Christianity from this American experience was to show how much political influence a well-organized Christian cadre could exert in a modern democratic nation, but also to show how dangerous the fusion of political and religious goals could be.

In the midst of a more secular society, many life-giving rivulets continued to refresh the stream of practical piety. New Bible translations made the Scriptures more widely accessible in almost all of the Western languages; in English there is now a Bible for every taste. Reading that strengthened Christian belief and practice came from many points on the ecclesiastical compass. The Catholic theologian and all-round savant Hans Urs von Balthasar (1905–88) provided unusually weighty reflections for an audience extending well beyond the Catholic Church. The British writer C. S. Lewis (1898–1963) enjoyed an even broader audience with a wide range of books that included Christian apologetics, literary criticism, science fiction and children's literature. One sign of the times was that devotional and theological works regularly crossed the divide between Catholics and Protestants with a freedom unthinkable earlier in the twentieth century.

Day-to-day spiritual practice was shaped to some degree by the consumerism that became so pervasive in Western societies. Traditional denominational loyalties often meant less than finding a church or fellowship that addressed the individual's spiritual needs. Almost all Christian groups paid more attention to the power and work of the Holy Spirit, some by practising the sign gifts that included speaking in tongues and divine healing, others by renewed attention to prayer, fasting and the spiritual disciplines. Especially in some US churches, preaching that linked faith in Christ to personal prosperity became popular; this emphasis was only one of the ways in which certain aspects of American church life resembled religious life in the Majority World more than was the case in Europe.

✳ Conclusions

One of the best general interpretations of the broad sweep of Christian history from 1800 to the twenty-first century was provided by the British scholar and active Anglican David Martin (*A General Theory of Secularization* (New York, NY: Harper & Row, 1978)). In Martin's view, de-Christianization has usually followed the pattern of earlier Christianization. Thus, Russia's top-down, tsarist, state-sponsored monopolistic Eastern Orthodoxy gave way to a top-down, Marxist, state-sponsored monopolistic atheism. In Europe, the early pattern was set by the strong traditions of Christendom, where state and church were joined together into a common social organism. With more room for personal freedom than in Russia, there has been more freedom for Christian initiatives once European societies moved from Christendom towards secularism. Yet because Christendom represented a cohesive ideal of society, secularism has affected European life comprehensively.

Things were different in the United States, which developed a democratic and voluntaristic society where churches competed vigorously with one another even as they effectively spread Christian values. That former pattern has now been replaced by a pluralistic and voluntaristic democracy in which religious bodies still compete with one another, but also with all sorts of other organizations, including government – and on roughly equal footing. By comparison with Europe (and to some extent Canada as well), secularization in the USA has taken place *alongside* the churches. In Europe (and Canada) secularization has occurred more directly as a development *within* the churches.

At the start of the twenty-first century, Europe and North America no longer make up the heartland of Christianity. More than 60 per cent of the world's Christian adherents now live in the Majority World, and the driving forces of Christian expansion and Christian spiritual development exist outside the West. Yet despite a difficult period when warfare, church infighting, secularization and intense commercialism have worked against spiritual vitality, signs of Christian hope are far from absent. Under popes John Paul II, Benedict XVI (b. 1927) and Francis I (b. 1936) the Catholic Church has divested itself of some of its merely traditional baggage; with their focus on the person and work of Christ, the writings and speeches of these three popes have also become the clearest recent expressions of basic Christian teaching in the world. Problems abound for European and North American Catholics, not least the sex scandals that have undermined public confidence in many regions. But Catholic efforts that can be supported by non-Catholics have never been more significant.

Among Protestants, signs of life include the faithfulness of traditional believers in many parts of Europe and some of the megachurches that have attracted vast numbers in several locations in the USA. Christian immigrants from Asia and Africa have breathed new life into many Protestant churches throughout Europe and North America. Lay Christians enjoy ever-increasing resources for strengthening biblical understanding and going deeper into spiritual life.

Yet throughout Europe and North America, as indeed throughout the rest of the world, the most basic reasons for hope in the continued relevance of Christianity come from the most basic realities. Individuals, families, communities and churches in Europe and North America struggle against doubt, personal failings and the distractions of worldliness. They have entered a much more secular era. But as European and North American believers experience the shocks of modernity, they are still being supported by acts of kindness in the name of Christ, faithful testimonies to God's transforming mercy, and regular renewal from the Scriptures and the varied but potent spiritual rituals maintained in a myriad of churches. Here, as in the rest of the world, it is possible to paraphrase what the apostle Paul wrote in Romans 5.20 (NRSV): 'where sin [and secularism] increased, grace abounded all the more.'

? DISCUSSION QUESTIONS

1 What were the major challenges facing the European and North American churches in 1800? Which were most successfully met, and why?

2 Compare Catholic and Protestant responses to the great changes that took place in European society in the nineteenth century.

3 How has the history of Christianity in North America been different from that in Europe?

4 When did Pentecostalism arise, and what has been the effect of Pentecostalism on Christian life in North America and Europe?

5 What did Europe and North America contribute to the missionary movement, and what major changes took place in missionary history over this period?

6 What effect did the First World War and the Second World War have on the churches?

7 What is meant by 'prisoner of the Vatican', and why was it important for the Catholic Church that this status came to an end?

8 Why was the Second Vatican Council such an important event in the recent world history of Christianity?

9 How might the interaction of religion and politics in the United States serve as a lesson to believers elsewhere in the world?

10 What is David Martin's general explanation for the process of de-Christianization in Western societies?

📖 Further reading

Chadwick, O. *The Secularization of the European Mind in the Nineteenth Century*. New York, NY: Cambridge University Press, 1975.

Christie, N. and Gauvreau, M. (eds). *The Sixties and Beyond: Dechristianization in North America and Western Europe, 1945–2000*. Toronto: University of Toronto Press, 2013.

Davie, Grace. *Religion in Britain: A persistent paradox*, 2nd edn. Chichester: Wiley-Blackwell, 2015.

Hatch, N. *The Democratization of American Christianity*. New Haven, CT: Yale University Press, 1989.

Knight, F. *The Church in the Nineteenth Century*. London: I. B. Tauris, 2008.

Lamb, M. and Levering, M. (eds). *Vatican II: Renewal within tradition*. New York, NY: Oxford University Press, 2008.

McLeod, H. *Religion and the People of Western Europe, 1789–1989*. New York, NY: Oxford University Press, 1997.

McLeod, H. *The Religious Crisis of the 1960s*. New York, NY: Oxford University Press, 2007.

Morris, J. *The Church in the Modern Age*. London: I. B. Tauris, 2007.

Noll, M. A. *A History of Christianity in the United States and Canada*, 2nd edn. Grand Rapids, MI: Eerdmans, 2019.

Stanley, B. *Christianity in the Twentieth Century: A world history*. Princeton, NJ: Princeton University Press, 2018.

Walls, A. *The Missionary Movement in Christian History: Studies in the transmission of faith*. Maryknoll, NY: Orbis, 1996.

2

Africa in the nineteenth century

Louise Pirouet (with revisions by Jehu J. Hanciles)

This chapter examines developments in the four major regions of Africa – North, West, South and East – in the nineteenth century. Egypt is geographically located on the African land mass, but it arguably forms an even more integral part of the Middle East, not least because it is the most populous country in the Arab world (see Chapter 9, therefore, for a discussion of

Africa

Egypt). This leaves us with Ethiopia and Sudan as the only other major sites of Christian development in northern Africa during this period. Ethiopia deserves special attention as the one place in black Africa where Christianity has had a continuous history since the early centuries of the Church, so it will be examined first. Then we look at three other major areas of nine-teenth-century Christian expansion: northward from the Cape of Good Hope at the southern tip of the continent; along the West African coast from Freetown in Sierra Leone; and inland from Zanzibar in the east. By the end of the century there were the beginnings of Christian witness in almost every country of Africa.

 Ethiopia

Ethiopia became largely Christian from the fourth century, but the spread of Islam in the seventh century made it isolated from most of the Christian world. In the centuries that followed, however, the Ethiopian kings gradu-ally extended their rule southward, and the peoples whom they conquered became Christians. The famous churches carved out of rock, which are among Ethiopia's greatest cultural treasures, are thought to date from the twelfth century onwards, and are associated with King Lalibela, who is hon-oured as a saint. There was a revival of literature and monastic life in the thirteenth and fourteenth centuries, and by the beginning of the sixteenth century Ethiopia was at the height of its power.

About this time Portuguese travellers first reached Ethiopia and were greatly impressed by both the wealth and the Christian devotion of the people. At first, relations were good, but efforts by the Portuguese to bring the Ethiopians into obedience to Rome (that is, make them Roman Catholic) bred strong disagreement between the two sides. The former wanted the Ethiopians to make sweeping changes in the liturgy, and said that the people should be rebaptized and the priests reordained. The Ethiopians were deeply insulted at this refusal to recognize them as true Christians. They rose in rebellion against King Susenyos (1572–1632), who had converted to Roman Catholicism and effectively made it the official religion. He was forced to abdicate his throne, but then told his people that he had misled them, and urged them to return to the Christianity of their ancestors. The Roman Catholics were expelled from the country, and it was a long time be-fore Ethiopians overcame their distrust of Western Christianity and culture.

By the nineteenth century the Ethiopian kings had lost their power and there was chaos in the country. The *abuna* (bishop), who by ancient custom came from Egypt, was unable to exercise any authority and the monaster-ies, which were the only places of education, were torn by theological con-troversy. However, the real strength of Christianity lay in the parishes. The people expressed their devotion by fasting, observing church festivals and obeying dietary rules like those in the Old Testament. Few of the clergy had much education, but the Church was at the centre of life, and the people were deeply loyal to what they knew of their faith.

When missions revived in the nineteenth century, their leaders looked for ways in which to help the Ethiopian Church, and a Roman Catholic mission had some success with this in the north of the country. A number of Ethiopian Orthodox priests and their congregations were brought into communion with Rome, but were allowed to keep their own liturgy and customs almost unchanged. Bishop Justin de Jacobis (1800–60), a French missionary, is still remembered for his saintliness by people in the area around Adwa and Adigrat where he worked. In the early 1860s, the work of the British and Foreign Bible Society led to a renewal movement in Eritrea, though the reformers were later forced into exile.

By the end of the nineteenth century Ethiopia had been reunited by forceful rulers who conquered large areas in the south, and efforts were made to evangelize the newly conquered peoples. Unlike the rest of Africa, Ethiopia was not brought under colonial rule. The Red Sea coast (Eritrea) was annexed by Italy, but the Ethiopians resoundingly defeated the Italians in 1896 when they tried to advance further. Africans elsewhere began to hear of this independent African country whose rulers and core culture were Christian, and Ethiopia became an inspiration to many, both because of its freedom from colonial rule and its ancient Christian culture.

 West Africa

New beginnings

The presence of Christians on the west coast of Africa dates to at least the late fourteenth century when Roman Catholic priests and Protestant clergy attached to trading posts (as chaplains) converted some Africans. A very early convert was Philip Quaque (1745–1816), born at Cape Coast, who became one of the first Africans to study in Europe. After ordination as an Anglican in 1765 – the first African to be ordained in the Anglican Church – he returned to the Gold Coast (now Ghana) where he worked as a chaplain and school-teacher until his death. His work was continued by a group of Africans trained in Britain who started a 'Bible Band' and asked the Methodist Missionary Society for help. The Methodist Church in Ghana is thus the end result of Quaque's work. But, for the most part, Christianity in West Africa had disappeared by the nineteenth century.

The re-establishment of Christianity in the region came not through European missionary efforts but from a completely unexpected source: black Christians from America. In the 1780s a group of philanthropists in England had identified a settlement in West Africa under a scheme to resettle newly freed African slaves on the continent. The settlement, which they named 'Province of Freedom', was part of present-day Sierra Leone. By this time, also, considerable numbers of African slaves in America who had fought for Britain during the American War of Independence (1775–83) found themselves homeless. The British had promised them their liberty and land to settle on (in America), but since Britain lost the war these 'Black Loyalists', as they were called, were dispersed. Some were shipped off to Nova Scotia where the harsh climate made life miserable. Eventually they agreed to be resettled in the Province of Freedom. In January 1792, 1,190 of these freed slaves set sail from Nova Scotia in five vessels. These Nova Scotian 'settlers' (as they became known) were all baptized Christians and they landed in the new settlement complete with their own churches and preachers. So began the first black church in modern Africa. A contemporary observer reported that:

> Their pastors led them ashore, singing a hymn of praise . . . Like the Children of Israel which were come out again of the captivity they rejoiced before the Lord, who brought them from bondage to the land of their forefathers. When all had arrived, the whole colony assembled in worship, to proclaim to the . . . continent whence they or their forbears had been carried in chains – 'The day of Jubilee is come; Return ye ransomed sinners home.'
>
> (C. Fyfe, *A History of Sierra Leone* (Oxford: Oxford University Press, 1962), p. 37)

The new settlers renamed the settlement 'Freetown'. Within a few years they were joined by another group of freed African slaves from Jamaica, known as 'Maroons', who numbered over 500. The settlement was a difficult place and both groups experienced many hardships and struggles. But the population of the colony and its prospects grew rapidly after 1808. This was the year in which administration of the settlement was taken over by the British Crown, making it the first Crown colony in Africa.

In 1807 Britain made it illegal for its citizens to engage in slave trading, but for years afterwards the trade continued illegally, so a squadron of warships was sent to stop it. When a slave-ship was caught, the slaves were set free in Sierra Leone. Under this scheme, tens of thousands of African slaves, collectively known as 'recaptives' (or 'liberated Africans'), were relocated in Freetown and villages established around it for the purpose. These recaptives, who numbered 18,000 by 1825 (and up to 67,000 by 1840), became the focus of evangelistic efforts by the black settler churches as well as European missionaries sent by British-based missionary societies such as the Church Missionary Society (CMS). Some of the recaptives were Muslim and remained so. But, displaced, destitute and grateful to their benefactors, the newcomers embraced the Christian faith in vast numbers. In what is considered the first mass movement to Christianity in modern Africa, tens of thousands were baptized, given 'Christian' (European) names and enrolled in schools.

Everywhere in the colony, church and school went together. The CMS took the lead in establishing primary and secondary schools where thousands of recaptives and their children (both boys and girls) were educated. In 1814 the Society opened a Christian institution to provide advanced training and religious instruction. Renamed Fourah Bay Institution in 1827, this establishment functioned as an important linguistic school and became a centre for advanced theological training. In time it produced a significant number of African teachers and clergy, some of whom went out as missionaries in the West African region and beyond. By the mid nineteenth century, about one fifth of the colony population was in school and no less than two thirds professed to be Christian. By the end of the century, former students of the many mission-founded schools held posts of responsibility in the Church, in education and in the civil service.

Henry Venn and the three-selfs strategy

Revd Henry Venn (1796–1873), CMS secretary from 1841 to 1873, emerged as one of the most visionary missionary administrators of the nineteenth century. At a time when all the major institutions in British colonies, including the churches, were under firm European control, Venn (who first encountered Africans as a child) was convinced that, given the right training, Africans were as capable as any European. By then he knew many Africans personally, and had great faith in the potential of the indigenous Church. He believed that the task of missions was to establish as quickly as possible churches that were self-supporting, self-governing and self-propagating (the three selfs). He saw this as the chief objective of a mission. Accordingly, he advocated the establishment of 'Native Pastorates' – the organization of indigenous congregations under well-trained 'native pastors' – to end the widespread practice whereby foreign missionaries became long-term pastors of local congregations. As it turned out, producing well-trained indigenous clergy proved much easier than convincing European missionaries to give up positions of control and notions of superiority.

Venn's scheme was first implemented in Sierra Leone – the CMS's first and most successful mission field – in 1861. A Native Pastorate was established with nine congregations placed under the care of African clergy, and a constitution was drawn up for their administration. The experiment faced much European missionary opposition even as it inspired African aspirations. After Venn's death, a new generation of missionaries emerged who had less faith in Africans and viewed the move towards an independent African church as highly premature. But, many struggles and challenges notwithstanding, there was no turning back the clock. By 1872 the Sierra Leone Native Pastorate comprised over 14,000 church members, 19 African clergy, nearly 60 catechists and over 100 Sunday School teachers. The future lay with African agency and initiatives.

The move eastward: Nigeria and the Gold Coast (Ghana)

By the 1840s many recaptives in Sierra Leone who were now educated and successful Christians began to make their way back to their original homelands in present-day Nigeria. Soon they were asking for teachers and pastors for themselves and their children, and both African and European missionaries were sent from Freetown in response to these requests. The hope that the Church in Sierra Leone would be the means of bringing the gospel to the whole of West Africa was now being fulfilled.

Samuel Ajayi Crowther (1806–91), later bishop, was one of the African agents sent by the CMS from Sierra Leone to Nigeria as a missionary. Enslaved as a teenager, he had been dramatically rescued from a slave-ship and brought to Freetown, where he embraced the Christian faith and excelled in school. He was ordained an Anglican priest and, in 1864, became the first African to be consecrated as an Anglican bishop. In CMS employ as a missionary bishop in the Niger region, he orchestrated one of the most notable periods of Christian expansion on the African continent in the nineteenth century. African ministers trained in Sierra Leone were his co-workers in this Niger Mission. This extensive all-African mission also represented the first sustained Christian missionary engagement with African Islam. While he championed Western civilization and made the founding of schools central to his missionary approach, Crowther also appreciated African values and strongly endorsed the translation of the Bible into African languages. He was arguably the most influential African Christian of the nineteenth century.

Revd Thomas Birch Freeman (1806–90), born in England to an English mother and an African father, was another pioneer missionary in the Gold Coast. For 52 years, from 1838 to 1890, he led the Methodist Church whose seeds had been sown by Philip Quaque. Freeman selected and trained African pastors, and arranged with African chiefs for these pastors to work in their territories. In 1849 he sent teachers to help Methodist Christians in Nigeria. From the Gold Coast, Methodists went inland to Kumasi, capital of the powerful Asante kingdom. Though he never learned to speak the local language, Freeman sustained a dynamic ministry in difficult circumstances and made the church popular in Fanteland. He retired after acting as the principal preacher at the jubilee celebrations of the Gold Coast Methodist Mission in 1885.

German missionaries from the Swiss-based Basel Mission began work in the Gold Coast in 1828. After much death and failure, Basel missionaries returned in 1843 with a group of black Moravian Christians from Jamaica who formed the nucleus of the church at Akropong. The Basel Mission work focused on economic development, education, church planting and Bible translation. Among other achievements, the missionaries introduced cocoa production in Ghana and translated the Bible into Ga and Twi (two of Ghana's main languages). However, in a misguided effort to limit the influence of African religious life and traditional practices, the German missionaries encouraged converts to settle with them in separate Christian communities known as 'salems'. The separation of Christians from the rest of society delayed African expressions and appropriation of Christianity;

but, in time, Ghanaian Christians contributed much to the expansion of Christianity in West Africa.

New developments

The revival of Roman Catholic missions

By the mid nineteenth century, a number of important changes had begun to occur. First, new life in the Roman Catholic Church in France led to a revival of Catholic missionary work. In 1861 the newly founded Society of African Missions arrived to start work in Dahomey (Benin). They were helped by Bishop Kobes (1820–72) of the 'Holy Ghost Fathers', who were already training African priests and sisters in Senegambia. The new missionaries settled at Ouida on the coast where there was a mixed population of Dahomeans – the descendants of Dahomeans who had married Portuguese traders – and freed slaves from Brazil. Some people in the latter two groups knew a little about Christianity. The missionaries began to teach, but it was a long time before the king of Dahomey allowed them to make converts among his subjects.

Nigeria became another centre of Roman Catholic missionary work. In Lagos, as in Dahomey, the missionaries found a group of former slaves from Brazil. They continued to practise their faith under the leadership of a man called Pa Antonio (*c.*1800–*c.*1880) who had been rescued out of slavery in Brazil and raised by one of the Catholic orders there. In Lagos Pa Antonio built a bamboo church where he gathered these Brazilian former slaves. He baptized dying children, blessed marriages and prayed with those who were dying, but stopped short of saying the prayers of the Mass. In 1878 the missionaries began to build a cathedral in Lagos to seat 2,000 worshippers, but it was soon too small. It was in Nigeria that Catholics first felt that they were securely on the way to planting the Roman Church in West Africa. In the meantime the Holy Ghost Fathers established missions in Guinea, Sierra Leone and Liberia, and to the east of Nigeria in Cameroon, Gabon and Congo.

Contact with Islam

As noted above, Bishop Crowther's Niger Mission, which encompassed predominantly Muslim territory, represented significant missionary engagement with Islam. By the 1880s Roman Catholic missions had also reached those parts of French West Africa known today as Niger, Chad and the Central African Republic. All these countries were sparsely inhabited, mostly by Muslims. By the middle of the century Islam had spread southward and westward from the semidesert interior of the continent, and had already reached the coast in some places at about the same time as Christian missionaries. One such area was Senegambia, where Christian missions were only successful on the coast. In Ghana and Eastern Nigeria the missions had much greater success because the advance of Islam had been slowed up by strong tribes living to the north. Overall, Christian missions had very little success in converting Muslims. Indeed, partly due to the fact that it depended on local Muslim rulers for economic and political stability, British colonial policy often prevented Christian missionary access to major Muslim areas.

The scramble for Africa

European colonization of Africa was a gradual process. But it culminated in the late nineteenth century with a competitive and haphazard grabbing of vast territories that one British newspaper dubbed 'the scramble for Africa'. The effects on Africa and African societies were traumatic and far-reaching. For the most part, colonialism aided European missionary expansion, and the numbers of European missionaries increased considerably. In areas with a large Muslim population, such as northern Nigeria, colonial policy usually denied Christian missionary admittance in order to avoid instability. But generally, colonial expansion gave European missionaries greater access to most regions and often provided the protection they needed to do their work, which focused primarily on building schools and Bible translation. Christianity spread even more rapidly than before, but mainly through the work of African missionary agents.

The Holiness movement

A notable development in the recruitment of European Protestant missionary personnel was recruiting individuals who had been influenced by Holiness teachings. The Holiness movement, which had roots in Methodism, was linked to a series of major revivals in the United States, known as the Second Great Awakening (1800–1830s). In Britain, Holiness teachings were championed by the Keswick movement. This Holiness movement laid great stress on personal prayer and Bible-reading, divine healing, evangelism, and sanctified or holy living – members were encouraged to give up drinking alcohol, smoking, dancing and other 'worldly pleasures'. The movement produced many dedicated missionaries, who set high moral standards both for themselves and for others. But their high ideals also bred critical intolerance. Some of the new generation of missionaries were harsh and unforgiving of what they took to be sin in African Christians. It was a group of such missionaries whose damaging condemnations of the Niger Mission overshadowed the final years of Bishop Crowther's life and gave impetus to an African independent church movement in Nigeria.

By then, Henry Venn had died (in 1873) and, while the CMS leaders who succeeded him did not immediately abandon his vision of African churches, they were far less convinced that Africans were ready to take over the highest positions of leadership in the Church. Roman Catholic missions were equally dedicated to planting an indigenous church, but they too drew back. The Holy Ghost Fathers gave up the attempt to train African sisters and priests, and decided, like the Protestants, that the time was not yet right.

At the same time, the colonial powers justified their empire-building by a doctrine of racial superiority. White people began to think of themselves as having a natural ability to rule people of other races, and many European missionaries shared such attitudes. European domination and control in the Church (and African society) led to increasing problems. Many capable African Christians felt discriminated against, and many church structures often seemed foreign to their culture or imposed upon them. The strained relations created by these tensions led to the formation of the first independent African-led churches in West Africa in the 1890s (see Chapter 3, under 'African renewal movements').

✳ Southern Africa

The Cape of Good Hope (on the southernmost tip of the continent) was the starting point for both colonial expansion and Christian missions throughout southern Africa in the nineteenth century. Dutch settlers, who called themselves 'Afrikaners', had been at the Cape since 1652. They were members of the Dutch Reformed Church who had fled the Netherlands to avoid persecution under Spanish rule. The rest of the population included the indigenous Khoisan (whom the European settlers called 'Hottentots' and 'Bushmen'), Bantu tribes such as the Zulus and Xhosas, Africans from Madagascar and other parts of the African continent, an Asian (mainly Indian) community and the 'coloureds' (peoples of mixed descent). Until the early nineteenth century, Africans and Asians in the Cape Colony formed a slave population that served white settler needs.

As colonists, the Afrikaners saw themselves as representatives of white Christian civilization in a land of heathen darkness. They also believed that Africans were condemned by God to servitude, and rejected the idea that they could become Christian. In reality, the Afrikaners needed cheap labour for economic reasons and they justified their exploitation of blacks with religious ideology. They also regarded themselves as a 'chosen people' who, like the Ancient Israelites, must separate themselves from the heathen who already lived in the land. Such notions of religious purity and racial dominance gave birth to the system of *apartheid* (meaning 'separateness').

The beginning of the nineteenth century was a turning point in the history of southern Africa. First, in 1806, the British succeeded the Dutch as rulers of the Cape Colony and implemented anti-slavery policies almost immediately. Second, missionaries of many nationalities came to South Africa as the modern missionary movement got under way. Third, conflict between the white colonists and the Bantu-speaking Nguni (comprising the Zulu, Xhosa, Swasi and Ndebele peoples) to the east intensified. The next half a century or so was marked by a series of bitter, sporadic wars in which the Nguni were gradually dispossessed and displaced, or forced into servitude.

When the Emancipation Act of 1833 was passed by Britain, it ended slavery in all British dominions, including the Cape Colony. For the Afrikaner population, already resentful of British rule, this development was the final straw. Thousands of Afrikaners joined a migration movement from the colony into the interior to establish new settlements beyond British control and away from a society were all persons were treated equal. These *voortrekkers* (as they were known) set up their own republics where citizenship was confined to Europeans.

Missionary beginnings

Since the Afrikaners rejected the possibility of salvation for African peoples, they resisted all missionary outreach. Missionary work among the indigenous inhabitants and the coloured community of the Cape Colony began with the arrival of Moravian missionaries and agents of the London Missionary Society (LMS). These European missionaries established settlements (or 'mission villages') where people could support themselves by agriculture or trade. Within a few years the LMS settlement at Bethelsdorp had several hundred settlers and a Christian community of 100 church members with their own deacons and deaconesses. There was daily as well as Sunday worship, and on moonlit nights and at sunrise people would sometimes slip out into the bush and kneel to pray. This practice was probably adapted from their African religious heritage.

In 1815 James Read (1777–1852), an LMS missionary at Bethelsdorp, enraged the Afrikaners by bringing 36 charges against them of murdering or using violence against coloured people. Twelve of the charges were proven and the guilty sentenced. The Afrikaners were furious, and never forgave the LMS for 'blackening their name', as they put it. British missionaries were not welcome in Afrikaner areas. During the next 20 years, Dr John Philip (1775–1851) of the LMS led the missionary campaign on behalf of non-whites. Due to his efforts, the British government issued an order (in 1826) that gave the Khoisan 'freedom and protection' and allowed them to own land. But while the missions played a leading role in securing Khoisan rights, few questioned the system of colonialism itself, which was based on the subjugation of people in their own land and the gross exploitation of their resources. There was not much to distinguish foreign missionary from colonialist; both belonged to the dominant class.

In the meantime, the Khoisan and coloureds converted to Christianity in significant numbers. Many also flocked to the mission villages to escape abuse and ill treatment from Afrikaners. By 1850 there were over 30 mission stations in the Eastern Cape with up to 4 per cent of the African population (about 16,000 people) living in them. In 1829 the colonial government also granted the Khoisan their own independent settlement in the fertile Kat River valley, and thousands of them made it their home. The settlement flourished under the leadership of James Read, with its own schools and churches; and the work of Khoisan evangelists even produced religious revival. It became the first independent African Christian initiative in South Africa. Unfortunately, the settlement was eventually destroyed (in 1851) by the devastating frontier wars between the British and the Nguni.

Christianity in the Eastern Cape and Natal

From 1818 to 1819 the Nguni were in a state of upheaval because the Zulus (one of the Nguni peoples) had embarked on wars of expansion under the leadership of a powerful warrior-king named Shaka Zulu (c.1787–1828). Shaka's push collided with the outward expansion of colonists from the Cape, resulting in bloody conflict and widespread chaos. Christian missions also began to move into the area about this time. The missionaries made their first converts among the Mfengu ('beggars'), the mass of refugees who had fled the bloody destruction created by the Zulu armies. Not for the first time in the history of Christian expansion (in Africa and other parts of the world), the earliest converts came from among the dispossessed and displaced. Here too the European missionaries used the mission village model; but, since they found the indigenous languages difficult to master, Khoikhoi Christian agents featured prominently in the spread of the gospel.

The southernmost Nguni were the Xhosa. They had allowed many Mfengu to settle among them. But they too were threatened by the advance of the colonists, as well as by internal tensions. Having been defeated by his uncle Ndlambe (c.1740–1828), Chief Ngqika (c.1775–1829) turned to the British for support. In contrast, Ndlambe supported the prophet–diviner Nxele (c.1790–1820), who adopted some elements of Christian teachings and incorporated them into a theology to resist the colonists, leading his people to war against them. His rival, Ntsikana (c.1760–1820), a famous singer of Xhosa songs, advised Ngqika against war. Ntsikana had been exposed to the teaching of missionaries and had experienced visions (around 1815), which he interpreted as a calling from God. As a result, he adopted Christian beliefs, including the doctrine of salvation through Christ, and implemented Christian practices such as regular meetings for worship and prayer. Unlike the majority of African converts, however, Ntsikana continued to live among his own people and did not take a 'Christian' name. His movement was independent of European missionary control, and he also incorporated Xhosa tradition in his ministry. His 'Great Hymn', for instance, used the structure of a Xhosa praise poem and African imagery to present a biblical message. Here is a paraphrase of part of it:

> It is he, the great God, who is in heaven!
> It is you indeed, our true shield;
> It is you indeed, our true fortress;
> It is you indeed, the true forest where we can take refuge.
> He who created life below also created life above.
> It is that same creator who made the heavens and the stars.

A star flashed forth – it was telling us;
The hunting-horn sounded – it was calling us;
In his hunting he hunts for souls.
It is he who reconciles enemies;
He, the leader who has led us,
He, the garment we put on.
Those hands of yours, they are wounded;
Those feet of yours, they too are wounded;
Your blood, why is it flowing?
Your blood was shed for us.
You paid the great price; and we didn't even ask you.
You made a home for us, before we even knew we wanted it.

(Originally published in John Knox Bokwe, *Ntsikana: The story of an African convert* (Lovedale: Lovedale Press, 1914), p. 31)

Ntsikana attracted many followers among the Xhosa who were drawn to his form of African Christianity. The Xhosa insist that he was converted before he ever met a missionary. He is remembered as a poet and prophet who made many correct predictions, and he is commemorated annually on 10 April as a saint and as a forerunner of African nationalism.

Tragic experience taught the Xhosa that it was impossible to defeat white colonizers by force, and many embraced Western education. Revd Tiyo Soga (1829–71) perhaps symbolized the outlook of a later generation of Christians. Soga was educated by the LMS, and when war disrupted the area, he was taken to Scotland to finish his education. He also received ordination and married the Scot Janet Burnside (1827–1903), before returning to Africa. He spent much of his life at Mgwali, where he built a large church and trained catechists to help him evangelize the area. Like the white missionaries, he found the Mfengu more receptive to the gospel than anyone else. Within ten years he had a congregation of 350, and his wife's sister had joined him and was teaching nearby. The best known of Soga's writings are his translation of *The Pilgrim's Progress* and his many hymns, some of which are still sung. Soga suffered from living in two worlds: he and his wife Janet were never fully accepted by either whites or blacks. But his pioneering achievements in education, literature and the Church blazed a trail for others to follow.

The school where Soga started his education was Lovedale (in South Africa), begun in 1841 by Scottish missionaries. In 1855 industrial training was added, and girls' education a little later. Under Revd Dr James Stewart (1831–1905, principal of the school from 1870 to 1905) there was great expansion. In 1872 there were 300 students; by the time of the school's golden jubilee in 1891 there were 650, and numbers continued to rise. Many eminent South Africans of all races were educated at Lovedale.

In 1857 many of the Xhosa were persuaded that if they destroyed their crops and sacrificed their cattle, the ancestors would rise from the dead and help them drive the whites out of the land. Starvation and terrible suffering followed the cattle-killing. The churches were massively involved in relief work during this catastrophe, and their members reported that after this tragedy people were more willing to listen to their teaching.

Ten years later diamonds were discovered, and then gold. This transformed the economy of South Africa, and more and more blacks left home to become migrant workers. Schools began to be seen as a way into the new society that was developing, but just when blacks were beginning to demand education, ideas about the kind of education suitable for them began to change. African education was redirected so as to enable them to serve their own people and the needs of white-dominated society, rather than as a means of bringing about greater equality.

From the 1840s the American Board Mission started work among the Zulu people, but there was little response. Very few Zulus became Christian, though Zulu kings were eager to take advantage of the services of European missionaries. In 1879 the Zulu were finally defeated by the Afrikaners, and it was at this critical point in their history that the Roman Catholic Mariannhill Mission was founded to work among them. By 1909 the Mariannhill missionaries had some 20 stations. Schoolwork dates from 1884 and the Mariannhill schools offered a high standard of education, both academic and practical. It is worth mentioning, however, that denominational rivalries and the competing claims of Protestant and Roman Catholic missionaries often baffled African rulers and peoples and, on occasion, hindered the establishment of Christianity.

The Tswana and Sotho

The pioneer missionary to the Tswana was Robert Moffat (1795–1883), an LMS missionary who worked in South Africa (at Kuruman) for 50 years. Moffat reduced the Tswana language to writing and translated the whole Bible, printing it on the Kuruman Press. He helped to establish missions to the north, partly through his good relations with chiefs. His daughter married the great Scottish missionary traveller Dr David Livingstone (1813–73), and Moffat helped him on his journeys. Livingstone was a complex figure. Driven by zealousness for missionary expansion, he preached the gospel to more African tribes than any previous missionary but made few Christian converts. Yet his writings transformed European views of Africa and Africans, and were immensely important in publicizing the needs of missions in Africa.

In 1833 Chief Moshweshwe (c.1798–1870) of Lesotho invited the Paris Evangelical Mission to his country, in part because he was looking for European allies. He had just become chief, and faced a difficult task because the Sotho (the people of Lesotho) had suffered greatly as a result of the Zulu wars. Moshweshwe encouraged his people to attend the mission and by 1848 there were 2,000 baptized Christians, 1,000 catechumens, 600 pupils in school and 6 mission stations. However, the missionaries had taught that accepting Christianity brought peace and prosperity, so when peace was disturbed and prosperity threatened by white people who also claimed to be Christians, many Sotho became angry. They said the mission had cheated them, and for a time Christianity suffered a setback.

In 1862 Roman Catholic missionaries reached Lesotho and, as elsewhere, this created new divisions. Catholics called their mission Motsi va Ma-Jesus (Village of the Mother of Jesus), but Protestants nicknamed it 'Roma', and the nickname stuck. Moshweshwe supported the spread of Christianity but, like many African rulers, he found monogamy an obstacle to joining the Church. He desired baptism on his deathbed but died before he could be baptized. Today, Catholic Christians are in a majority in the country.

The Ngwato are a northern branch of the Tswana. In 1860 a chief's son called Khama (1837–1922) was converted to Christianity. In 1875 he succeeded to the chiefdom, and in the interests of unity among his subjects he allowed no mission other than the LMS in his country. He was greatly respected by both blacks and whites. 'Khama was a gift of God to the people,' said Tsogang Sebina, a retired teacher who remembered his reign. 'He was not educated . . . He had only a Tswana education, but he was, in religion and rule, what they call a sage' (quoted in Bessie Head, *Serowe: Village of the rain wind* (London: Heinemann, 1981), p. 23). Both Khama and Moshweshwe resisted domination by Afrikaners and submitted to British annexation. The northern Tswana kingdom became modern Botswana. Both Botswana and Lesotho became independent nations in the 1960s, with largely Christian populations.

Independent churches

Foreign missions in South Africa were particularly slow to give black and coloured people responsibility in the churches, and Christianity remained strongly European in form and expression. Racial inequality, cultural rejection, denial of leadership responsibilities, as well as African instincts for religious innovation, all contributed to the emergence of independent church movements in South Africa and elsewhere. In 1884 Revd Nehemiah Tile (d. 1891), a prominent African leader, left the Methodists to found an independent church, the Tembu National Church, with the chief of the Tembu people as its head. A spate of secession movements followed. One strand emerged as Ethiopianism, an intertribal movement that stressed African identity and self-determination based on key biblical texts such as Psalm 68.31 (AV) which declares that 'Ethiopia [black Africa] shall soon stretch out her hands unto God'. Another strand emerged as Zionism, mainly centred among the Zulus, which emphasized an earthly Zion or 'Holy City', and espoused faith healing and Pentecostal practices within an African framework.

These new African churches rejected white missionary control and strove for a form of Christianity that consciously introduced or emphasized African cultural elements. Their emergence reflected deeply rooted dissatisfaction with Western missionary Christianity. Such movements appeared in many parts of Africa – indeed the earliest appeared in Sierra Leone in the late 1860s – and expanded rapidly in the early twentieth century.

By the end of the nineteenth century the thrust of the missions based in the Cape had taken them as far north as the present countries of Zambia and Zimbabwe, in both of which work had just begun. In the east and west, Roman Catholic missions had come to life again in the Portuguese territories of Mozambique and Angola, and Protestant work had just begun in these countries. German Lutherans were at work in what is now Namibia, Scottish missions in Malawi and the Baptists in Congo.

East Africa

Freed slaves on the east coast

By the middle of the nineteenth century the east coast slave-trade had reached huge proportions. Slave-traders coming down the Nile from Egypt and those working their way inland from Zanzibar had almost linked up. A little further south, Arab traders had made their way as far inland as Lake Tanganyika. They made alliances with militarily stronger peoples such as the Ngoni and Nyamwezi of Tanzania, encouraged them to raid their neighbours and organized slave caravans to the coast.

Dr David Livingstone, who travelled widely in southern and central Africa, drew the attention of Europe to the extent of the slave-trade, and to its cruelties. He was a strong advocate of the view that it could only be stopped if legitimate trade was introduced as an alternative. His writings caught the attention of missions and attracted them to the area; and the British tried to make Barghash bin Said (1837–88), the Sultan of Zanzibar, declare the trade illegal. The sultan was unwilling to do so because the economy of Zanzibar depended on slave labour. However, by 1873 he was forced to outlaw the trade, although, as in West Africa, it continued illegally for some time.

Before 1873 freed slaves on the east coast were resettled in India because of the risk that they would be recaptured if allowed to return to their homes in Africa. They lived in 'Christian' settlements similar to those in Sierra Leone, and were educated in the hope that one day they would return to Africa as evangelists. After 1874 some of these 'Bombay Africans' returned to work among other freed slaves near Mombasa, where the CMS had opened two settlements with up to 2,000 inhabitants at most. As elsewhere, such settlements provided security for the new converts, but they also reflected the belief that Christianity was incompatible with African traditions. Only African Christians could disprove this. William Jones (*c.*1840–1904) and Ishmael Semler (*c.*1840–*c.*1930), who had been brought up in India, and David George (d. 1884), a local catechist, became the leading African Christians on the Kenya coast, and worked as evangelists and teachers. Within a few years a mature church developed near Mombasa, and its leaders persuaded the people of the Taita Hills to accept evangelists – the missions had been unable to win their confidence. It seemed as though an independent pastorate might come into being on the lines of the one in Freetown, with Jones as a prospective bishop.

But in the 1880s a new breed of European missionaries attacked the work of the African Christians in much the same way that Bishop Crowther's work in West Africa had been attacked. European racism and paternalism caused much bitterness; but the experienced missionary William Price (1826–1911), sent to investigate, praised the work of the African leaders and advised that several of them should be ordained. When James Hannington (1847–85) arrived in 1885 as the first bishop of the newly formed Diocese of Eastern Equatorial Africa (comprising Uganda, Kenya and Tanganyika), he ordained William Jones and Ishmael Semler, but David George had died the previous year.

Roman Catholic missions were also at work in East Africa. The Holy Ghost Fathers started in Zanzibar, moved to the mainland in 1868, and founded Christian villages where freed slaves were trained as artisans and catechists. An attempt to train priests and sisters in the 1870s was not successful. The mission hoped that the orderly and prosperous life of the villages would attract others and make converts. By 1886 six settlements had been founded, but they did not attract the surrounding villagers, except in times of danger or hunger, when people turned to them for help. Perhaps they were run too much like monasteries to be suitable for lay people. The greatest success of the Holy Ghost Fathers in the nineteenth century was to train catechists, who went and established schools in the interior among non-Muslims who were more open to the gospel.

Anglican missionaries of the Universities' Mission to Central Africa (UMCA) also helped freed slaves whom they hoped would evangelize the interior. They too began work in Muslim Zanzibar, but in 1875 and 1876 they moved to the mainland and set up missions at Masasi and Mbweni. A few years later, in 1882, Masasi was attacked by the Ngoni in a raid for slaves, and many people were carried off. Charles Sulimani (1859–99), a freed-slave catechist, helped to get some released, but others were never seen again. The mission withdrew for safety, but Sulimani stayed on working as a catechist.

In spite of some success, freed slaves in East Africa did not take Christianity as far or as widely as freed slaves had done in West Africa. The coastal people of East Africa were mainly Muslims and so were hostile to Christianity. The economy depended on slaves, and the missions' campaign for their emancipation only increased Muslim hostility to Christianity. Work was therefore very slow. Unlike in the west, the freed slaves did not make their way back to their original homes as traders. So the plans made by the missions did not fully work out. Instead, as many became Christians, they were employed by the missions as catechists, and when work began further inland, they began to meet with more success.

The move inland to Uganda

It was in Uganda, however, that the East African missions met with their most spectacular success. Islam, brought by Muslim traders from the coast, had penetrated the Buganda kingdom in the mid nineteenth century and won converts from among the ruling class. But in the mid 1870s it was reported that Mutesa (1837–84), the *kabaka* (king of Buganda), wanted Christian missionaries. The king's desire was politically motivated. His country was threatened by Egypt, whose traders were advancing down the Nile in search of ivory and slaves and were approaching his northern borders. European influence and technology, not religion, was his main interest. Anglican missionaries of the CMS arrived in 1877 in response to his appeals, and Roman Catholic White Fathers two years later.

Mutesa was disappointed when he found that the missions were not willing to supply him with firearms, and the missions were equally disappointed to find that he was more interested in guns than in the gospel. Meanwhile, the Baganda (the people of Buganda) were now confronted with four commonly antagonistic religious systems: Protestant and Catholic Christianity, Islam and African religion. The years that followed were marked by incessant religious debates at the royal court. Christianity eventually gained the upper hand, both because of its associations with technology and literacy, which were understood as symbols of power and so prized within indigenous thought, and because it introduced new religious ideas that converts found compelling, for example the end times. It can also be argued that Islam paved the way for Christianity by introducing the concepts of monotheism, a holy day and a sacred book, and generating strong interest in literacy. Many Baganda found Christianity attractive and a number of the most intelligent young men from the court attached themselves to the missions. Until the White Fathers abruptly withdrew from Buganda in 1882 Catholic missionaries enjoyed greater influence at the royal court than Protestants.

Mutesa's successor was a young man called Mwanga (1868–1903), who came to the throne in 1884. Two years later he unleashed brutal persecution of both Protestant and Catholic Christians. The immediate reason was the refusal of some of his pages to participate in homosexual practices. But, like his father, Mwanga was also threatened by the realization that his Christian subjects had primary loyalty to church authorities in distant Europe. Meanwhile, powerful factions at his court, including strong supporters of traditional religion and Muslims, joined forces to oppose Christians as a political danger. The greatest slaughter took place on 3 June 1886, when 31 young men and boys were burned alive at Namugongo. The victims also included a number of minor chiefs. The youngest martyr, Kizito, was 14 years old. As many as 200 may have died altogether. No foreign missionary was killed.

The leader of those who died at Namugongo was Charles Lwanga (*c.*1860–86), a palace official who had become a Roman Catholic and who baptized several of the martyrs the night before they were led away to execution. He died alone before the others. One of the leading Protestants was Robert Munyagabyanjo (?1836–86). He encouraged the others in words which the Ugandan historian James Miti has recorded thus:

> I appeal to all of you gathered here to have firm minds. Never fear those who kill the body but cannot kill the spirit. We sympathize with those of you who are going to remain in this world of extreme hazards. We are happy because in a short time we shall be in this place which Jesus Christ has prepared for us, not by ourselves, but with all those who love him and happily await his coming. You who have seen us, go and tell our brothers that we have broken Satan's chains, and that we shall soon be with our Saviour.
>
> (Cited in Louise Pirouet, *Strong in the Faith* (Mukono: Church of Uganda Literature Centre, 1969), pp. 45–6)

In 1964 the Roman Catholic martyrs were recognized as saints by their church, and the first visit ever made by a pope to Africa was by Pope Paul VI in 1969 to do honour to the 'Uganda Martyrs'. Protestants and Roman Catholics joined together for part of these celebrations in much the same way that the martyrs from both groups had been connected 80 years before in suffering and martyrdom. St Charles Lwanga and his companions are commemorated on 3 June each year.

Only four years after these martyrdoms, a revolution took place in Uganda. Christian leaders seized power after both they and the Muslims had been further threatened by Mwanga. After that, anyone who wanted to be successful in Buganda had to be literate, and that meant being a Christian. It is sad that in the political strife of the 1890s bitter rivalry grew up between Catholics and Protestants, and Muslims were pushed into third place and acquired genuine grievances which were to have serious results later.

The new Christian leaders in Buganda encouraged evangelism and made themselves responsible for building churches and providing land for catechists. Political and religious motives were often mixed with their passion for evangelism. They used the churches to strengthen their own positions, and even to spread the influence of Buganda into other areas of Uganda, but many also had a deep personal commitment to Christianity. They set the pace in the evangelism of Uganda, and the white missionaries found it difficult to keep up with all the demands made on them.

One of the best-known Ugandan Anglican missionaries was Revd Apolo Kivebulaya (1864–1933). Baptized in 1894, he went as an evangelist to western Uganda the following year, and then on to the Congo (now the Democratic Republic of the Congo). There he worked among the Batwa of the Ituri Forest and translated part of St Mark's Gospel into their language. He was loved by all who knew him, and radiated happiness. He received only a tiny salary and gave away most of what he possessed. He died in 1933 and his saintly life has been an inspiration to many. Yohana Kitagana (1858–1938) was a Roman Catholic missionary catechist who was contemporary with Kivebulaya. He too worked in western Uganda, and then went south to the border with Rwanda. Like Kivebulaya he was a pioneer in places where no white missionary had been. Kitagana is remembered for his zeal and devotion, and for caring for widows and orphans. He was decorated by the British for his services to the people of Uganda.

Stanislaus Mugwanya (1849–1938) was one of the greatest of the Christian chiefs, and he represents another aspect of the Christian impact on Uganda. He was baptized as a Roman Catholic in the year of the martyrdoms and became one of the most powerful men in Uganda. He was a leading supporter of Catholic schools, and he paid the fees of many poor pupils. He also initiated the growing of cotton and coffee. In 1914 he travelled extensively in Europe, as well as visiting the Holy Land and the headquarters of the White Fathers Mission, which was then in Algiers. Like many Ugandans he was a writer, and he published a book describing his travels. He was honoured by both the British government and the Roman Catholic Church.

The impact of Christianity in Uganda was often divisive and its spread contributed to messy political developments that culminated with British colonization of Uganda. But, by 1900, Christianity was in the ascendancy, associated with the structures of political power, and destined to take firm root under the influence of Christian chiefs and indigenous evangelists.

 ## Conclusion

In all, there were three main lines of Christian advance in Africa in the nineteenth century: from Sierra Leone in the west; from the Cape in southern Africa; and from the East African coast. In most of the countries of modern Africa the Church had been founded by the end of the century, though in several only a very small beginning had been made, and many of the peoples of Africa had not been reached at all. Only a tiny part of the population was Christian, even where Christianity had been present longest. No one could possibly have guessed at the transformation which was to take place in the next century. But already, by the end of the nineteenth century, hundreds of Africans were dedicated to spreading their new faith. These included the Sierra Leoneans who evangelized the Niger Delta under the leadership of Bishop Crowther, the rising class of African clergy (some highly educated), catechists, schoolteachers, prophet-healers and ordinary believers (such as the chiefs of Uganda).

Admittedly, European colonialism was part of the story, and many aspects of African church life reflected European forms. But Christianity in Africa was already experiencing those transformations that would reshape it into an African religion. As we shall see in the next chapter, the future of African Christianity lay less with European designs and initiatives, missionary or otherwise, than many imagined in 1900.

? DISCUSSION QUESTIONS

1 In what way has the history of the Church in Ethiopia been different from its history in all other countries of Africa?

2 Give a brief description of the events which explain why Freetown in Sierra Leone came to be founded and why it was given that name.

3 Henry Venn believed the task of missions was to establish local churches which could run and support themselves, and then to move on quickly to evangelize new areas. Others believed that new churches needed continuing missionary control, coupled with the training of indigenous catechists and teachers to carry on the evangelizing. What is your opinion? How far do you think the choice of such policies should depend on local circumstances?

4 How did the following affect Christian missionary work:

   (a) the spread of Islam south and west from the Sahara;

   (b) the establishment by European powers of colonial governors to protect their trading interests in Africa;

   (c) the recruitment by Protestant missions in Britain and Europe of people influenced by Evangelical revival and the Keswick movement?

5 Approximately when, and why, did Dutch colonists (Afrikaners) first come to settle in South Africa?

6 (a) Which were the first missionary societies to work systematically in the Cape, and what form did their work take?

   (b) What was the relationship between these missions and the Afrikaners?

7 What was the effect on people's lives, and on the work of missions, of each of the following events in South Africa during the nineteenth century:

   (a) the Zulu wars of expansion;

   (b) the discovery of diamonds and gold?

8 What were the chief reasons for the founding of independent churches in South Africa? Why did some of them include the word 'Ethiopian' in their titles?

9 Give a brief account, with dates, denomination and sending countries, of the early work in East Africa of each of the following:

   (a) the Holy Ghost Fathers;

   (b) the Universities' Mission to Central Africa.

(c) For what chief reason was their work on the east coast of Africa less successful at first than it was later on?

10 In what ways did the early development of the Church in East Africa in the second half of the nineteenth century resemble that of the Church in Sierra Leone and neighbouring West African countries in the first half of the century?

Further reading

Baur, John. *Two Thousand Years of Christianity in Africa: An African history*. Nairobi: Paulines Publications Africa, 1994.

Isichei, Elizabeth. *A History of Christianity in Africa: From antiquity to the present*. London: SPCK, 1995.

Kalu, Ogbu (ed.). *African Christianity: An African story*. Trenton, NJ: Africa World Press, 2007.

Sanneh, Lamin. *West African Christianity: The religious impact*. New York, NY: Orbis, 1983.

Shaw, Mark. *The Kingdom of God in Africa: A short history of African Christianity*. Grand Rapids, MI: Baker, 1996.

3

Africa in the twentieth century

Louise Pirouet and Jehu J. Hanciles

In 1900 there were an estimated ten million Christians on the African continent, roughly 9 per cent of the African population. This included around four million Christians in Egypt and Ethiopia. Taken as a whole, African Christianity was fragile. In much of the continent, there was no identifiable Christian presence and, with the exception of Ethiopia, Christian communities existed as minority groups. In sharp contrast Islam, though largely confined to the northern (and eastern) regions, was a thriving faith. All in all, Muslims outnumbered Christians six to one. Many European observers were convinced that Africa was destined to become a Muslim continent. Foreign missionary societies depicted Africa as a continent where millions of souls were trapped in 'degraded paganism' and increasingly prey to energetic Muslim evangelists.

This assessment ignored African Christian initiatives or movements. Only a few decades earlier, leading missionary thinkers such as Henry Venn of the Church Missionary Society (CMS) had implemented policies intended to replace European control with increasing African leadership and ownership. By 1900 that vision had evaporated, replaced by the unshakeable belief within European mission agencies that the fate of Christianity in Africa rested squarely on the resources and designs of European powers and foreign agents. The shortsightedness of this understanding only became obvious much later.

In the opening decades of the twentieth century, European projects seemed to carry the day. Colonialism was at its height, and with it came economic reorientation, the building of new infrastructure and a greater penetration of African societies than ever before. The new situation greatly bolstered the European missionary effort. Colonial administration facilitated missions because it provided improved security and stimulated an increasing demand for literacy. New medical breakthroughs – in the treatment of common diseases such as malaria and yellow fever, for instance – and major technological advancements also allowed foreign missionaries to serve in greater numbers and travel between Europe and Africa with greater ease. Mission stations multiplied, mission-run hospitals and clinics expanded, and the demand for mission-run schools grew tremendously. Most importantly, the number of European missionaries on the continent increased in unprecedented fashion.

Between 1890 and 1925 the total Protestant foreign missionary force in Africa grew by 81 per cent, from roughly 1,171 to 6,289. Half of these came from Britain and the majority were still drawn from the Evangelical tradition. The much smaller Roman Catholic missionary contingent also increased significantly. By 1920 there were 1,950 foreign Catholic priests, 800 brothers and 4,000 sisters on the continent. From the turn of the century, single women missionaries constituted a rapidly growing number of the foreign missionary force, and their work among the female population greatly expanded the reach of missions. The members of this new generation of foreign missionaries were generally more educated than their predecessors; but, with few exceptions, they were more critical and intolerant of African beliefs and values. In any case, the increased number of foreign agents meant that missionary control of churches and Christian institutions became even more entrenched.

The remarkable dedication and sacrificial service of countless European missionaries is an important part of the story of African Christianity. But the widespread tendency to elevate the influence and impact of foreign missionaries over that of African agents and initiatives greatly distorts the narrative. There were rare instances, of course, when active collaboration between indigenous Christian leaders and European missionary agents ignited a major movement. But the establishment of Christianity in Africa is much more an African story than is generally recognized.

For one thing, the majority of Africans had only minimal exposure to a white missionary. The dramatic growth in the numbers of European missionaries in the first three decades of the twentieth century was accompanied by even more remarkable increases in the number of African agents associated with Protestant missions. The number of African agents rose from 22,279 (compared to 3,335 foreign agents) in 1903 to 43,181 (compared to 6,289 foreign agents) in 1925. The average ratio was six to one. Throughout the subcontinent, it was African Christians serving as priests (there were over 2,000 ordained African priests in 1925), catechists, schoolteachers and interpreters, or dispersed as traders and labour migrants, who formed the forefront of Christian expansion. Their stories overlapped with that of the more conspicuous prophet-healing movements that reshaped the African Christian landscape. Some estimate that as much as 90 per cent of all conversions in Africa up to 1960 resulted from such diverse indigenous efforts. To put it simply, most Africans have heard the gospel from other Africans. Furthermore, significantly, African Christianity experienced its most significant growth from the 1970s, after the European missionary movement had waned.

✳ Ethiopia

In 1900 the Church in Ethiopia was more than 1,500 years old, with a strong theological tradition and deep roots in the African soil. But it was in great need of reform. It was historically dependent on the Coptic Church for consecration of bishops; church and state were welded together; priests were largely illiterate and poorly trained; religious texts and liturgy were composed in Ge'ez, a dead language with an ancient script; and, although Ethiopians were deeply religious, Mass was poorly attended. Steps towards reform began in the late nineteenth century under emperors Yohannes IV (r. 1872–89) and Menelik II (r. 1889–1913): the organization of the church was strengthened, missionary activities (including outreach to Muslim areas) were encouraged and many new churches were built. In 1881 four bishops were consecrated by the Patriarch of Alexandria, the first time in over 400 years that Ethiopia had more than one bishop. But, since all were Egyptians, the church remained under foreign control. Indeed, the four bishops were not replaced when they died.

In 1929 a new *abuna* (bishop) was consecrated, and the Patriarch agreed to consecrate five Ethiopians to serve under him. For the first time dioceses were demarcated, and a bishop was placed in charge of each. This was a first step towards better church administration. It also deepened the desire among Ethiopians for an end to foreign control of the church.

Further reforms in church and state were disrupted in 1935 when the Italians invaded the country (the first such attempt in the 1890s had ended in their defeat) and annexed it as a colony. There was strong resistance, and the Italians had great difficulty in imposing their rule on the church. Bishops Mikael (d. 1936) and Petros (1892–1936) were executed for their opposition, and many monks and clergy were massacred on suspicion of resistance. Abuna Qerillos VI (c.1880–1950) refused to cooperate with the Italians and returned to Egypt. The aged Bishop Abraham was made *abuna* in his place, and the Italians forced him to declare the Ethiopian Church independent of Egypt. He and those who cooperated with him were ex-communicated by the Patriarch of Alexandria because of this. Ordinary Ethiopians were divided, but many welcomed greater independence from Egypt. Abuna Abraham (*fl.* 1937–9) and his successor Yohannes XV (*fl.* 1939–45) were able to consecrate several Ethiopian bishops and ordain some 2,000 priests. The Italians also tried to win the support of the Muslims – who were almost as numerous as the Christians but had little power or influence – by granting them favours and opportunities which they had not possessed before.

Ethiopia was liberated in 1941 with British help. The following year, Abuna Qerillos returned and was reinstated, and all Ethiopian Christians were restored to the fellowship of the Coptic Church. But the clock could not be put back, and the Ethiopian church leaders insisted that greater independence from Egypt was needed. After years of debate an agreement was reached in 1948 and five Ethiopian monks were consecrated as bishops in Egypt. It was also agreed that the next *abuna* would be an Ethiopian with power to consecrate bishops, thus ending dependence on the Patriarch of Alexandria. In 1959, under Emperor Haile Selassie (r. 1930–74), Archbishop

Basilios (1891–1970) was consecrated *abuna*, the first time an Ethiopian had occupied this office in 1,600 years.

Better education for the clergy was also introduced, with help from trained Egyptians. A theological college was started in Addis Ababa in 1962 and later became the theological faculty of the university. Priests now received a general as well as a theological education. The church's finances were put on a better footing, and Amharic (the language of the dominant Christian ethnic group) began to be used in worship along with the ancient liturgical language, Ge'ez. The Bible was translated into Amharic and other vernaculars, which helped to increase people's understanding of the Scriptures.

Foreign missionary societies were permitted to work in Ethiopia, but only under strict controls. In the Christian areas of the country they were allowed to do medical and educational work, but they were not supposed to convert people away from the national church. The missions had considerable success among the followers of the indigenous religions, such as the Oromo people of the south-west where Lutherans were at work. The Mekane Yesus Church which they founded there had about half a million members by 2000.

✳ New missions and more missionaries

The revival of Roman Catholic missions in Africa had already begun in the later part of the nineteenth century. Roman Catholic missionaries soon began to equal Protestants in number, and then to overtake them. Many new missions were set up specifically to work in Africa, such as the Society of African Missions, begun in 1856 to work in West Africa. Ten years later Italian missionaries, who had tried for years to establish missions along the Nile Valley, were reorganized as the 'Verona Fathers', and worked in Sudan and Uganda. The first White Fathers had arrived in Africa in 1869, working in North, East and Central Africa. The Italian Consolata Mission arrived in Kenya in 1900. Each of these societies had a related congregation of missionary sisters. Propaganda Fide, the department of the Vatican responsible for missions, directed the societies to different areas so that there should be no overlapping.

New Protestant missions were also specially founded to work in Africa. Among these were the South Africa General Mission (1889), the Africa Inland Mission (1895), and the Sudan United Mission (1902) which worked throughout the Sahel, the region just south of the Sahara Desert. All were interdenominational, and their purpose was to evangelize individuals rather than to plant denominational churches or become involved in 'secular activities' such as running schools or hospitals. They were often deeply suspicious of the older denominational missions, based on a perception that their missionaries were not properly converted. Before long, however, the newer missions realized that they could not avoid establishing churches, and that if they did not provide schools and hospitals, their converts would go off to other missions which did.

Protestant church development was less orderly than that of the Roman Catholic Church because there was no overall authority to direct the Protestant missionary effort. Missionaries often competed with one another, though in some places they entered into what were known as 'comity' agreements among themselves, committing to work in separate areas; in other places, governments forced such agreements upon them. Roman Catholics rarely entered voluntarily into such agreements with Protestants, but occasionally they were imposed, as in the Sudan. Since there were never enough missions and missionaries to work everywhere on the continent, it was often a matter of geographical accident rather than choice that determined which church African Christians belonged to.

Countless Africans responded to the message of salvation, but many struggled with the missionaries' insistence that they reject the old ways and customs. Furthermore, Christian missions were all too strongly tied to the colonial structure. In terms of land grabs, foreign missionaries seemed little different from other white (or colonial) settlers. Catholic monasteries in Africa, for instance, were often 20 to 40 times the size of those in Europe. But if Christian mission embodied the structural inequalities of the period, it also exemplified the processes of modernization and globalization that marked the new order.

Schools

It is impossible to overemphasize the importance of the educational and medical work of the Christian missions in Africa for the growth of the Church. The school, in particular, was the chief instrument of mission. In Freetown, Sierra Leone, and elsewhere on the West African coast where people had been in contact with European traders for a long time, education was in demand from the early 1800s. Nearly everywhere else people initially resisted education because they could see no point in it, and because they thought (quite correctly) that it would disrupt their society. However, when they saw that change could not be resisted, they demanded education because schools offered a way into the new society that was emerging. With a little education a person might become a clerk in government service, a teacher or nurse, or find his or her way into other paid employment.

The missionaries looked at education from a different point of view. For Protestants, the basic reason for providing schools was so that people could learn to read the Bible. But education could not stop there. Through the schools they also hoped to train Christians who would become the leaders of their society as well as pastors and teachers. Roman Catholics, like Protestants, wanted to train Christian leaders, but they also needed to train indigenous priests. Since all Catholic priests, whether African or European, had to have the same level and kind of training, this meant establishing seminaries and a network of schools which would provide candidates for them. The seminaries in fact fulfilled a dual role. Some students who entered them were eventually ordained, but the majority were not. Their education was not wasted, since it enabled them to take their place among the lay Christian leaders of their communities.

The missions found it difficult to meet all the requests they received for teachers and schools. Sometimes Africans benefited from the rivalry between missions and played one off against another in order to get the education they wanted. A striking example of this was in Eastern Nigeria, where the Igbo were willing to convert to whichever branch of Christianity would provide them with schools. Most Igbo became Roman Catholics because Father (later Bishop) Joseph Shanahan (1871–1943) and the Holy Ghost Fathers succeeded in establishing the most schools.

Most of the schools which the missions managed were small village primary schools where reading, religion, and perhaps writing and a little arithmetic were taught. In the early years the teacher was usually an African catechist; and when in the 1920s the roles of catechists and teachers were separated, the catechists continued to teach reading and writing to those who wished to be baptized. The primary school buildings were usually of mud and wattle with a thatched roof, and were put up by the local people. Equipment and furniture were almost non-existent, and children and adults sometimes studied together. Central schools at mission stations offered a more extensive education for the most able pupils from the village schools, and taught geography and history (of Europe, not Africa!), a European language, arithmetic, and perhaps woodwork and some agriculture. Religion was at the centre of the syllabus.

There was much discussion about the sort of education that should be given, in particular whether education should be mainly literary or mainly practical. For a time some students at Livingstonia in Nyasaland (now Malawi) took an advanced Arts course which included philosophy and ancient and modern European languages and literature. The teacher was a gifted enthusiast, and some of the students found the course greatly stimulating. But for the most part, Livingstonia concentrated on training people in practical trades, which enabled them to find work with European employers, mostly in South Africa. It is not clear that this sort of practical training contributed anything to the development of Nyasaland as it was intended to do.

In the 1920s surveys were made of both Protestant and Roman Catholic schools. The Phelps-Stokes Commission of 1924 reported on Protestant schools and praised them for their work, while also offering searching criticisms. It called on governments to give more assistance to education so that better standards could be reached, particularly in the village primary schools, which were often substandard. The Commission thought that the schools were too 'bookish' and recommended that much more attention should be paid to training in agriculture. The missions welcomed the report, and the governments increased their grants, but the schools were not successful in promoting agriculture. People came to school to escape from agriculture, not to return to it.

In 1927 Monsignor (later Cardinal) Arthur Hinsley (1865–1943) was also sent from Rome to tour the Roman Catholic mission schools. He too urged cooperation with government and told the missions to accept all the government help they could get. The missions were gaining most of their converts from among those being educated in their schools, so Hinsley's advice to the missions was, 'Where it is impossible for you to carry on both the immediate task of evangelization and your educational work, neglect your churches in order to perfect your schools' (Roland Oliver, *The Missionary Factor in East Africa* (London: Longmans, Green, 1952), p. 275). The schools were proving to be the main evangelistic agencies. All the missions agreed that teachers needed to be better trained, and training colleges were opened.

Girls' education generally lagged far behind that of boys, and girls-only schools were lacking. The Annie Walsh Memorial School in Sierra Leone, started by the CMS in 1849, was an early exception. It provided secondary education for girls almost a century before any other school in Africa. St Monica's Girls' School at Onitsha in Eastern Nigeria had its roots in a school started in 1895 by Edith Warner (1867–1925) of CMS. Like most girls' schools before the 1940s, it concentrated on homecraft and childcare. At Mbereshi in Northern Rhodesia (now Zambia) a remarkable LMS missionary, Mabel Shaw (1889–1973), ran a girls' school and worked to help Lunda women and girls in the 1920s and 1930s. She had a most unusual appreciation of African cultural values, which she deeply respected. In a book called *God's Candlelights* (1942), she gives a sympathetic account of aspects of Lunda culture and tells of her efforts to express Christianity in Lunda terms in school.

The 1940s saw the beginnings of secondary education for girls in most parts of Africa. Mother Kevin (1875–1957) of the Franciscan Missionary Sisters founded Mount St Mary's School in Uganda in 1940 as a full secondary school. Among its former pupils was the first African woman in East Africa to gain a science degree (also the first woman doctor in East Africa), Dr Josephine Namboze (b. 1934).

Hospitals

The missions pioneered medicine throughout Africa. Most missionaries thought of hospitals as opportunities for evangelism; and, in truth, disease epidemics invariably produced a flood of conversions. But few foreign missionaries recognized or valued the religious dimensions of healing that marked the African understanding. Most derided traditional medicine and its rituals, unable to see positive aspects. Africans were quick to take advantage of Western medicine, but they seldom gave up traditional medicine entirely. African attitudes to sickness and health were part of their whole philosophy of life, part of a world view that perceived all of reality as spiritual and thus was strongly preoccupied with the powers behind the visible order. Africans appreciated the effective medical treatment and the good nursing care available in mission hospitals, and many patients were converted, but the emphasis on spiritual power meant that Western scientific explanations or solutions were not always satisfactory.

The best-known mission hospital in Africa was probably Lambarenc in Gabon, run by the brilliant German theologian, musician and doctor Albert Schweitzer (1875–1965). At the age of 30, Schweitzer decided to study medicine in order to become a medical missionary to Africa. The hospitals which made the greatest contribution to African development were those that pioneered the training of nurses and medical orderlies. Kikuyu Hospital in Kenya started training Africans in 1911, and when the First World War broke out in 1914 it was the one hospital in East Africa able to provide trained African medical personnel for the forces. Roman Catholic training of nurses was somewhat hampered until 1936 by a rule which prohibited nuns from practising midwifery. One of the first Roman Catholic lay missionaries was Dr Evelyn Connolly (1892–1974), who started training nurses in Uganda in 1921 because the nuns were not able to do so. When the ban was lifted in 1936 a new era began for Roman Catholic hospitals. With the help of specialist societies such as the Medical Missionaries of Mary, founded in 1937, they soon caught up with the Protestants. In medicine, as in education, the missions were able to meet a felt need, and hence were successful.

Training church leaders

Some missions began to train African clergy very early. We have already seen examples of that in Freetown (Sierra Leone) and Lovedale (South Africa). Even then, European domination remained entrenched. For the most part, Protestant missions were slow to train African clergy and did not attempt to provide the same sort of training that European missionaries had received. Some European missionaries argued that it was sufficient for aspiring clergymen to be filled with the Spirit; others insisted that too much education 'spoiled' Africans (that is, made them overly ambitious, even arrogant); and still others doubted that Africans had the ability to cope with advanced training. These same arguments explicitly justified foreign missionary control, since it was too risky to hand over administration to undereducated men. This was a source of great frustration for African agents. Roman Catholic policy, on the other hand, was to give African priests just the same kind of training that priests anywhere in the world were given, even though this meant learning Latin and spending 20 years in the seminary. The Protestants were able to ordain far more Africans than the Roman Catholics, but African Catholic priests were the intellectual equals of missionary priests in a way that African Protestant clergy were not.

The first African Roman Catholics were ordained in Uganda in 1913. Fathers Brazilio Lumu (1875–1946) and Victoro Mukasa (1882–1979) had entered the seminary just outside Masaka in 1893, the year of its foundation by Bishop Streicher (1863–1952), who had gone ahead with plans for an indigenous clergy in spite of the doubts of some of the other White Father missionaries. In 1939 the Masaka District of Uganda was placed under an African bishop, Monsignor Joseph Kiwanuka (1899–1966), the first Roman Catholic to be consecrated. He had a staff of 33 priests, 43 brothers and 262 sisters, all of whom were Africans. But it was a long time before any other area was treated in the same way. By 1950 some long-established African dioceses still remained without any indigenous priests at all, and for a long time Monsignor Kiwanuka remained the only African Catholic bishop.

The Roman Catholic Church had far more African sisters than priests, and again Uganda was in the lead, having the oldest congregation of African sisters, the Bannabikira (Daughters of the Virgin). This sisterhood was founded in response to repeated requests from African women and girls. The first Bannabikira made their preliminary vows in 1910, and in 1924 Mother Cecilia Nalube (profession 1912) became the first African superior general of her congregation. The blue-clad sisters soon became a familiar sight in Masaka District, and the success of this congregation led to the foundation of others. In West Africa, the Little Sisters of the Poor was founded in Eastern Nigeria in 1913, and the 1920s and 1930s saw the founding of many other congregations, often at the request of a bishop who realized how much African sisters could offer to the life of the Catholic Church.

One group of church leaders, the catechists, received less and less training during the period from 1900 to 1950, yet it was they who kept the Church in existence in the villages of a continent that was still very largely rural. African catechists taught the rudiments of literacy and religion, they visited the sick, they led daily prayers in the village churches, and on Sundays they either led worship themselves or escorted their congregations to worship at the central mission church. They often made no conscious attempt to indigenize, but the whole atmosphere of the prayers and worship which they led was unmistakably African, even where they used a set liturgy. Furthermore, an unnoticed process of adaptation went on in their preaching and teaching. Village congregations were lucky to receive one visit a year from an ordained clergyman; some were never visited by a white missionary at all. To missionary eyes, village Christianity seemed uninspiring, and there were large areas of African life and thought which remained untouched by Christianity, but often the catechist and his church blended into the rural background in a way that was far from alien.

Some catechists were more aggressive in enforcing norms dictated by Western missionaries. They had themselves made a clean break with much of the traditional way of life and they demanded that their congregations should do the same. In *The River Between*, Kenyan novelist Ngugi wa Thiong'o (b. 1938) described such a catechist in the person of Joshua, a man whose uncompromising attitudes did more harm than good. African catechists and Protestant pastors who had little education themselves often went to great lengths to secure a good education for their children, and many leading Africans of the next generation were the children of such men. President Kenneth Kaunda (1924–2021) of Zambia, son of a Presbyterian minister, comes immediately to mind.

✳ African renewal movements

The developments in education and medicine, and the beginnings of African sisterhoods, were responses by missions to African demands. But the pattern and framework of all these activities were provided by the missions and based on European models and assumptions. Almost from the start, however, African Christians themselves wrestled with the claims of the gospel and sought to apply their new faith to African questions and concerns. This effort was evident not only in the work of catechists, who consciously or unconsciously indigenized Western norms and practices, but also in the emergence of nineteenth-century movements such as Ethiopianism and Zionism, which challenged European control and established separate 'African' churches.

In the opening years of the twentieth century, prophet-healing and Charismatic movements, led by dynamic African leaders, became more widespread. Insofar as these movements rejected or challenged existing forms of Christianity and the structures of control associated with them, they can be seen as protest movements. But they are best understood as renewal movements, marked by religious innovation and radical reform in which great emphasis on spiritual power was the centrepiece. Most called people to repentance and holy living and proclaimed the supremacy of the Christian God. All aimed at bridging the gap between mission-established Christianity and the African religious world.

The nature and impact of these movements varied from one context to another depending on the form of colonial rule, the extent of vernacular translation, the size of the European population, the duration of the European missionary presence, the proportion of educated African Christians and the extent of white domination in church and society. But everywhere, the breakdown of communal life (worsened by social catastrophes such as famine or disease epidemics) and vernacular translation of Scripture were important factors in their emergence.

Traditional African life revolves around the extended family; difficulties are shared and decisions are taken by the community. If Africans were to feel at home in the Church, they needed to experience something of the closeness of the extended family within the Christian family, and too often this did not happen. During the worldwide influenza epidemic of 1918, Nigerian Christians felt keenly the need for prayer and fellowship to see them through this time of trouble, and people who felt the need most were the poor and illiterate who did not count for much in the mission-founded churches. They began to pray in small groups, meeting together out of doors near their own homes. In these groups everyone felt free to take part, and they shared the burdens of life. At first the prayer groups were additional to church worship, but as more and more people joined them who had no previous connection with the churches, the groups tended to become churches. These independent Aladura (meaning 'praying') churches spread throughout West Africa.

A similar need for fellowship arose in South Africa. There it became the custom for the churches to hold women's fellowship meetings on Thursday afternoons, and these 'manyanos', as they were called, met the same needs for South African women as the Aladura churches for people in West Africa, through the same means of praying and sharing one another's burdens. For women in South Africa the problems were particularly acute, since racial discrimination and economic repression were destroying family life. The East African Revival, which started in the Anglican Church in Rwanda and Uganda in the 1920s and 1930s (in the wake of a great famine), shared many of the same characteristics. Revival produced a close-knit fellowship of those who confessed their sins and could testify to being 'born again', and it reached across tribal and natural boundaries, as did the Aladura churches. It quickly spread to other churches throughout the region in Burundi, Kenya, Uganda, Congo and Tanzania. Most of the members remained in their churches, often forming a self-righteous elite who became known as Balokole ('the saved ones'). The Revival demanded high ethical standards, encouraged evangelism and brought new life to congregations which had lost their first zeal. In its close fellowship, people who felt adrift in a rapidly changing world could find reassurance and a strong community spirit such as had characterized the extended family.

From the start, Protestant missions in Africa embarked on extensive efforts at translating the Bible into vernacular languages. By 1966 translations into African languages accounted for one third of all translations worldwide. Vernacular translations of the Bible furnished Africans with an independent source of authority apart from the European missionary, allowed them to see the striking similarities between the biblical and African worlds, and fostered greater confidence in an African Christian identity. Based on research in the 1960s, American missiologist David Barrett concluded that, in societies where the New Testament was available in the vernacular, there was a 67 per cent probability of the emergence of an African independence and renewal movement; and if the whole Bible was translated the probability rose to 81 per cent! This helps to explain why the vast majority of these movements emerged out of Protestant missions or churches and why so few were of Roman Catholic origin – since Roman Catholic missions placed less emphasis on translating the Scriptures. However, it needs to be said that denominational and sectarian divisions among Protestants also favoured the creation of new movements or initiatives.

Throughout the African subcontinent, the same pattern of explosive Charismatic movements headed by prophet-healing figures (both male and female), usually members of mission-founded churches, recurred with astonishing regularity from the early 1900s. Almost all of them integrated distinctive African elements, emphasized healing and divine power and incorporated ritual practices drawn from the Old Testament. Many also adopted distinctive robes and produced new liturgy or hymns.

Prophet-healing movements proliferated most in West Africa. In 1909 William Wadé Harris (1865–1929), a member of the Grebo tribe in Liberia and a former catechist in the Anglican Church, experienced a divine visitation while in prison for sedition. On his release, he preached for two years (1913–15), mainly in Ivory Coast, then a French colony (Côte d'Ivoire). Whole villages embraced Christianity, and over 100,000 Africans were reportedly baptized in 18 months. Unnerved by his influence, the French colonial authorities promptly deported him. There are still 'Harrist' churches today in Ivory Coast, Liberia and Ghana, notable for their hymn production. About 1,300 miles to the east in the Niger Delta, Garrick Sokari Braide (c.1882–1918), a newly baptized Christian in the Anglican Church, also had a visionary experience in 1912 and embarked on a prophet-healing ministry that produced revival and mass conversions, severely stretching the resources of the local churches. Both Harris and Braide demanded the destruction of all idols and traditional shrines, healed the sick, cast out demons, banned drinking alcohol, preached strict sabbatical observance, condoned polygamy and promptly baptized those who confessed their sin. Both were persecuted by colonial authorities.

The movement that emerged in Western Nigeria between 1918 and 1930 became the most prominent. Its most powerful branches include the Christ Apostolic Church and the Cherubim and Seraphim Church which claimed about 83,000 and 50,000 members respectively by 1960. A third major branch, the Church of the Lord, founded by a young Anglican teacher in 1930, quickly transcended ethnic and national boundaries, growing from three congregations in 1931 to 72 branches (in Ghana, Ivory Coast, Liberia, Sierra Leone and Guinea) by 1961.

In the vast Belgian colony of Congo, Simon Kimbangu (1887–1951), a catechist in the Baptist Mission, experienced divine commissioning during the 1918 flu epidemic. From 1921 his ministry as an itinerant evangelist who performed miraculous healings galvanized a mass movement that filled Protestant churches with new members. But the fact that Catholic churches were being deserted led the colonial authorities to take action. After barely six months of ministry, Kimbangu was arrested, tried before a three-man military tribune, charged with sedition and sentenced to death. At the intervention of King Albert I of Belgium (1875–1934), his sentence was commuted to life imprisonment with 120 lashes. He spent the remaining 30 years of his life in prison completely isolated from his family and followers. With the support of European missions, the Belgian colonial government cracked down on the movement. Persecution and mass deportations drove the movement underground and caused it to spread across the country and beyond. The Church of Jesus Christ on Earth, as the movement became known, was granted official recognition in December 1959, six months before Congo gained independence. By 1996 there were an estimated seven million Kimbanguists, making it the largest of all the original prophet-healing movements.

Women featured prominently in the new movements and many of the new prophet-healers were young women. The Cherubim and Seraphim Church, one of the main Aladura branches, was founded in 1925 by a 15-year-old Anglican girl, Christiana Abiodun Akinsowon (1907–94) and an illiterate prophet, Moses Orimolade Tunolase (1879–1933). In 1955, Alice Mulenga Lenshina (1920–78) founded the Lumba Church in northeastern Zambia. Within five years of its founding, the Lumba movement had grown to 150,000 members, alarming the colonial government. In 1963 two lay Catholic Luo Christians in Kenya, Simeon Ondeto (1920–91) and Gaudencia Aoko, a young woman (1943–88), led the largest secession from the Roman Catholic Church in Africa. By the 1990s this Maria Legio (Legion of Mary) movement had a membership estimated between 250,000 and two million.

Some prophet movements in southern Africa focus on a sacred place, often called 'Zion'. Two Shona prophets who had had deep religious experiences emerged from eastern Zimbabwe in the early 1930s at a time of great social and economic deprivation. Both Johane Maranke (1912–63) and John Masowe (1914–73) modelled themselves on John the Baptist, preached repentance and baptism, cast out evil spirits, adopted white garments and travelled throughout southern, central and eastern Africa. The churches they founded are collectively known as Vapostori ('apostles' in the Shona language) and grew to about one million in total.

In South Africa Isaiah Shembe (c. 1870–1935), the most prominent Zionist prophet, was already famous as a healer by the time he broke away from the African Native Baptist Church to establish the Church of the Nazarites ('Ama-Nazaretha') in 1911. Amanazaretha worship, with beautiful hymns set to Zulu tunes, recaptures for the worshippers some of the past glories of the Zulu kingdom. Like all Zionist movements, the idea of a holy city or 'Zion' – in this case the city of Ekuphakameni 18 miles north of Durban – is a central feature. Whether or not Shembe was a messianic figure remains a matter of debate. By 1970 the movement had some 70,000 adherents.

These African-instituted renewal movements incorporated African world views and cultural practices more substantially than mainline churches. Healing practices, for instance, typically included the use of symbolic objects such as blessed water, ropes, staffs, papers, even ash. To reiterate, all emphasize spiritual power. Accusations of 'syncretism' typically ignore their vigorous confrontation with traditional religion, including a stance against witchcraft, idol worship and spirit possession. Attitudes to other

African practices such as ancestor veneration and polygamy also vary. In truth, some became so radically African in their expressions or veered so deeply into traditional religious mysteries that biblical authority and orthodox Christian identity were displaced. But, as a distinct alternative to the Europeanized Christianity that prevailed in mission-founded denominations, these African renewal movements represented a vibrant and popular form of African Christianity with extraordinary appeal among youths, women, and marginalized or displaced groups. In addition to the appeal of African spirituality, the extensive migration movements engendered by the colonial economy contributed greatly to their ability to evangelize new areas and make new converts. By the 1980s they accounted for 10 to 25 per cent (estimates vary) of the African Christian population.

✳ Decolonization and the African Church

By 1970 the number of African Christians had increased from around ten million in 1900 to roughly 117 million. Christians were still a tiny minority in many areas, but this represented phenomenal growth. It defied the generally pessimistic concerns about the future of African Christianity in Western missionary reports in the opening years of the century. Importantly, the two world wars, which saw the deportation or withdrawal of many European missionaries and the eclipse of the British missionary movement, did nothing to slow the expansion of the African Church. In fact, the sharp decrease in the number of foreign missionaries highlighted the indispensable role of African agents in the life of the church. Within Catholic missions the rapid growth of churches, combined with the dwindling number of (mainly European) priests, galvanized efforts to train an African leadership. Between 1920 and 1960 the number of African Catholic priests rose from 50 to 2,000; half of them were ordained in the 1950s. On the face of things, most churches in Africa remained under foreign control; but by the late 1950s, on the eve of decolonization, Christianity in Africa was well on its way to becoming an African religion.

In the wake of the Second World War (1939–45), foreign missions were able to reassert their control of churches, mainly due to their monopoly on education. Both Protestant and Catholic missions flourished. But the currents of revolutionary change were detectable under the surface. The Second World War profoundly affected the thinking and expectations of African peoples. The use and availability of radios, the recruitment of Africans to serve in the armies of colonial powers and the establishment of university colleges (mainly in British colonies) exposed Africans more thoroughly to the wider world and increased consciousness of a worldwide struggle of oppressed peoples to win their freedom.

The establishment of university colleges – in Khartoum (Sudan) in 1902; Makerere (Uganda) in 1923; Ibadan (Nigeria) in 1948; and Legon (Ghana) in 1948 – produced a rising class of highly educated Africans whose desire for greater participation in economic and political life grew with each passing decade. Neither European missionaries nor colonial officials anticipated that the members of this growing African class would become the most vocal critics of Western missions and prominent leaders in the nationalist movements that would bring colonial rule to an end. Generally speaking, by the mid twentieth century there were ample signs that African tolerance for Western cultural and political domination was waning more than ever before. As the stories of Wadé Harris and Kimbangu illustrate, even the prophet-healing movements threatened colonial power and foreign control in their own way. They did so by creating alternative communities that addressed widespread suffering through spiritual power, vibrant worship, healing and home-grown welfare systems. These were mass movements under African control and mainly dependent on indigenous resources, whose very existence challenged notions of white supremacy.

The colonial powers scrambled out of Africa from the 1950s to 1970s. The close relationship between European missions and colonial governments meant that decolonization had far-reaching implications for the Western missionary project. The story is complex. Many of the new African leaders were educated in mission schools. But for them, appreciation for this education and the benefits of modernization was mixed with strong opposition to continued domination of Africans in church and society. By the end of the 1950s most denominations in Africa were autonomous – at least in theory. The Roman Catholic Church led the way. A local hierarchy was established in British West Africa in 1950 and in British East Africa and South Africa the following year. On the Protestant side, the Anglican Province of West Africa was inaugurated in 1951 and that of East Africa in 1961. In Cameroon the Presbyterian Church became autonomous in 1957, three years before the country gained independence. Still, many foreign mission agencies were reluctant to cede complete control of their operations to Africans.

All said, the period leading up to and immediately following political independence in Africa was marked by a fracturing of relationships between African Christians and foreign agents. To start with, the majority of European missionaries and white settler populations were strongly opposed to the African nationalist movements. In African countries with substantial white settlement, the demand for independence led to violent and protracted liberation struggles that pitted white-dominated denominations and foreign missions against African Christians and clergy involved in nationalist movements. Virtually everywhere, the transition to African political self-rule was marked by ill feeling and widespread anti-missionary (even anti-Christian) sentiments. Throughout the continent, political independence brought determined efforts to end foreign control of schools and churches. Mistrust and resentment hardened when the newly independent African countries and African-led churches found themselves in a new global order dominated by Western nations and institutions – a state of affairs that preserved old structures of control and dependency.

Extreme reaction produced calls for a moratorium on the sending of foreign missionaries and money to Africa. But most African Christian leaders (and their Western counterparts) saw greater possibilities in reconciliation, partnership and interdependence. By the 1990s there were still 30,000 to 40,000 Protestant and Catholic expatriate missionaries in Africa. The older, Europe-based missionary societies had declined, giving way to a massive influx of American Evangelical missionaries. But new shifts related to processes of globalization were already changing the contours of global Christianity and altering the shape of the global missionary movement.

✳ African Pentecostalism and African migrations

Throughout Africa the decades following political independence were marked by widespread political chaos and long-term economic crises. In most newly independent African states, the survival of whole populations was threatened at one time or another. The numerous catastrophes afflicting the continent contributed to the emergence of two significant developments with far-reaching implications for the growth and expansion of African Christianity: first, a new African Pentecostal–Charismatic renewal movement from the 1970s that formed a new cutting edge of Christian growth; second, a massive tide of migrations of Africans, within and from the continent, that gave African Christianity a global reach.

The emergence of the new Pentecostal–Charismatic movement

The origins of the new Pentecostal–Charismatic churches that now dominate the African Christian landscape are complex. Like the earlier prophet-healing movements, their emergence is linked to the many acute problems plaguing the continent, combined with new foreign influences. In this case outside stimulus came from the healing and deliverance practices and prosperity doctrines disseminated by American television evangelists such as Oral Roberts (1918–2009), German-born mass evangelist Reinhard Bonnke (1940–2019) and South Korean megachurch pastor David Paul Yonggi Cho (1936–2021). In Nigeria, the earliest manifestations occurred in 1970 among university students involved in British-based Evangelical organizations such as Scripture Union and the International Fellowship of Evangelical Students. Nigerian evangelist Archbishop Benson Idahosa (1938–98), a gifted evangelist who established over 6,000 churches throughout Nigeria and Ghana in the 1970s and founded the popular All Nations for Christ Bible Institute, was one of the early leaders of the new movement.

While these new Pentecostal Charismatic churches can be found all over Africa, the greatest numbers are in West Africa. Key characteristics include strong emphasis on the power and manifestations of the Holy Spirit, the practice of spiritual gifts in the lives of individual believers, prominence of healing and deliverance ministries, a major focus on teachings related to prosperity and success in the life of the believer and church services marked by vibrant worship and innovative use of modern media technologies. The leaders or founders are generally men and women in their thirties and forties who have a gift for charismatic leadership and are relatively well educated. By and large, their churches and ministries appeal most strongly to upwardly mobile, formally educated young people and middle-class professionals. Female involvement in leadership positions is also much more extensive than in the older African-instituted churches or mainline denominations. A fervent commitment to outreach ministries and evangelistic campaigns is perhaps the most important single feature of the movement.

Among the most notable and influential of these fellowships are Deeper Life Bible Church, established in 1973 by Nigerian William Kumuyi (b. 1941), then a mathematics lecturer at the University of Lagos; Winners Chapel, established in 1983 in Ilorin (Nigeria) by David Oyedepo (b. 1954), a graduate of civil engineering and former member of the Cherubim and Seraphim (Aladura) Church; the Back to God Evangelistic Association, founded in 1983 by Peterson Sozi (b. 1953), former moderator of the Reformed Presbyterian Church in Uganda; Rhema Bible Church in Randburg (South Africa), founded by Ray McCauley (b. 1949); the Central Gospel Church, established by Ghanaian Mensah Otabil (b. 1959) in 1985; the True Church of God, founded by Nestor Toukea, a francophone Cameroonian (c.1935–2020); and Nairobi Chapel, led since 1990 by Oscar Muriu (b. 1961).

Membership in many of these churches runs into several thousands and most have extensive international ministries. Relations between the new movements and the older prophet-healing movements are complicated. Both movements reflect the African emphasis on spiritual power, and some of the older prophet-healing movements recreated themselves as new Pentecostal–Charismatic churches. At the same time, the latter generally promote individualistic, urban lifestyles, and their members generally have strongly negative attitudes towards traditional religion. Significantly, the new Pentecostal–Charismatic movement has had a much greater impact on the mainline churches, Catholic and Protestant, than the older prophet-healing movements – so much so that Charismatic practices or emphases have proliferated in Anglican, Baptist, Presbyterian and Methodist denominations, as well as Catholic churches, throughout the subcontinent. Indeed, some mainline churches can easily be mistaken for Pentecostal–Charismatic churches. All of this has led some scholars to talk about the 'Pentecostalization' of African Christianity. That said, African Christianity remains both vibrant and diverse, and multiple membership (among churches and ministries) is fairly common.

Between 1970 and 2000 the number of African Christians grew by 195.5 per cent, from 117.5 million to over 340 million. In all, the growth of African Christianity in the twentieth century is unparalleled in Christian history. Much of this growth occurred in the postcolonial period, with the energetic evangelism of the new Pentecostal–Charismatic movement playing a major role. It is estimated that this movement accounted for 11 per cent of the entire African population (roughly 90 million members) by 2000. Generally speaking, mainline denominations in Africa have also enjoyed considerable net increases. It is noteworthy that roughly 44 million African Anglicans account for more than half the membership of the worldwide Anglican Communion, with Nigeria home to more practising Anglicans than any other country (including the UK). By most accounts the Church is growing faster in Africa than anywhere else. The *World Christian Encyclopedia* (2001) pinpointed the rate of increase within African Christianity at 23,000 new believers a day.

Migration and the new African missionaries

An often overlooked factor in the expansion of African Christianity during the final decades of the twentieth century is the unprecedented rise in its migrant population. Human migration has historically played a major role in the spread of Christianity. Christian immigrants invariably establish new churches in the countries they migrate to, and Christian groups in receiving countries instinctively seek to evangelize migrant and refugee populations in their midst. As noted above, one reason for the rapid growth of prophet-healing movements was the rise in the migrant population stimulated by the colonial economy. The voluminous flow of migrants in the postcolonial era also contributed to the spread of Christianity in Africa. Between 1970 and 2005 the volume of African migrants rose dramatically as escalating conflicts, brutal regimes and economic collapse induced unprecedented displacements of peoples. By 1995 Africa was home to about a third of the world's refugees and asylum seekers. At the same time, unprecedented numbers of Africans fled the continent in search of better opportunities or a better life elsewhere.

By 2000 African migrants were widely dispersed among the wealthy industrialized countries in Europe and North America. And everywhere they went they established new Christian congregations. In effect, African migrations have provided a vital stimulus for missionary expansion. It is important to bear in mind that, while most Christian missionaries are migrants in some sense, every Christian migrant is a potential missionary. Most of the new Pentecostal–Charismatic churches have expanded their ministries to other parts of Africa by utilizing migrant networks and the movement of their members to other countries.

Interestingly, Christianity in Africa has been experiencing extraordinary growth at precisely the same time that Christianity in Europe and

North America has been experiencing dramatic decline. As a result, African Christian migrants in the West often develop a missionary consciousness about the societies in which they find themselves; however, initially at least, they are more successful in reaching other migrants like themselves than the native population. In any case, churches and congregations formed by African immigrants have exploded in number within major cities in the Western world. In most countries, such immigrant churches form the cutting edge of Christian growth. In Europe in particular, their vitality is in sharp contrast to the waning home-grown congregations around them. Today for instance, the largest Baptist church in the UK is the Calvary Charismatic Church, led by Ghanaian pastor Francis Sarpong (*fl.* 1994 onwards); and it is well known that the largest church in Europe is the 25,000-member Embassy for the Blessed Kingdom of God to All Nations, located in Kiev (Ukraine) and founded in 1993 by Nigerian pastor Sunday Adelaja (b. 1967). In the USA too, African churches, mainly Pentecostal–Charismatic types, have expanded rapidly since the 1980s, and many have used the USA as a base to extend outreach into other countries.

Needless to say, not all African Christian migrants establish separate centres of worship. Countless thousands become members of established denominations and churches where they often take up important ministries. But the missionary function and vision of the rapidly expanding African congregations in Western societies is undeniable. In important ways, this remarkable development shows how the missionary movement has come full circle. The seeds sown by European missionary endeavour have helped to produce African churches that have in turn generated a missionary movement engaged in meaningful outreach to European lands. This is not to suggest that the Western missionary movement has ended. In fact, the world's Christians now find themselves in an extraordinary historical moment when international missionary outreach is no longer the privilege of one or two regions but an enterprise shared globally in multiple directions. Nevertheless, the African element in this development remains one of the most remarkable and prominent.

❓ DISCUSSION QUESTIONS

1 What were some of the changes and reforms in church organization and practice effected in Ethiopia between liberation from Italian occupation in 1941 and the appointment of an Ethiopian as *abuna* in 1959?

2 In what important ways did Roman Catholic missions operating in Africa during this period differ from the Protestant ones?

3 What were some of the many different reasons why Protestant and Roman Catholic missions were anxious to provide education; and what were

the main reasons Africans themselves overcame their own resistance to mission education and eventually came to demand it?

4 What was the chief difference between the aims and methods of Protestant missions in training African clergy and church leaders, and those of the Roman Catholics, especially in the training of women?

5 Describe the main contribution mission hospitals made to the development of Africa. What was the general attitude of Africans in the early twentieth century towards the treatment offered by these hospitals?

6 How critical was the work of catechists for the establishment of Christianity in the colonial period? What made them effective?

7 What circumstances and particular needs helped to give rise to 'independent' churches? In what ways could these be considered reform or renewal movements, and how would you describe their impact?

8 Briefly describe the particular characteristics which distinguish the independent churches as they developed:

(a) in West Africa;

(b) in southern Africa;

(c) in the form of 'revival' in East Africa.

9 Describe briefly, with dates, the aims and achievements of each of the following, and the particular practices of their followers and the churches they founded:

(a) William Wadé Harris;

(b) Simon Kimbangu;

(c) Isaiah Shembe.

10 Explain the role which education played in:

(a) the establishment of African Christianity in the colonial period;

(b) the relationship between mission-founded churches and colonial governments;

(c) the movement towards political and ecclesiastical independence in Africa.

11 What are some of the factors that have influenced the rise of Pentecostal–Charismatic movements (from the 1970s), and how are these new churches or ministries different from the earlier independent church movements?

12 How has the huge migration of Africans since the closing decades of the twentieth century contributed to the worldwide spread of African Christianity? What is your assessment of the missionary potential of growing African churches in Europe and North America?

Further reading

Anderson, Allan H. *African Reformation: African initiated Christianity in the 20th century.* Trenton, NJ: Africa World Press, 2001.

Baur, John. *Two Thousand Years of Christianity in Africa: An African history.* Nairobi: Paulines Publications Africa, 1994.

Isichei, Elizabeth. *A History of Christianity in Africa: From antiquity to the present.* London: SPCK, 1995.

Kalu, Ogbu (ed). *African Christianity: An African story.* Trenton, NJ: Africa World Press, 2007.

Sanneh, Lamin. *West African Christianity: The religious impact.* New York, NY: Orbis, 1983.

Shaw, Mark. *The Kingdom of God in Africa: A short history of African Christianity.* Grand Rapids, MI: Baker, 1996.

4

North-East Asia

Julie C. Ma and Angus Crichton

This chapter covers the historical movement and development of Christianity in populous countries in North-East Asia. The region under consideration includes China, Japan and Korea. The message of the gospel arrived in each of these countries in different time periods, brought by Roman Catholic and Protestant missionaries from Western nations. The only exception is the

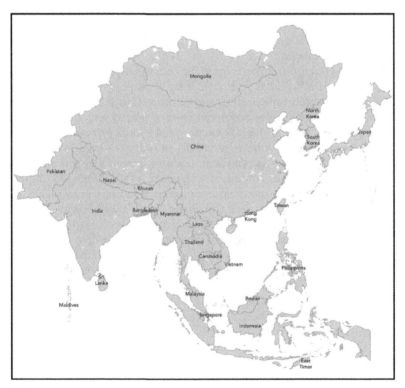

Asia

Korean Church, born as a result of indigenous rather than external agency. These missionary initiatives varied considerably in terms of strategy and impact, but the overall objective of spreading the Christian faith remained the same. Almost everywhere the missionary effort encountered formidable obstacles and newly established Christian communities often faced strong persecution; but, through sacrificial foreign missionary labour and courageous witness by indigenous believers, the churches survived and the gospel bore fruit.

 # China

Catholic continuation and Protestant beginnings

Two interlinked issues characterize the Chinese Christian story in all periods. The first is the degree to which the Christian faith has been articulated and appropriated in ways that resonate with Chinese sensibilities and aspirations. The second is the Christian churches' relationship with the Chinese state, particularly the degree to which Christianity is seen as an external and even threatening religious movement that must therefore be controlled, even suppressed. Our period begins in the middle of one of those state-ordered suppressions (since 1724); yet despite this, the Roman Catholic Church had put down strong roots in the countryside of eastern and southern China. From its ranks had come a small number of Chinese priests, and a greater number of catechists and Christian virgins (women who took a vow of celibacy, but not additional vows of poverty and obedience, for entrance to the religious life). These provided a more permanent presence than European priests, who were usually in hiding or exile. Without the support of these clergy, lay Christian leaders nurtured their communities and also allowed for the continuing adaptations of Christianity to Chinese culture, for example the use of ancestor tablets at funerals, but with altered words. The similarities between Christianity and banned religious groups led state authorities to group the two together when the latter provoked the state's anger. So after the Three Trigrams Society Rebellion of 1813, the churches experienced a wave of persecution that produced the martyrdoms of the priest Augustine Zhao Rong (1746–1815), the catechists Peter Wu Guosheng (1768–1814) and Joseph Zhang Dapeng (1754–1815), and the Christian virgin Agatha Lin Zhao (1817–58). However, such waves were periodic rather than sustained and were often fuelled by local rivalries.

Into these pre-existing Catholic Christian communities arrived Protestant missionaries, whose access to China was closely tied up with unequal treaties between Western powers and China. When the first of these, William Morrison (1782–1834), arrived in 1807 he was only allowed to reside within a restricted area in Guangzhou for the short trading season and had to spend the rest of the year in Portuguese-controlled Macau. This kind of limitation characterized the experience of Western missionaries for the next 30 years, during which some 50 Protestant missionaries wrestled with the complexities of learning Chinese, produced tools to help others do so and translated the Bible. In these activities they were assisted by Chinese colleagues, and from their ranks were drawn the first generation of Protestant converts, probably numbering fewer than 100 in the first 30 years. Notable among these was Liang Fa (1787–1855) who assisted Morrison and other missionaries with language-learning, translation and printing, was ordained to the role of evangelist and wrote *Good News to Admonish the Ages* (*Quan Shi Liang Yan*). This substantial text was probably circulated originally as a series of separate pamphlets, whose subjects included a description of his conversion and a critique of Chinese religions and culture, the latter inspiring Hong Xiuquan (1814–64), the leader of the Taipings (see below), to whom Liang handed some pamphlets in 1834. While Protestant and Catholic missionaries in China usually dismissed each other's version of the Christian faith, Chinese enquirers were now faced with two competing versions of Christianity.

The unequal treaties, the Taipings, expansion and the Boxers

In 1842 China entered into the first of a series of treaties with different Western countries that opened the country up to greater external trade, residence and influence, including that of Western missionaries. These unequal treaties were extracted from China after a series of conflicts between 1839 and 1860, which on the surface were over the right of Western traders to sell the illegal substance opium into China and which culminated in 1860 with British and French forces sacking the Chinese emperor's palace outside Beijing. By 1860 Western missionaries had secured free travel throughout the interior of China, as well as the right to rent or purchase land and put up buildings, and to remain under the legal system of their home governments. Practising the Christian faith was legalized for both foreigners and Chinese. Church properties confiscated after 1724 were to be returned. The Western missionary movement saw these clashes as the means to open up the interior, with some missionaries actively involved as translators and advisers in the subsequent negotiations. This wider access initiated a wave of institution-building, alongside a more united approach to Bible translation among the Protestants. The resulting Delegates Version, completed in 1854, was produced by representatives from different Protestant missionary societies and Chinese colleagues. Henry Medhurst (1796–1857), Karl Gützlaff (1803–51) and Wang Tao (1828–97) were the principal architects, with the latter probably bearing substantial responsibility for the translation's elegance. Like their Catholic predecessors from the seventeenth century, the translators wrestled with how to render key theological terms in Chinese, not least the name for God. The sustained disagreement between the translation teams and the wider missionary community was in part fuelled by differing views as to whether or not the Creator God had revealed himself not only to the Israelites but also to the Chinese in the first two millennia BCE. Some found support for such parallel revelations in the apostles' use of Greek divine titles in their explanation of Hebrew monotheism to non-Jewish audiences. One choice by Bible translators for the name for God in Chinese was to have a literally revolutionary impact on Hong Xiuquan and the Taipings (see below).

A similar wave of new Catholic missionary priests came from Europe in the wake of these treaties, sometimes supplanting long-serving and effective Chinese colleagues such as Joseph Han (1772–1844) and Matthew Xue (1780–1860), as well as religious orders competing with one another. While the treaties now gave the missionaries the power to purchase land or reacquire former church properties, this also pitched them into conflict with local government officials and generated hostility among the surrounding population, which could be exploited to generate local waves of periodic persecution. During population upheavals and land hunger in southern and eastern China during the second half of the nineteenth century, Catholic migrants and priests established Christian villages in new locations such as Central Asia and Inner Mongolia. While adopting the Christian faith was a requirement to join these villages, so that initial professions included a pragmatic response to the entrance requirements set, the practice of Christian rituals over generations produced communities of genuine and profound faith that weathered the persecutions of the twentieth century and continued to produce vocations to the priesthood.

In 1837 a young schoolteacher from the minority Hakka ethnic group collapsed after again failing the entrance examination for the imperial civil service. He had already received a copy of Liang Fa's *Good News*. In his resulting fevered state, Hong Xiuquan was swept up to heaven where he encountered his heavenly Father and his elder brother Jesus. Six years after this, Hong, together with his cousin Hong Rengan (1822–64) and fellow schoolteacher Feng Yunshan (1815–50), baptized one another and gathered other Hakka around them. This group grew into a powerful movement generally referred to now as the Taipings. Hong's Christian influences were enlarged by receiving the Protestant Delegates Version of the Bible, together with two months of instruction with an American missionary in Canton. By 1853 this religious movement had also become a political kingdom that had wrested south-east China from imperial control, with the Delegates Version providing the major catalyst, adapted to accommodate Confucian concerns. The Chinese emperors appropriated the title Shangdi (Lord on High) for themselves in the third century BCE onwards. Yet Hong was reading a Bible where 'Shangdi' was used for the one who made heaven and earth and whose name was not to be taken in vain. The political consequences were explosive: the emperor's claim to the title Shangdi was blasphemous and so his rule must be overthrown. The Ten Commandments were central to Taiping worship and practice, fuelling a monotheism that destroyed imperial political and religious images and personnel, and introduced a radical moral and economic order which others were invited to join.

The resulting 'heavenly kingdom', centred on Nanjing, lasted until 1864, when it was as violently overthrown as it was set up. In the eyes of China's political establishment, the Taipings had developed out of existing Christian groups, and so the latter were just as prone to political and religious rebellion after the extinction of the former. In contrast, Protestant and Catholic missions showed little desire to learn from the Taipings' appropriation of Christianity, one that used indigenous terminology and drew on Chinese culture and history. Instead they continued to hitch their wagons to Western imperialism and culture.

The second half of the nineteenth century saw an unprecedented expansion of European and North American missions in terms of numbers, missionary methods and theological diversity. The number of Protestant missionaries increased from around 100 in 1860 to just below 3,500 in 1905. Founded in 1865 by J. Hudson Taylor (1832–1905), the China Inland Mission (CIM) contributed over 20 per cent of missionary personnel by 1905 and pursued a rigorous focus on evangelism beyond the cities, while devoting fewer resources to social-service institutions. Alongside CIM, an increasingly diverse array of more theologically conservative missionaries and societies flocked to China through the second half of the nineteenth century; such missions were often small, even consisting of a single individual. By the start of the twentieth century, these were joined by Pentecostal missionaries, whose ministries were often one of the sparks leading to the formation of independent Chinese Christian groups. Like the CIM, these groups tended to focus on evangelism at the expense of social-service ministries.

In contrast, the more established missions, both Catholic and Protestant, invested heavily in educational, medical, humanitarian and publishing ministries. While, for many missionaries, conversion to Christ also required conversion to the Euro-American 'Christian' civilization promoted through these institutions, a minority discerned a Christ-shaped imprint among the religious traditions of China, as did Chinese Christians. An example was the Benedictine monk Dom Lu Tseng-tsiang (1871–1949), whose meditations on John's Gospel led him to discern:

> In the beginning was the *Tao* and the *Tao* was with God and the *Tao* was God. Jesus Christ is the *Tao* made flesh, coming to reveal to us the life of God and to unveil his human heart and the filial piety that he shows to his father.
> (Lou P. Tseng-Tsiang, *La Rencontre des humanités et la découverte de l'évangile* (Bruges: Desclée de Brouwer, 1949), p. 61; trans. in Jean-Pierre Charbonnier, *Christians in China: A.D. 600 to 2000* (San Francisco, CA: Ignatius Press, 2007), p. 413)

The desire to access the fruits of modernity through Western learning brought the Chinese elite into contact with Christianity on a wider scale than ever before. By the end of the nineteenth century, programmes of modernization and reform suggested by some missionaries had been taken up by a section of the elite at court and provided the seedbed for the nationalist movement in the following decades. Publications by both Protestant and Catholic presses provided a key means of sharing Western scientific and educational insights. In 1882 the Jesuit priest Li Wenyu (1840–1911) established the weekly *Yiwen lu* (Record of Useful News) on these topics, which ran under several different titles until his death; alongside this successful endeavour, he was the author or translator of 60 books. However, in more rural locations, the elite was often threatened by and resented the arrival of Christian missionaries, who offered an alternative power structure and who laid claim to privileged rights under the treaties Western powers had wrung from China. These tensions generated anti-Christian pamphlets misrepresenting Christian practices and periodically escalated to violence, while the return of property to the missions produced a steady stream of court cases. In 1900 famine, flood and drought brought population upheaval and extensive suffering, all of which accelerated the anti-Christian 'Boxer' movement into an all-out attack on missionaries and Chinese Christians in northern China (the term 'boxer' was created by Westerners, referring to the group's practice of martial arts). Foreigners in Beijing only survived by barricading themselves within the foreign quarter of the city, while 250 of their number beyond the city perished, alongside 30,000 Chinese Christians, with the Catholic Church experiencing the greatest loss. A multinational force was mobilized to invade northern China. The Chinese court fled before this eight-nation Western army, which occupied Beijing and then moved against suspected Boxers far inland in a campaign stretching into the following year and possibly killing more Chinese than the Boxers did.

Yet despite this elite suspicion of Christianity, the Chinese Church grew in numbers, with Catholic Christians numbering 700,000 to 800,000 and Protestants around 100,000 by 1900, the latter representing a significant growth rate from a few hundred converts four decades before. Some Chinese joined the Christian community for material gain: employment in the expanding missionary institutions or in a missionary household; access to missionary famine relief; and medical or legal assistance. For others occupying a marginal position in Chinese society, Christian social structures opened new doors of opportunity, including for female converts. Yet others discerned a truth and power within Christianity that they had hitherto not encountered in their own religious journeys. So converts such as Huang Naishang (1849–1924) and Liang Fa saw in Christianity resources to lead the moral life as espoused in the ancient Confucian texts. Others experienced greater supernatural power than they had hitherto found in popular religious practice to ward off life-denying forces and secure this-worldly blessings. In drought-stricken Fuzhou during 1877, this led Xu Bomei (b. 1827) into a direct confrontation with the local deity and its representatives as to whether that god or Xu's Christian God would bring rain. The situation was reminiscent of the contest between the priests of Baal and the Israelite prophet Elijah (see 1 Kings 18).

The road not taken: nationalism, modernity, communism and Christianity

The first decades of the twentieth century witnessed both the enthusiastic uptake by China's nationalist elite of the missionary movement's modernizing programme and the rejection of Christianity in favour of communism as the dynamo to drive that programme. It was a period of seeming triumphs – the president of the year-old republic asked Christians to pray for this new government on Sunday, 27 April 1913 – and of unforeseen peril – revolutionary troops attacked a number of Christian institutions and personnel in the late 1920s. Marx, not Christ, emerged as the more attractive replacement for Confucius. After 1900 the imperial and then republican governments ended dependence on Confucian-based education for entry into public service. Consequently, the well-developed Christian school and college system, particularly on the Protestant side, was strategically positioned to deliver the modern education desired by these governments. This system also generated upward mobility for the mainly rural Protestant population of modest means. The graduates of these colleges went on to staff the Protestant missionary institutions or to fund them through success in business. As in other regions, missionaries were slow to extend genuine partnership in leadership to their Chinese counterparts. However, the latter forged federations of churches not under missionary control in several major cities, a process facilitated by new legal rights granted by the republican government for Chinese Christians (not just foreign missions) to construct and own church buildings. In contrast, the Catholic Church retained its rural origins and, with a smaller investment in social-service provision, lacked a mechanism for encouraging social mobility into urban centres. Like the Protestants, the Catholic Church was too dependent on foreign clergy, who were slow to share power with their Chinese counterparts.

Resentment at Western interference in China's affairs boiled over into a series of widespread protests in the late 1910s and 1920s. The presenting issue was the failure in 1919 to return territory from Germany to China but instead to cede it to Japan, with underlying bitterness about the privileged status of Westerners in China together with the inadequacies of the imperial system and the selfish rule of the warlords. At that point, the Christian faith was not a direct target of these protests, but it soon became so. Its representatives were viewed as the servants of a Western imperialism that had exploited China, peddling a religion with unbelievable superstitions such as the virgin birth and the resurrection, despite the excellent moral qualities of Jesus' teaching. The missionary movement's readiness to avail itself of privileges under the unequal treaties, together with its extensive failure to share leadership with Chinese Christians, provided ready ammunition for

73

this attack. By the mid 1920s these sentiments had crystallized into joint demands from the republican and communist parties for increasing government control of the missionary education apparatus. As for the Chinese Christian leaders raised up through this system, it was all too easy to attach to them the label 'imperialist running dogs'. While the missionary establishment was granted a respite in the 1930s and 1940s under the nationalist government and the Japanese occupation, these sentiments returned with a vengeance when the communists came to power in 1949.

In this period a series of independent Christian movements emerged, such as the Jesus Family, the Spiritual Gifts Society, the True Jesus Church and the movement founded by Ni Tosheng (Watchman Nee 1903–72). The shared feature of these movements was a desire to work out the Christian faith in the Chinese context beyond Western missionary control. Their founders usually had significant exposure to Protestant missionary Christianity, while its Pentecostal dimension often provided the starting point for a new trajectory. However, these imported expressions were deemed deficient and founders established new movements, often characterized by equality among members in contrast to the hierarchical church structure of some Western denominations, an emphasis on the imminent return and reign of Christ, and various forms of ecstatic experience and revelation. So while Wei Enbo (1876–1919) may have received healing prayer for his tuberculosis from a Swedish Pentecostal missionary, the resulting True Jesus Church was shaped by Wei's own intense religious experiences of being swept up to heaven during a 39-day fast. In this, as in other independent groups, there are clear echoes of earlier movements such as the Taipings, which similarly drew upon traditional Chinese religious concerns. Other individuals such as Dora Yu (1873–1931) pursued successful itinerant ministries rather than founding movements. The very nature of the Catholic Church prevented Chinese Catholics from pursuing independent ministries such as these.

As China entered the whirlwind of the Japanese invasion (1937–45) and the continued civil war in its aftermath (1946–9) leading to the communist victory at its end, four different categories of Chinese Christians can be discerned based on their engagement with the surrounding socio-political turmoil and their readiness to entrust leadership to Chinese Christians. At one end of the spectrum were the established Protestant churches and missions that had for four decades pursued greater unity (more or less successfully). These churches had a strong history of social and political engagement which encouraged some, by 1949, to consider communist rule as the means to address the socio-economic challenges that had for so long preoccupied them. The exodus of missionaries during the Japanese occupation had thrust Chinese Christians into more leadership positions. However, their extensive social and educational infrastructure was badly damaged in the conflicts and also attracted communist critique. In contrast, the more theologically conservative missions such as CIM and its many smaller counterparts focused more exclusively on personal salvation, but were similarly slow to share leadership power in practice. The independent churches, with minimal infrastructure, proved adept at slipping under the radar screen of official notice and needed no wartime severing of ties with the West to school them in self-support. Their numbers swelled in response to their end-times preaching and the practical help they offered to displaced multitudes, fuelled by their radical egalitarian ethos. By their very nature their leadership was entirely Chinese. Finally, the Roman Catholic Church was characterized by marked hostility to the incoming communist regime, emanating from the papacy itself, and by unfortunate entanglements with US intelligence. Only 19 per cent of its key leadership roles were held by Chinese clergy, despite the move in 1926 to ordain the first six Chinese Catholic bishops.

The Chinese Church in the communist era

Some Protestant leaders, led by the Young Men's Christian Association secretary Y. T. Wu (1895–1979), were willing to work with the incoming communist government, which itself needed to control all non-party groups, particularly those with extensive foreign ties such as the churches. This co-operation came to be expressed through the Three-Self Patriotic Movement (TSPM), to which all Protestant churches were strongly encouraged to affiliate. While not a church in its own right, by 1954 it had become the official structure by which the Protestant churches related to the Communist Party, with its name appropriated from the holy trinity of nineteenth-century Anglo-American mission theory: the view that newly established churches were to become self-supporting, self-governing and self-propagating. Advocates for TSPM from within the churches were quick to highlight the churches' ties to Western imperialism, while non-compliant leaders were denounced; however, some individuals in the former group found themselves in the latter within just a few years. International tensions between China and the USA on the Korean Peninsula in the early 1950s only increased pressure on the churches to cut international ties and affiliate to the TSPM. The collapse of international money transfers between the two countries effectively ended the work of foreign missionary personnel and funding for the churches' social-service institutions, which therefore fell under state control. Increasing government pressure on foreign missionaries resulted in nearly all leaving by 1955, either by choice or by order. However, some found significant ministries among the Chinese Diaspora elsewhere in Asia and beyond, where they were joined by Chinese priests who were unable to return to China. Taiwan and Hong Kong were key centres of this Chinese Christian Diaspora, ministering to exiles from the Mainland, wrestling with a Chinese appropriation of Christianity (encouraged by the Second Vatican Council (1962–5) on the Catholic side), and in subsequent decades sharing information on and resources with the churches on the Mainland.

While several key independent church leaders helped to establish TSPM, by the mid 1950s the leaders of the Little Flock, the Jesus Family and the

True Jesus Church had been denounced and their congregations scattered, although these movements continued throughout the rest of the twentieth century. The Catholic Church faced the same pressure to come under state control, deemed to be even more necessary because of its large land-holdings, foreign leadership, the Vatican's consistently anti-communist stance, and its extensive unregistered lay groups, such as the Legion of Mary. Again the Korean War increased government control, with Shanghai – as the seat of Chinese Catholicism – providing the stage for the most intense confrontation. This culminated in the arrest and imprisonment in 1955 of Bishop Gong Pinmei (1901–2000), several hundred clergy and over a thousand lay people, as well as the continuing denouncement and expulsion or arrest of foreign personnel. Bishop Gong, alongside 13 others, was finally tried and sentenced to life imprisonment in 1960 after he refused to take the Shanghai Catholic Church into the Chinese Catholic Patriotic Association (CCPA, the equivalent of the TSPM for Roman Catholics) and sever ties with the Vatican. When, in 1958, the relevant organ of the Communist Party began to appoint Catholic bishops, Pope Pius XII (1876–1958) was quick to respond with the encyclical *Ad apostolorum principis*, warning that sacraments administered by such bishops were 'gravely illicit'. While some priests refused these government appointments, over the next five years more than 50 accepted, caught between their loyalty to Rome and the pressing need of their dioceses. However, Catholics flocked to attend secret masses celebrated by a priest connected with the Vatican, while avoiding those held in CCPA churches.

As China's Christians, along with the entire population, were hurled into a series of disastrous mass social, economic and political experiments, from the Anti-Rightist Campaign of 1957–8 to the Cultural Revolution of 1966–76, many predicted the end of Chinese Christianity. The Protestant churches under state control were characterized by bland assemblies, formulaic services, and an ageing and non-replaced leadership, with its Catholic counterpart sharing many of these features. The majority of church buildings were closed, and pastors and priests were either sent to work in the fields or interned in labour camps. The conditions in the latter were grim, so that many inmates did not survive, while others were not released until the 1970s. Yet even in the camps, some Christians maintained their faith and witness, such as a group of Shanghai Catholic priests who carved a sacred response in wood to atheistic materialism. During the Cultural Revolution even official church structures were swept away, as all religions were outlawed and the remaining churches closed. Yet the internal convulsions of this period effectively neutralized the state organs that monitored the churches to enforce their compliance, creating an extraordinary space for growth. Prior distinctions between state-registered and informal churches disappeared as all now had to occupy the latter space. The inheritors of the theologically conservative missions and Chinese independent churches thrived within this space, with their millennial message, radical egalitarianism and Pentecostalizing empowering gifts, multiplying in number five- or sixfold until their numbers were similar to or greater than the Catholic population of five to six million. Church statistics in this period are a matter of best guesses. Shorn of Western finances, personnel and infrastructure, the Chinese Church reverted to a more basic expression of the Christian faith and grew.

The churches emerged on the other side of the Cultural Revolution into government oversight structures similar to those in the 1950s, while internally the pressures of the preceding period intensified the long conversation between Christ and the religious traditions of China. The reforms introduced from 1978 onwards liberalized large sections of life from government control, religious belief being but one, alongside substantial economic reforms. The TSPM and CCPA were reintroduced, along with new parallel intermediary structures for Protestants and Catholics, creating links between these former entities and local congregations. Yet for many Chinese Christians these structures and their personnel were compromised by their too-close relationship to the government. These systems had facilitated state oppression from the 1950s to 1970s and state control from the 1980s, thus undermining the authority of Christ and, for Catholics, his representative on earth, the Pope. Faced with other, greater national and international challenges, the government itself became less concerned with what its citizens believed, as long as they did not pose a threat to the state. This position crystallized into the official 'Document 19', issued by the Central Committee of the Communist Party in March 1982, which accepted the reality of religious belief within China, while still allowing for the government to move against 'abnormal' religious expressions, a right it exercised with the suppression of the Falun Gong in 1999.

In this liberalized environment, churches were reopened and repopulated at an explosive rate throughout the 1980s. This happened among Protestants more than Catholics, but was a rural phenomenon for both. Both faced challenges of congregations without church leadership and buildings, the Catholics dealing with the continuing complexity of two parallel church hierarchies whose appointments were made either by the Vatican or by the Communist Party. As prosperity returned to the rural areas so did the evangelists and evangelistic media, often from independent streams of Christianity with bases in Hong Kong and Taiwan. As seen before, the emphasis on a coming millennial rule ushered in by a saviour figure and access to tangible this-worldly power to ward off misfortune and bring blessing, found fertile ground among the rural Chinese population. Some of the most significant groups to emerge in the 1980s were the Huhan pai (Shouters, the inheritors of Watchman Nee's mantle), the Kupai (Weepers) of the China Gospel Fellowship, and the Fangcheng Church. Other groups hived off into more questionable beliefs and practices. For example, the members of Kuangye zhaimen (Narrow Gate of the Wilderness) understood its founder, Ji Sanbao (1940–97), to be the Saviour; as part of his assumed role, Ji commissioned 12 disciples and predicted a series of world-endings, which had to be revised as prior ones failed to materialize. Some of these groups, such as the Huhan pai and the Kuangye zhaimen, were deemed by TSPM and the government to express 'abnormal' religious beliefs, which earned them a place on the officially banned list of *xiejiao* (evil cults). Similarly, rural Catholic communities, which still formed the bulk of the Catholic population, expressed their Christian faith shaped by the same millennia-long concerns of China's agricultural communities.

China's 1990s economic boom, focused in cities on its eastern seaboard, produced a massive rural-to-urban migration of perhaps 100 million people. Thus, Christians from the expanding rural churches of the 1980s moved to the cities in the 1990s, triggering urban church growth as a result of this migration as well as from conversion. With incomes rising and converts now coming from higher socio-economic groups, these urban churches launched significant social welfare programmes as well as evangelistic ministries. They caught the attention of China's intellectuals, who started to ask if Christianity could be less the opiate of the people and more an ethical bedrock to counter widespread corruption in public life.

During the two centuries considered here, the relationship between church and state in China ranged from outright repression through careful control to potential embrace, particularly if the Church was perceived as a motor for modernization. The Chinese state, be that the Qing Dynasty or the Chinese Communist Party, was consistently anxious about any networked structure with alternative loyalties, particularly when, as was the case with the churches, these networks reached beyond China. In this regard, Chinese Christians are descendants of the first-century network of Christian communities on the coast of modern-day Turkey – groups of believers who were reminded by the apostle John in his Apocalypse that Christ and not the emperor (or the party) is Lord. In a similar way to John's readers, Chinese Christians have expressed their faith within the pre-existing religious and cultural milieu, be that the moral priorities of Confucianism or the millennial expectations and quest for power of popular religious concerns.

✳ Japan

An underground church

At the start of the nineteenth century, Christianity was still banned by the Japanese government, based on a series of edicts dating from the later sixteenth century. Nagasaki, heartland of the underground Christians, witnessed state-sponsored round-ups in 1842, 1856 and 1865–8 in which thousands were exiled and hundreds martyred. By the 1850s European priests had been allowed back to Japan after the country made trade treaties with Western powers. These priests first made contact with the Nagasaki Christians in 1865. The edict banning Christianity was only finally lifted in 1873, allowing some 10,000 Christians to return to the Roman Catholic Church. However, others chose to remain within their communities, becoming known as the Kakure Kirishitan (Hidden Christians) and retaining their distinctive form of Christianity, which had developed through more than two centuries of isolation. The yearly requirement to tread on an image of Christ or Mary generated not only appropriate prayers of repentance after the event, but also an understanding of God less as a judging father and more as a tender, merciful mother.

Diversity through an influx of external agents and local appropriations

Propagating Christianity gradually became more possible in Japan through the second half of the nineteenth century, culminating in the right to freedom of religion enshrined within the Meiji Constitution of 1889. Unlike in the sixteenth century, missionaries came from a broad range of both European and North American countries and confessional loyalties. Inevitably, some Catholic missionaries focused their efforts on the Kakure Kirishitan in and around Nagasaki, while others wanted to take advantage of the desire for Western learning among ex-samurai in Yokohama, as did Protestants. Catholic missionary work predominated among the former rather than the latter. By focusing on the more religiously conservative countryside, the Catholic Church was less able to take advantage of the openness to new ideas in the urban areas. It was less engaged with the tensions between Christianity and loyalty to the emperor, and also with movements of social reform. By 1912 six Catholic dioceses had been created across Japan.

Given its small number of missionary personnel, the Russian Orthodox Church's mission to Japan gained a considerable number of converts. By 1900 the Orthodox had nearly half as many converts as the Catholics. Nikolai Kasatkin (born Ivan Dimitrovich Kasatkin (1836–1912)) pioneered Orthodox Christianity in Japan, arriving as chaplain to the Russian Embassy in Hakodate in 1861. However, the bulk of the church's leadership was Japanese, with Swabe Takuma (1833–1913) becoming the first priest to be ordained in 1875. As with Protestantism, converts to the Orthodox faith from the former samurai class were attracted by its connections beyond Japan. Its more distinct features were its ornate buildings, particularly its cathedral in Tokyo, and its detailed rituals, perhaps suggesting parallels with Buddhism.

Protestantism, in contrast to Catholicism, focused more on the urban areas and on providing access to Western education. This proved to be particularly attractive to former samurai. They had lost many of their privileges with the end of the rule by warlords and the restoration of the emperor in 1868. Some encountered Protestant missionaries and their emerging educational facilities, which promoted Western technology and institutions as fruits of Christianity. As these former samurai converted at a particular Protestant educational institution, they formed 'bands' committed to the expansion of the Church across Japan, and it was from these that the first Japanese Protestant leaders were drawn. For example, the 15 students at Sapporo Agricultural College became Christian under the leadership of the American William Clark (1826–86). They then influenced students in the second year to convert. From the 'Sapporo Band', Nitobe Inazō (1862–1933) and Uchimura Kanzō (1861–1930) emerged as significant Christian leaders, with the latter forming the first independent Japanese Christian movement, the Non-Church Movement (Mukyōkai) in 1901. Within Christianity, these former samurai found a high ethical ideal similar to what they had enjoyed in Confucianism. Devotion to their feudal lord was replaced with devotion to God, whom they identified with the Confucian concept of heaven (*tian*) and so emphasized how expectations in the Confucian texts were fulfilled in the Christian faith. *Seikyō Shinron* by Kozaki Hiromichi (1856–1938) was the first publication to take this approach, produced in 1886. This first generation of converts had a disproportionate impact on wider Japanese society in this period. For example, Yusa Jirō (1851–1932) and Shimada Saburō (1852–1923) were elected to lead newly forged political institutions. The former campaigned against prostitution, while the latter advocated for the first labour union, formed in 1897.

These appropriations of the Christian faith by Japanese Protestants from the samurai class have been understood as a 'top-down' approach. The founders of these bands, reading their Bibles for themselves, noticed the gaps between the Christ recorded in the biblical texts and differing representations within the large number of imported denominations. The latter were described as *batā-kusai* (literally 'reeking of butter'). Missionary personnel often took a negative view of Japanese culture and religious heritage. This, together with a sometimes patronizing attitude towards Japanese converts, fuelled tensions and resulted in Japanese Christians founding new groups. Uchimura stated that Christianity was like other foreign imports: 'before it can be acclimatised in Japan, it must pass through great modifications in the hands of the Japanese' (Mark R. Mullins, Susumu Shimazono and Paul L. Swanson (eds), *Religion and Society in Modern Japan: Selected readings* (Berkeley, CA: Asian Humanities Press, 1993), p. 272). He resented the missionaries' labelling of his Japanese Christianity as 'nationalistic' while refusing to recognize their own similar approach. In his defence he asked: 'Do not these very missionaries uphold sectional or denominational forms of Christianity which are not very different from national Christianity?' (Mark R. Mullins, *Christianity Made in Japan: A study in indigenous movements* (Honolulu, HI: University of Hawai'i Press, 1998) p. 37). For these converts, their Christian faith fulfilled religious impulses that they had already experienced within Confucianism. Growing nationalism within Japanese society only provided further impetus in this direction.

Other Japanese converts noted the experiential aspects of the biblical narratives, which they observed were missing from missionary Christianity and yet spoke to their own world populated by spiritual beings. Murai Jun

(1897–1962) founded the Spirit of Jesus Church in 1937, which turned the ancestors towards Christ through an innovative rite of baptizing a living individual on behalf of a deceased relative. Kawai Shinsui (1867–1962) founded the Christ Heart Church in 1927 and saw parallels between his own ministry, which had moved beyond missionary Christianity, and the ministry of the apostle Paul initiated through direct experience independent of the Jerusalem church: 'As Jehovah appeared to Moses in thunder on Mt. Sinai, and Christ called to Paul in lightning in the neighbourhood of Damascus, God renewed all things in me through sacred Mt. Fuji' (Kawai Shinsui, *My Spiritual Experiences* (Tokyo: Sacred Heart Church, 1970), p. 12). Forming a new group beyond Western missionary control was characteristic of Protestant rather than Catholic or Orthodox Christianity.

The rise of state-sponsored Shinto and the churches

While the Meiji Constitution granted freedom of religion, the same period also witnessed the renewal of connections between the Japanese state and Shinto. While its origins are lost in Japanese prehistory, Shinto is the indigenous religion of the Japanese people. At the start of our period, most Japanese practised a mix of Buddhist and Shinto rituals at family and community level. During the second half of the nineteenth century, the Japanese government raised Shinto ritual to a national level as a means to forge national unity and demonstrate increasing imperial confidence. This initially involved reviving the role of the emperor as both head of state and chief priest of Shinto state rituals, which were celebrated at a unified network of Shinto shrines. In 1890 copies of an edict were introduced into all schools, highlighting the divine origins of the emperor's ancestry and the loyalty of Japanese people to the state. By the 1930s, as Japan's imperial possessions increased, attendance at Shinto shrines moved from being encouraged to being a test of a citizen's loyalty to the Japanese state. The relationship between the Japanese state and Shinto was itself complex and varied, with Shinto priests at times challenging co-option by the government. This revival of Shintoism was in part linked to the impact of Christianity in Japan, as Christianity was seen as one of a number of external influences to be countered.

A minority of Christians were deeply troubled by participation in these rites. In 1891 Uchimura Kanzō, while on the teaching staff of a Tokyo school, found himself unable to bow before a copy of the 1890 edict alongside his fellow teachers. Outcry in the media at this unnationalistic behaviour led to Uchimura's resignation, which was tragic for a man who would go on to state: 'I love two Js and no third; one is Jesus, and the other is Japan. I do not know which I love more, Jesus or Japan' (Miura Hiroshi, *The Life and Thought of Kanzo Uchimura 1861–1930* (Grand Rapids, MI: Eerdmans, 1996), p. 52). Protestant and Catholic church leaders published in 1917 and 1918, respectively, statements in which they raised serious concerns about Christians participating in rites at Shinto shrines. Even in the 1930s students at the Catholic Jōchi

University and staff at the Protestant Dōshisha University resisted attempts by military officers to impose elements of shrine worship at their institutions.

Other Christians responded to the trauma of Japan's rapid modernization by becoming involved in movements of social and political reform and in social ministries to ease the hardship that accompanied this modernization. The young Kagawa Toyohiko (1888–1960) abandoned his seminary dormitory and moved to the urban slums of Kobe and so experienced poverty first-hand. There he learned that, while inhabitants supported one another in the face of poverty, it required change in their working conditions to bring transformation. And so he began four decades of involvement in both urban and rural labour unions and in cooperative unions. Yoshino Sakuzō (1878–1933), a professor at Tokyo Imperial University, was at the forefront of the movement for parliamentary democracy. By the 1920s such social and political activism shifted towards inner, spiritual concerns.

However, the most common route taken in this period was cooperation with the state authorities. As Japan gained imperial territories in Taiwan (1895), Korea (1905), the Pacific Islands (1919) and Manchuria (1931), the Japanese state co-opted the churches to project a Japanese version of Christianity into these territories. In response, the use of indigenous forms of Christianity became associated with resistance to Japanese rule. By the 1930s first Catholic and then Protestant authorities shifted from their previous position to state that rituals at Shinto shrines were civic rather than religious, thus cutting the ground from under, for example, the protesting students at Jōchi University. During the Second World War, most churches supported the state's demands for spiritual resources to be mobilized behind the war effort. In the 1940s the government required the majority of Protestant churches to form the Nihon Kirisuto Kyōdan, a single unified church that had to accept the rituals of state-sponsored Shintoism. Those that were perceived to question this, for example the Holiness Church, were banned and their members persecuted.

The churches in the post-war period

The end of the Second World War brought a dramatic shift in the political and religious landscape of Japan. The close link between the state and Shinto ended, with the Japanese emperor renouncing his divine ancestry and freedom of religion being included within the 1947 constitution. In the immediate aftermath of the war, the churches made a significant contribution to relief work, paving the way for a rise in the number of Japanese turning to Christianity. However, this growth slowed into the 1950s and 1960s as the churches struggled to offer a credible alternative vision to those on offer in the mainstream of Japanese society. They were hampered from doing so both by their perceived foreignness, coming from their close association with Western churches, and by their reluctance to address their support for the Japanese state in the 1930s and 1940s.

Western missionaries, particularly from North America, flooded into Japan in the post-war period. They tended to come from the newer inter-denominational agencies, with a theology that emphasized the interior spiritual life but was weaker on political and social engagement. While Japan had initially looked to North America as a model for its rebuilding, this approach became less necessary as Japan became a successful consumerist culture in its own right and as disillusionment grew with US military involvement in East Asia. The churches, with strong links to North America, found themselves on the wrong side of this distancing from the USA. The deficit in their imported theology, with its characteristic division between the material and spiritual, was exposed in the face of the more integrated spirituality of so-called 'new religious movements' such as Risshō Kōseikai and Sōka Gakkai. Between 10 and 20 per cent of the population had links to these groups, while Christian affiliation stubbornly remained at less than 1 per cent. In marked contrast to the churches, new religious movements attract those of a lower rather than higher educational level, are experiential rather than intellectual in their spirituality and address the concerns of this world rather than those of the next.

The churches' relative success in the immediate post-war period discouraged reflection on their legacy from before the war. This continued as the economic prosperity of the 1960s brought with it a renewed confidence in the wider society that made examination and apology harder. It was only in 1967 that the leadership of the Kyōdan issued an apology for the church's past support of the government's military and imperial activities. As members of the next generation entered adulthood, they became increasingly impatient with their elders' shelving of this difficult past, which overflowed into student protests at seminaries. During the 1980s the Kyōdan addressed the Japanese imperial legacy by establishing ties with denominations in its former colonies of Korea and Taiwan, and built further links with other Pacific Rim countries. Throughout the 1970s and 1980s both Roman Catholic and Protestant denominations made united protests against the state's action in retaking control of the Yasukuni Shrine, the major Shinto shrine that was a key focus of Japanese militarism in the 1930s and 1940s.

Despite their minority status, Japanese churches have a disproportionate reach in the wider society. Schools founded by Catholic and Protestant missionaries in the late nineteenth and early twentieth centuries have flourished to become colleges and universities. Christian institutions now outstrip their Shinto and Buddhist counterparts and are some of the most prestigious and highly sought-after establishments in the country. The churches have a similarly impressive range of social institutions. For example, the Catholic Church operates over 500 social welfare and over 30 medical institutions. The theologian Kuribayashi Teruo (1948–2015) challenged the church in its commitment to the Burakumin, the 'outcasts' of Japan, understanding Christ to be the one who suffers alongside the Burakumin and also brings liberation from oppression.

While Japan has produced significant Christian thinkers such as Kitamori Kazoh (1916–98), with his significant reflection, *Theology of the Pain of God*, it is perhaps the novelist Shūsaku Endō (1923–96) who brought Christian thought to the attention of a wider audience, both in Japan and globally. In his novels *Silence* and *Deep River*, Endō explored distinctly Japanese understandings of the divine, rooted both in the specific experience of the Kakure Kirishitan under persecution (see above) and wider trends in Japanese religious ideas, as he observed in a short story:

> Many long years ago, missionaries had crossed the seas to bring the teachings of God the Father to this land. But when the missionaries had been expelled and the churches demolished, the Japanese *kakure*, over the space of many years, stripped away all those parts of the religion that they could not embrace, and the teachings of God the Father were gradually replaced by a yearning after a Mother – a yearning that lies at the very heart of Japanese religion.
>
> (S. Endō, 'Mothers', in S. Endō, *Stained Glass Elegies*, trans. Van C. Gessel (London: Peter Owen, 1984), p. 135)

As in other Asian countries, the Church has developed Christian rituals that address the central Japanese concern for the ancestors. Early converts were urged not to participate in ancestral rituals, usually resulting in division and considerable pain within families. In contrast, the Catholic Church issued guidelines in 1985 that encouraged church members to conduct ceremonies to remember the deceased before family altars. If the Church has to accommodate to Confucian and Buddhist influences in funeral rites, marriage rites have become a growing Christian preserve in the wider society. In 1982, 90 per cent of weddings were conducted according to Shinto rites, with only 5 per cent conducted within churches. By 2005, 70 per cent of weddings were Christian in comparison to only 20 per cent Shinto. While this has become something of a 'business', it remains to be seen whether it will translate into church membership and Christian commitment. At the end of the twentieth century, the percentage of Christians in Japan still remained at less than 1 per cent. This, coupled with Japan's low birth rate, means that in practice many congregations are increasingly ageing and denominations are facing a shortage of ordained clergy. The exception is the Catholic Church, whose foreign membership is now greater than local, a result of immigration into Japan from Pacific Rim countries with larger Catholic populations.

Korea

Catholic missions

Since the early seventeenth century, Korean diplomats had met Jesuit priests annually at the Chinese court in Beijing. The following century allowed more extensive contact between these diplomats and Christians in China.

By the late 1770s a group of scholars at the Buddhist temple in Jueosa gathered to study Christian texts brought back from Beijing. One of these, Lee Seung-hoon (1756–1801), was baptized in Beijing in early 1784 and, on his return to Korea, baptized other members of this study group in the same year, including Yi Byeok (1754–85), who became a key exponent of the new Christian faith. This event in 1784 marks the launching of Christianity in Korea. In 1845 Andrew Kim Tae-goon (1821–46) was the first Korean to be ordained a priest in Shanghai, by the French bishop Jean-Joseph Ferréol (1808–53). Born to Christian parents – his father became a Christian martyr – Tae-goon was baptized at the age of 15 and studied at a seminary in the Portuguese colony of Macau, China. After ordination, he returned to Korea to preach and evangelize. This was during a time when Korean Christians were experiencing fiery persecution by the Joseon Dynasty. In 1846, at the age of 25, Tae-goon was tortured and beheaded near Seoul on the Han River. His last words were:

> This is my last hour of life, listen to me attentively. If I have held communication with foreigners, it has been for my religion and for my God. It is for Him that I die. My immortal life is on the point of beginning. Become Christians if you wish to be happy after death, because God has eternal chastisements in store for those who have refused to know Him.
>
> (Nicholas Patrick Wiseman, *The new glories of the Catholic Church, translated from the Italian by the fathers of the London Oratory, at the request of the Cardinal Archbishop of Westminster* (London: Richardson & Son, 1859), p. 118)

State persecution of Roman Catholic Christians occurred from time to time over a number of years. It caused immense suffering, and by 1865 the Catholic Church in Korea had almost been wiped out. French and other European Roman Catholic priests entered Korea secretly, but the majority of them were found, tortured and beheaded. The number of martyrs during the first century of Christianity in Korea is estimated to be around 10,000.

Beginning of Protestant missions

In a similar way to Catholicism, Protestantism first entered Korea in the form of Chinese Christian literature that Protestants were pioneering in China (see above). Two European missionaries, Karl Gützlaff (1803–51) and Robert Thomas (1840–66), distributed this literature down the west coast of the Korean Peninsula in the 1830s and 1860s respectively. The latter lost his life, along with the rest of his shipmates, when their American armoured merchant ship was stranded and attacked near Pyongyang in 1866. Regrettably, these attempts at mission took place during a period when Western powers were forcibly advancing their own economic, military and political interests on the Korean Peninsula and elsewhere in East Asia, producing severe persecution for Korea's Christians between 1866 and 1873.

The distribution of Christian literature was pursued more successfully in the following decade by the Scottish missionary John Ross (1842–1915) and the group of Korean translators and couriers that gathered around him in north-east China. Ross's initial struggle to learn the Korean language was finally overcome with the assistance of Yi Eung-chan (d. 1883), who agreed to teach him in secret because Grand Prince Heungseon Daewongun (1820–98) had warned his subjects about mixing with outsiders. Ross and his team produced translations of first Luke and John in 1882 and subsequently the entire New Testament in 1887. Korean couriers then circulated these among the Korean community, first on the Chinese side of the border and then into Korea itself. From Ross's team came the first Korean Protestants to be baptized, in 1879: Yi Eung-chan, Kim Jin-gi, Baek Hong-jun and Yi Seung-ha (*fl.* 1870s) and the planters of the first Protestant churches in Korea itself. The travelling literature-distribution work of the last two led to a Protestant community within Korea with 18 members at Uiju by 1885. However, two brothers, Suh Sang-ryun (1848–1926) and Suh Sang-u (*fl.* 1880s), had already established a community at Sorae the year before, the former continuing his travelling ministry, the latter pastoring the new community. Just as with Catholic Korean Christianity, Protestant communities were founded not by Western missionaries but by Korean Christians migrating from China into Korea with their new faith and gospel tracts.

Throughout the 1880s individual Western powers concluded a series of treaties with Korea, allowing their missionaries to settle in the country, alongside Korean reformers requesting assistance in encouraging modernization. The first generation of missionaries consequently established hospitals and schools as openly evangelistic activity was still illegal. The earliest of these workers to arrive, the Presbyterian Horace Allen (1858–1932), a medical doctor, saved the life of Min Yeong-ik (1860–1914), a member of the royal family, during an abortive coup by progressives. This secured royal favour for the American missions – even though their progressive associations were discredited after the coup – and so allowed Allen to open a mission hospital in 1885. Many of the Koreans baptized and appointed as elders by these Western missionaries had already learnt the faith from Suh Sang-ryun and Baek Hong-jun in Sorae, including four Korean women baptized in 1888. It was these early male and female converts who facilitated the missionaries' entry into segregated outer quarters of Korean households. Protestant schools swiftly followed, with the Presbyterians founding Jeongdong Yeohakang (Chungshin Girls' School) in 1887 for girls, and the Methodists Paichai Hakdang (School for Cultivating Talent) in 1886 for boys. Literature ministries continued with further translation work, the establishment of presses and publishing ministries, and the production of Bibles, tracts and Christian newspapers. The 1887 New Testament brought out by Ross and his Korean colleagues was foundational until a new translation was completed in 1906, followed by a Korean version of the whole Bible in 1911.

The growth of Catholic and Protestant churches

As with the United States, France's treaty with Korea in 1886 ended state persecution of Catholics and allowed priests to reside again within the kingdom. Like their Protestant counterparts, institutions swiftly followed: a parish school (1882), an old people's care home (1885) and an orphanage (1888). By 1888 the Vicariate Apostolic of Korea was established, in 1896 three Korean students were ordained, and a cathedral in Myeong-dong was dedicated in 1898. By the 1890s both Protestant and Catholic missionaries were working and residing in the interior, often playing catch-up to the initiative of Korean believers who had consciously moved to new areas and gathered enquirers. This indigenous agency was facilitated by the Protestant missionaries' commitment to the 'three-self' principles for their churches, while they occupied a more detached and supervisory role. The 'three selfs' of missionary thought in this period were that newly established churches were to become self-financing, self-governing and self-propagating. The path to and beyond baptism was rigorous, requiring the acquisition of literacy and biblical knowledge and renouncing external activities such as gambling and drinking alcohol. Ancestor veneration and marriage practices, as elsewhere, proved contentious, eased by the reformers' disillusionment with Confucianism. While the missionaries distanced themselves from the issue of spirit possession, Korean believers, faced with pastoral realities and examples in the New Testament, exorcized spirits in the name of the more powerful Holy Spirit. Christianity changed the status of Korean women as they acquired literacy, new networks and enhanced roles. Chun Sam-deok (1843–1932), one of the first Protestant women to be baptized, led some 600 people to faith. She was but one of a number of Korean 'Bible women' who travelled to remote villages, shared their new-found biblical knowledge and offered the Holy Spirit's protection against a hostile spirit world.

Japanese encroachment and revival

As elsewhere in the region, political and economic turmoil marked the turn of the century, culminating in Korea coming under Japan's influence after the former's defeat of China in 1895 and finally being annexed as a territory of Japan in 1910. As a result, Confucian structures and influences were removed from many areas of life. In many ways Protestant Christianity filled this vacuum, offering the following alternatives: an unquestioned, sacred text in the Bible, a philosophy in Christian theology and a moral community in the Church. For members of the elite such as Yun Chi-ho (1864–1945), Western education, accessed through mission schools and publications, was the avenue for Korea to modernize and so meet other nations on a more equal footing. For the Korean masses, Christianity, particularly its Protestant expressions, grew in appeal because it offered them both social and spiritual uplift: the former through its social institutions and its missionaries' international connections; the latter through its modernizing influences and future hope in unstable times. Pyongyang and its surrounding area became a strong centre of Korean Protestantism, with the independent mindset of its small farmers and traders finding a ready echo in the three-self formula. Gil Seon-ju (1869–1935) received an ascetic upbringing within Buddhist and Taoist circles. He experienced both the national trauma of occupation and the personal trauma of near blindness. These factors in his life were to be key in shaping the strict devotion of Presbyterian Christianity in Pyongyang. Converted in 1897 after reading *The Pilgrim's Progress*, Gil developed a religious practice that included rigorous prayerfulness at meetings with fellow believers at dawn, throughout the night and on mountaintops; the renouncing of alcohol, tobacco and any form of depravity; and the self-giving of time and resources. In the wake of the Japanese occupation, he adopted the manner of an Old Testament prophet as he called the Korean people to turn back to God. Resistance to Japanese rule showed itself among Koreans in the form of resigning from government posts, emigrating, joining resistance movements or even committing suicide.

The revival that swept through Korea from 1903 to 1907 was in part a response to the crisis of occupation. Starting in Wonsan, Songdo and Seoul, this wave of renewal spread out across the country with its characteristics of communal repentance, simultaneous praying and ecstatic experience. This Protestant revival had widespread appeal, as it reflected traditional religious practices and allowed expression for the anguish of occupation through personal confession. However, other Christians advocated active resistance to Japanese occupation, such as Ahn Chang-ho (1878–1938), while Ahn Jung-geun (1879–1910) went so far as to assassinate a leading Japanese official, Itō Hirobumi (1841–1909). By the end the 1900s, Protestant Christianity had become deeply rooted in Korean soil through its choice of the indigenous term for God, its commitment to the three-self formula, the appointment of Korean clergy, and the start of the Korean missionary movement to the Korean Diaspora and beyond.

Japanese colonialism and independence

In 1910 Korea formally came under Japanese rule. Christians were forced to worship at the Shinto shrines. Christians also suffered harshly for taking part in a nationalist independence movement in 1919. During the Second World War Koreans suffered severely as Japan took as many resources as possible to support its war efforts, while putting down any move for independence. At the end of the war, the country was divided between the Soviet-controlled North and the American-occupied South.

The believers in North Korea, under the newly established communist regime, encountered incredible challenges as they struggled to retain their Christian faith. During the Korean War (1950–3) many Christians were martyred, while the majority of Christians escaped to the South. The South was only saved by the intervention of the United Nations. The two Koreas are still divided and technically in a state of war.

From the late 1960s South Korea suffered under the military dictatorship of former president Park Jung-hee (1917–79). Korean Christians raised their voices in strong objection to government policies, including the imposition of martial law in 1972 and the creation of a new constitution which allowed the president almost unlimited powers. Church leaders also condemned the abuse of state power and violations of human rights. In 1971 the Roman Catholic bishops issued a mutual letter entitled 'Let's defeat today's injustice', in which they addressed the corruption and brutality committed by the government. Many Christian leaders were imprisoned, often without trial, and given long-term prison sentences. In 1975 the Catholic poet Kim Chi-ha (b. 1941) candidly criticized the government for executing many political prisoners and was issued a life sentence. Ironically, during this period until the 1980s, the Korean Church achieved remarkable growth in numbers.

Currently, there are many Bible colleges and seminaries in South Korea, along with Christian elementary, middle and high schools and universities. Christianity has become a major influence in every sector of public life. Christian radio stations broadcast the gospel and have a reputation for balanced reporting of news. Christian chaplains serve in the armed forces. About 25 per cent of South Korea's 44 million people are Christians. South Korean believers are proud to make up the second largest missionary-sending church, while the largest congregations in the world are also located in Korea.

By 2005, according to one estimate, there were around 500 house churches in North Korea, with some 10,000 believers. There are several churches in the capital city of Pyongyang. Bongsoo Protestant Church and Chang-choon Catholic Church were established in 1988 and Chil-gol Protestant Church was built in 1990. These churches hold regular worship services on Sundays, with 150 to 300 believers attending.

❓ DISCUSSION QUESTIONS

1 Compare and contrast the role played by indigenous Christians in establishing Christianity in China, Japan and Korea.

2 Describe how Christians in North-East Asia identified resources within their own religious heritages to appropriate the Christian faith in ways that were meaningful to them. Describe both top-down, elite approaches and bottom-up, grassroots approaches.

3 Referring to the Christian faith, Uchimura Kanzō stated: 'before it can be acclimatised in Japan, it must pass through great modifications in the

hands of the Japanese.' Describe both how Christianity was presented as a foreign import and ways in which it was acclimatized to local needs.

4 Describe the relationship between Western missions and Western imperialism. What were the consequences of this relationship for Christ's kingdom in the region?

5 Describe how the churches cooperated with, were co-opted by, or confronted political power. What lessons have you learned from the churches for your own context?

6 How did the introduction of Christianity change the position of women in the region?

7 What role did translation of the Bible and the production of Christian literature play in the appropriation of the Christian faith?

Further reading

Bays, Daniel H. *A New History of Christianity in China*. Chichester: Wiley-Blackwell, 2012.

Charbonnier, Jean-Pierre. *Christians in China: A.D. 600 to 2000*. San Francisco, CA: Ignatius Press, 2007.

Clark, Allen D. *A History of the Church in Korea*. Seoul: Christian Literature Society of Korea, 1971.

Hunt, Everett N., Jr. *Protestant Pioneers in Korea*. Maryknoll, NY: Orbis, 1980.

Kim, In Soo. *Protestants and the Formation of Modern Korean Nationalism, 1885–1920: A study of the contributions of Horace G. Underwood and Sun Chu Kil*. New York, NY: Peter Lang, 1996.

Kim, Sebastian C. H. and Kim, Kirsteen. *A History of Korean Christianity*. Cambridge: Cambridge University Press, 2015.

Mullins, Mark R. *Handbook of Christianity in Japan*. Leiden: Brill, 2003.

Paik, L. George. *The History of Protestant Missions in Korea: 1832–1910*. Seoul: Yonsei University Press, 1970.

5

The Indian subcontinent, Sri Lanka and Nepal

George Oommen

Christianity on the Indian subcontinent has followed complex trajectories leading to a wide variety of manifestations in local society. This chapter highlights some of the major historical processes involved in the shaping of the Christian movement from the 1800s, especially capturing some crucial developments and groups in its historical narrative. While analysing the movement, the fundamental approach will be to argue that Christianity in India and in the wider subcontinent has carved out an authentic and distinct space and identity of its own, at times resisting Western impositions and models.

 India

Prior to the 1800s

The Indian subcontinent has a rich and unique history of Christian presence dating back to the first century (CE). By 1800 this history had produced three distinct Christian 'families' in India with varying degrees of interconnections: the Orthodox, the Roman Catholics and the Protestants. The Orthodox branch traces its roots back to the migration of clergy and lay Christians in the fourth century from Edessa in ancient Syria, from which it has gained its Syrian liturgical and ecclesial traditions. The arrival of Portuguese traders at the very end of the fifteenth century paved the way for Portuguese colonization focused on Goa and with it two centuries of vigorous Roman Catholic expansion in India. Although colonial powers from Protestant European countries were present in India from the beginning of the seventeenth century for commercial purposes, it was only in 1705 that the first Protestant missionaries arrived in India at Tranquebar (Tarangambadi) in Tamil Nadu on the south-eastern coast.

Impact of Christianity

The systematic spread and impact of Protestant Christianity with a pan-Indian vision, however, is linked to the well-known names of William Carey (1761–1834), Joshua Marshman (1768–1837) and William Ward (1769–1823). These three men, known as the 'Serampore Trio', arrived in India at the turn of the nineteenth century and founded a mission just north of Calcutta (now Kolkata). Their advent marked a new epoch in the history of Indian Christianity, a period in which the work of Christian mission became indelibly linked to the British consolidation of colonial power over the Indian subcontinent through the East India Company.

William Carey, the leading personality behind the formation of the Baptist Missionary Society, arrived in Bengal with his famous two-point vision: 'Expect great things from God; attempt great things for God.' Despite the lack of support or permission from the East India Company to go to its territories, William Carey landed at Calcutta in November 1793 via the Hooghly River, thus inaugurating one of the most historically significant eras in the development of modern India: its Christianization, and with it the advent of Western science, the English language and the gradual transference of Western ideas. Joshua Marshman, an educator, and William Ward, a printer, joined Carey in 1799. They worked together in subsequent decades on several ambitious projects, including translating the Bible into several Indian languages, printing magazines and founding educational institutions.

By 1801 the Bengali New Testament was printed and published. Soon Carey was appointed as Professor of Bengali in the College of Fort William, Calcutta. With his exceptional linguistic abilities, Carey was further asked to teach Sanskrit and Marathi. He was responsible for Bengali, Hindi, Sanskrit and Marathi translations of the Bible. The project was so extensive that many local Hindu *pandits* (scholars) were part of the team. In 1811 Ward, writing to a relative of Carey, described the scene of translation as follows:

> As you enter, you see your cousin, in a small room, dressed in a white jacket, reading or writing, and looking over the office, which is more than 170 feet long. There you find Indians translating the Scriptures into the different tongues, or correcting proof-sheets. You observe laid out in cases, types in Arabic, Persian, Nagari, Telugu, Panjabi, Marathi, Chinese, Oriya, Burmese, Kanarese, Greek, Hebrew and English. Hindus, Mussulmans [Muslims] and Christian Indians are busy – composing, correcting, distributing. Next are four men throwing off the Scripture sheets in the different languages; others folding the sheets and delivering them to the large store-room; and six Mussulmans do the binding. Beyond the office are the varied type-casters, besides a group of men making ink; and in a spacious open walled-round place, our paper-mill, for we manufacture our own paper.
>
> (S. Pearce Carey, *William Carey* (London: Hodder & Stoughton, 1924), p. 283)

With such laborious processes in place, six versions of the entire Bible and 23 of the New Testament had been completed by the time Carey passed away in 1834.

The Serampore Trio also pioneered the printing of Indian scripts and the publication of newspapers in Indian languages. By the 1820s missionaries were publishing *Dig Darshan*, a monthly magazine in Bengali; *Samachar Darpan*, a weekly newspaper also in Bengali; and *The Friend of India*, an English journal and forerunner to the modern *Statesman*. In 1818 they launched themselves into the educational field in a significant way by founding the Serampore College. This opened a new chapter in the Christian involvement in modern education in India.

The Serampore Mission established its stations in various parts of North India, including such significant centres as Benares, Agra and Delhi, although its impact was stronger in Bengali society. As a result of the renewal of the East India Company Charter by the British parliament in 1813 a diocese of Calcutta was founded by the Anglican Church (Church of England), and the presidency centres of Bombay and Madras were also brought under its ecclesiastical jurisdiction.

In 1833 the whole of India was opened up to non-British Protestant mission societies, thus widening the scope and impact of Protestant churches' involvement. British missionaries had already established missionary stations in several regions in South India, such as Travancore-Cochin, Tirunelveli, Madras and Tiruchirapalli. Famous missionaries such as Robert Caldwell (1814–91) were not only involved in religious activity but were also making creative contributions to the development of South Indian languages. His *Comparative Grammar of the Dravidian Languages* (1875) was one such distinguished and systematic work. Thus, during the first decades of the nineteenth century, Protestant Christianity was not only having an impact on the wider society but also bringing significant numbers of Indians into its fold, cutting across castes and regions. Several high-caste Hindus responded positively to Protestant Christianity in major centres such as Calcutta, Bombay and Madras. Approximately 91,000 Protestant Christians were present in India in 1851, the majority of whom were from South India.

However, the role of the local Indian leadership was pivotal in most of these conversions. Without the translation of the gospel and its transmission in the local idiom to reflect everyday reality, and without potential converts absorbing it in indigenous categories, conversions would not have taken place. For instance, Maharasan Vedamanikam (1772–1827), from Myiladi near Cape Comorin, was instrumental in bringing large numbers of low-caste people, particularly the Shanars of South India, into the Christian fold. He was an influential socio-religious leader who was attracted to Christianity particularly through the work of W. T. Ringeltaube (1770–1816) who worked for the London Missionary Society. Vedamanikam's oratory style and preaching appear to have enhanced the missionary movement.

Although the attraction of the upper classes of Indian society towards Christianity continued during the whole of the nineteenth century, it was more intense during this early period, when Christian missionaries introduced Western education to the young people of India, mainly those of the upper caste, in an unprecedented manner. In fact, Christian missionaries generally hoped that the Christian impact on the intellectual leadership of India would result in the collapse of Hindu society. They were confident that it would only be a matter of time before most of the educated youth turned to Christianity and Western culture. However, Christianity's impact was radically different from what the missionaries envisaged. The young men of the educated classes never considered Christianity a substitute for their traditional Hindu belief system. Instead, Christian ideas helped them to challenge and reform their own religion and society. This spirit of enlightenment and liberalism resulted in intellectual awakening and social reform, particularly within the higher classes of Hindu society.

Social reform and education

No impartial history of Indian society and religion can ignore the involvement of Christianity in the field of education and social reform during the first half of the nineteenth century. Protestant Christians were particularly critical of the dehumanizing aspects of Hindu religious customs and traditions. In Bengal, Protestant missionaries, with the help of liberal-minded and educated Hindu youth, attacked several Hindu religious practices. *Sati* (the burning of a widow on her husband's funeral pyre), infanticide and the plight of widows within Hindu society were perceived and presented by the Protestant missionary leadership as symbols of moral degradation and inhumanity within Indian society. With the aid of British liberalism and imperial power, missionaries and other like-minded reformers exerted mounting pressure that would result in far-reaching social changes.

Public opinion turned against the sacrifice of children and *sati* as a result of the Protestant campaign. The *Friend of India*, a Baptist Mission monthly publication, carried several articles supporting these missionary goals. Ram Mohan Roy (1774–1833), one of the most enlightened Hindus of the time, who eventually emerged as a pioneer of Reformed Hinduism, fought along with Protestant missionaries for the prohibition of *sati* in all territories of the East India Company, and in 1829 Governor General William Bentinck (1774–1839) abolished *sati*. Although the missionaries' ultimate aim was evangelism and the conversion of Hindu society to Christianity, they could see that the outcome of their involvement was being manifested in various ways in Indian society. To a great extent, humanitarian reforms brought about by their efforts gave them a deep sense of satisfaction and Christian fulfilment. It is a well-known fact that when Carey received a copy of the famous prohibition of *sati* by Lord Bentinck on a Sunday morning, he arranged for someone else to take the worship service so that he could work on the translation of the document without delay and see the changes quickly implemented, thus saving the lives of several widows.

The social involvement of Christian missionaries had several consequential dimensions, including humanitarianism, social activism and the transformation of religion and society. The undermining of the Hindu faith and its practices was integral to these activities, and missionaries hoped that it would ultimately bring about the success of their plan for Christian expansion.

Education was one of the top priorities of the Protestant and Roman Catholic missionaries. Until 1833 the Protestant Church saw the establishment and maintenance of elementary schools as one of its fundamental commitments. Indian languages were promoted in most of these schools. However, Alexander Duff (1806–78), a Presbyterian missionary sent by the Church of Scotland, became a prominent advocate of the promotion of English education in India, bringing a shift in the missionary approach. He and many other Protestant figures firmly believed that the introduction of the English language and the study of modern sciences, accompanied by Christian evangelism, would create a favourable atmosphere for the reception of the gospel and the collapse of Hinduism. In fact, soon after this shift, several educated young men, including Brahmins, converted to Protestant Christianity in Calcutta, and later became well-known leaders of the Christian Church in North India. Krishna Mohan Banerjee (1813–85), Lal Behari Day (1824–92), Mohesh Chunder Ghose (d. 1837) and Gopinath Nandi (1809–61) were some of the most influential high-caste converts.

To many of these young men, however, conversion to Christianity did not mean complete Westernization. In fact, despite their conversion, their sense of patriotism and commitment to Indian society and culture remained intact. The missionaries did not expect this. While they themselves were uncompromisingly critical of Hinduism, several of the converted youth defended Indianness and opposed the Westernizing tendency of Christianity. Sisir Kumar Das has this to say about two of the high-caste converts in Bengal:

> Both Krishnamohan and Lal Behari Day were fierce critics of Hinduism and yet they were intensely patriotic and loved their countrymen . . . Their love for their national culture assured them permanent places in the history of modern Bengal. Yet none of them could check the tide of neo-Hinduism or Hindu-revivalism that was started by Rammohan Roy. Yet the direct impact of Christian thought on Bengali society was made possible through them . . . Their lives proved that an Indian could remain an Indian in his social, cultural and political life, yet be a Christian by religion. The 'foreignness' of Christianity was disproved by them. They showed that Christianity could be an Indian religion by its own right.
>
> (Sisir Kumar Das, *The Shadow of the Cross* (New Delhi: Munshiram Manoharlal, 1973), p. 56)

The promotion of English education by the Christian missionaries prompted government educational policy to shift to a pro-English emphasis from 1835. In effect, Protestant missionary efforts played a definitive role in the emergence of the modern system of public education in India. By the mid nineteenth century there was a wide network of schools and colleges developing all over Indian towns and cities, under both government and private management.

Churches established numerous schools and several prominent colleges during subsequent years by making use of grants-in-aid from the government. Between 1833 and 1857 the most renowned Christian colleges were established, including St Stephen's in Delhi, John Wilson College in Bombay, Madras Christian College in Madras, Hislop College in Nagpur, Noble College in Masulipatnam and St John's College in Agra. This process continued with the founding of several women's colleges during the second half of the nineteenth century; among these were Women's Christian College in Madras, Isabella Thoburn College in Lucknow, Sarah Tucker College in Palayamkottai and Lady Deak College in Madurai. This extensive system of Christian schools and colleges would afford Indian Christians a leading role in India's educational sector.

Evangelization and the educational involvement of Roman Catholics continued to wane as a result of the ecclesiastical and jurisdictional power struggle between the Portuguese patronage system and the Propaganda Fide during the nineteenth century. Pope Leo XIII (1810–1903) established the episcopal hierarchy in India in 1886, restricting the power of the Portuguese monarchy. This paved the way for an extensive network of Roman Catholic evangelistic, social and medical activities in various parts of India, especially in Chota Nagpur and other tribal-dominated regions including West Bengal (now Bangladesh).

Missionary involvement in social reform and education, with the support of the colonial power, further enhanced the perception among the educated classes of Indians that Protestant missions were acting hand in glove with British colonialism. So, along with a yearning for the reform of Indian society, educated Indians became anti-Christian in their attitudes due to the denationalizing power of the Christian religion. The role of the missionaries in promoting the cause of the British Empire created further estrangement between Christianity and the educated classes. In essence, the relationship between Christian missionary activity and the British Raj, and the Indian people's negative perception of this relationship, hampered the growth of Protestant Christianity in India. This was particularly so among educated, upper-class Hindus. By promoting Western education, Protestant missionaries helped to further anti-Christian and nationalistic feelings.

Dalit and tribal response to Christianity

The missionaries' plan of evangelistic action envisaged a downward movement of Christianity – the Christianization of upper castes first, followed by lower-caste groups. But as we have already seen, the upper echelons of Indian society did not respond positively to Protestant Christianity for various reasons. To the amazement and surprise of the missionaries, it was the

Dalits (previously 'untouchables') and other downtrodden peoples of India who embraced Christianity and responded positively to the message of the gospel. This unprecedented movement of Dalits to Christianity began in the 1860s when Protestant missions in India were looking for a directional shift as a result of the 1857 Sepoy revolt against British rule. It was reported that there were 160,955 Protestant Christians in India in 1871; by 1900 this number had increased to 506,019. Presently, it is estimated that nearly 80 per cent of the Protestant community and 60 per cent of Roman Catholics are descendants of various Dalit communities.

The second half of the nineteenth century was a time of dramatic change for the Dalits. Several socio-economic factors provided the context within which this change could express itself. The most significant one was the introduction of a colonial economy. The new categories and patterns of land relations and agricultural activities altered the traditional system in an unprecedented way. This transforming environment also affected Dalits, who were caught up in the repressive patron–client system of the landlords; as a result of the socio-economic changes, they gradually gained more rights. This period was also a time of religious change. Among the most significant was the Shuddhi movement introduced by the Arya Samaj, a Hindu revivalist group. This movement, which arose partly as a response to Christian missionary involvement in charity and social reform, sent the message that Dalits were an important group in Indian society and that Hindus would like to continue to keep them within their fold. In South India also, several religio-cultural reform movements were emerging, especially during the last decade of the nineteenth century and the early part of the twentieth.

Historically, Dalits in India have used religious conversion to Buddhist and Islamic traditions as a means of liberation. But what was different about Dalit conversions in this instance was that it took the form of a mass turning to Christianity, and it was mainly to the Protestant churches that the people turned. The story of this group movement of Dalits in various parts of India to Protestant Christianity had certain unique characteristics.

The conversion of Dalits to Christianity, with its mass base, was particularly evident from the 1860s to the 1920s. It is not a historical accident that Dalits chose these crucial decades in the history of India – when census-taking and demography became political tools and the Gandhian movement was at its height – to make this en masse move to Christianity. In many places in fact, it was not the European missionaries who sought the Dalits but the Dalits who went after the missionaries, seeking baptism and schooling. The comparative rates of growth of India's religious communities during the period 1881–1931 demonstrate that the rate of growth among Christians was 338 per cent, which was the second highest among all communities.

Although Dalit communities were isolated in certain regions of India, particularly the southern states, a pan-Indian character was obvious in their movement towards Christianity. The churches of Punjab, and various Dalit peoples such as the Chamars of Uttar Pradesh and Delhi, the Mahars of Central and Western India, the Paraiyars and Chakkliars of Tamil Nadu, the Parayas and Pulayas of Kerala and the Malas and Madigas of Andhra Pradesh were involved in this conversion movement. One of the main features of the Dalit conversions was the group and community nature of their affiliation. In most places, people converted to Christianity as families, kinship units, even villages, thus maintaining their socio-cultural cohesion and communal structures.

It was natural for many observers, notably Mohandas Karamchand Gandhi (1869–1948), to dismiss these large-scale conversion movements as 'conversion for convenience'. As a result, the label 'rice Christians' was almost permanently attached to Christians in India. One of the main reasons for such labelling was the fact that Dalits were seeking so-called material benefits such as education along with their conversion and that, in some places, conversions occurred during famines. However, it would be naive on the part of any scholar to think that Dalits, who had their own strong religio-cultural beliefs and customs, could make such a shift in their affiliation primarily due to material motivations. Conversions were an expression of the cumulative effect of the changing situations in which Dalits found themselves.

An analysis of the major features of Christian mass conversion movements reveals that the sociological and psychological dimensions involved in such movements played a dominant role. First, it is argued that the underlying motivation in Dalit conversion movements to Christianity was 'the search for improved social status, for a greater sense of personal dignity and self respect, for freedom from bondage to oppressive land owners' (John C. B. Webster, *The Dalit Christians: A history* (Delhi: ISPCK, 1992), p. 57). Conversion to Christianity was an expression of a search for human dignity and better treatment from landlords and other members of the higher castes. In many cases, Dalit converts forced missionaries to intervene on their behalf when atrocities occurred as a result of conversions. Second, conversion was a form of protest, reflecting Dalit rejection of, and opposition to, the oppressive marginalization of the caste system. Third, Dalits used conversions to distance themselves from institutions and religious customs that denied them access to religio-cultural and social resources of power.

One of the main outcomes of this mass conversion of Dalits to Christianity was that the whole Indian political process began to give attention to them as an important socio-cultural constituent. Conversions brought Dalits to the centre of the Indian nation-making exercise. In this sense, it would be appropriate to state that Christianity, especially as represented by Protestant groups, played a vital historical role in shaping the Dalit liberation movement, particularly during the second half of the nineteenth century. The history of the Christian experience and its identity in the Indian subcontinent cannot be detached from the aspirations of Dalits, which found expression through ecclesial structures.

A similar mass conversion of 'adivasis' (meaning 'original inhabitants') or tribal peoples to Christianity in different regions of India occurred during the last decades of the nineteenth century. Significantly, it continued into the post-Independence period. In certain regions, for example Chota Nagpur and the North-East Indian states, entire tribes embraced Christianity. The Roman Catholic, Lutheran and Baptist missions were some of the major recipients of this large-scale tribal affiliation. In the 1860s Kols, Santals, Gonds, Bhills, Konds and Pans from the central provinces of India attached themselves to Christianity in large numbers. Exploitation by *Zamindars* (feudal landlords), socio-religious dislocation, cultural crises and the potential protection of the colonial systems constituted the context within which these religious conversions took place. The Chota Nagpur tribals found the cooperative credit movements, initiated by the Roman Catholic and Lutheran missionaries, particularly attractive. In several cases, tribal peoples became owners of land and were freed from bonded labour systems. Economic injustices were confronted, and Christianity offered them a position of assertion and a means to unshackle themselves from dehumanizing experiences. The work of Father Constant Lievens (1856–93), a Belgian Jesuit missionary among tribal people, helped to turn thousands of them to Roman Catholicism.

In the North-East Indian region, which consists of present-day states such as Nagaland, Manipur, Mizoram, Meghalaya and Tripura, large communities of the Garo, Naga, Khasi, Jaintia, Lushai, Ao and other tribes rapidly turned to Christianity in the twentieth century. Membership in the tribal Christian community of North-East India has increased by more than 170 per cent since political independence. Among the American Baptists alone, the number of tribal converts increased from 48,000 in 1918 to nearly 250,000 in 1941. In 1951 North-East Indian tribal Christians represented 7.8 per cent of the total Christian population of India and totalled 659,065. Roman Catholic expansion among the north-eastern tribes occurred comparatively recently. However, Catholics constitute 26 per cent of the Christians in the region. By 1990 they were operating 1,300 institutions, mainly educational.

Explaining the massive movement of tribal peoples in these regions to Christianity, Frederick Downs states that 'For the tribals, Christianity provided a means of preserving their identities and promoting their interests in the face of powerful forces of change' (*History of Christianity in India*, Vol. V, Part 5, *North East India in the Nineteenth and Twentieth Centuries* (Bangalore: CHAI, 1992), p. 7). He adds that entire tribes opted for Christianity because Christianization reinforced tribal identity and helped tribal groups to adjust to the changed context created by the coming of British imperialistic rule and the resultant imposition of new value systems among them.

Rather than displacing local culture, Christianity helped tribes maintain their culture and customs to a great extent. At a time when their socio-cultural life might have been severely disrupted or perhaps wiped out, their conversion to Christianity allowed them to keep many of their cultural practices by Christianizing them. In other words, the processes of inculturation and Christianization went hand in hand; for example, the missionaries accepted the people's belief in evil spirits, while also demonstrating the greater power of the Christian God. By affirming indigenous culture, 'Christianity liberated the people from a world-view in which they were socially and psychologically enslaved by the fear of spirits' (Downs, *History of Christianity in India*, p. 170). (For more on this, see the section on 'Village Christianity' below.)

Thus, the second half of the nineteenth century and the first half of the twentieth century was a time of considerable Christian expansion in India. This expansion, mainly among Dalits and 'adivasis' or tribal peoples, transformed both the nature of Christianity and its role in Indian society. As the restructuring of Indian religion and society increasingly became the preserve of Hindu reformers and Indian nationalists, Christianity became strongly associated with philanthropic activities such as the founding of orphanages, leper asylums, agricultural and industrial institutions and, more importantly, medical facilities. Protestant churches began to greatly emphasize rural education and reconstruction programmes. Groups such as the Young Men's Christian Association (YMCA), Young Women's Christian Association (YWCA) and the Student Christian Movement (SCM) contributed significantly to these efforts.

Involvement in medical work by Christian missions became most prominent in the final decades of the nineteenth century. The Zenana Bible and Medical Mission, for instance, played an important role in providing better medical care for the women and children of India. Large numbers of doctors and nurses were trained in Protestant and Roman Catholic medical institutions such as Christian Medical College and Hospital, Vellore; Christian Medical College and Hospital, Ludhiana; and St John's Medical College and Hospital, Bangalore, all of which symbolized the deep involvement of Christian medical work in India.

Women and conversion

The comparatively recent entry of gender into the discussion of Christian conversions in the historical narrative has greatly enriched our knowledge about nineteenth- and twentieth-century Christianization in India. The significant transformation brought about among women in Indian society through colonial interventions, conversion movements and the various Zenana educational and medical missions constitutes a glorious foundational building-block in the Christian influence in the region. Capturing the role of women and gender ideologies in the conversion process provides a more complete story of Indian Christianity. It demonstrates that not only did Christianity change the status, marriage rights and domestic roles of many women; it also 'radically transformed the style of femininity to which Indian Christian women were expected to conform' (Eliza F. Kent,

Converting Women: Gender and Protestant Christianity in colonial South India (Oxford: Oxford University Press, 2004), p. 4).

Female missionaries, high-caste educated women and numerous Bible women all had a significant role in this dimension of Indian Christianity. European female missionaries and several widowed high-caste Indian women tried to break new ground for women's liberated identity away from the confines of the socially and culturally prescribed boundaries, which included issues of status, clothing and the wearing of jewellery.

Pandita Ramabai

Pandita Ramabai (1858–1922) is a hugely important figure in the history of Christianity in India because of her multifaceted involvement prior to, but especially after, her conversion to Christianity. She was born into a high-caste Brahmin family. Her marriage to an educated Bengali at the age of 22 was non-traditional. However, she was widowed after two years of marriage by her husband's passing away. Her advanced learning in the Hindu Shastras, philosophy and the Sanskrit language eventually took her to Calcutta, a centre of learning and aggressive missionary presence during the defining period of the second half of the nineteenth century. In the 1880s her exposure to the teachings of the Brahmo Samaj led her to found the Arya Mahila Samaj (or Women's Society), demanding education for females and the training of female teachers. While studying medicine at Oxford, Ramabai converted to Christianity and was baptized, along with her daughter.

The conversion of women, particularly high-caste women and widows, caused considerable consternation in Hindu society. In 1889 Ramabai travelled back to Bombay and set up the Sharada Sadan (or Home for Learning) for higher-caste Hindu widows. Her Christian conversion and feminist movement played a key role in redeeming the Indian Christian's identity as fully Indian and Christian at the same time. Ramabai's leadership and impact went beyond these institutions and movements, shaping the fundamentals of women's emancipatory movements in India. Her conversion to Christianity in itself was groundbreaking for its wider socio-religious implications: she had an impact on the Hindu nationalist dialogue by reclaiming her 'Hindu' identity in spite of her conversion. Her resistance to the untamed behaviour of the Brahmin patriarchy and the consequent empowerment of women opened up a new era for women's liberation and Christianity in India.

Village Christianity

The mass appropriation of Christianity by Indians had both constructive and perplexing consequences. From a beneficial point of view, the situation of Christianity in the rural areas of India demonstrates that village Christians have, in their own way, evolved systems of existing peaceably in their socio-religious milieu. In other words, village Christians in India, through a process of accommodation and acceptance, allow various systems of beliefs and practice to coexist. Often, the essentials of Christianity are mixed with their pre-existing religio-cultural concepts and patterns. This results in harmonious relationships with their neighbours, who may belong to different faiths. In this mode of adaptation, Christian villagers participate in and contribute to local festivals.

Western Christian missionaries, in many instances, attempted a process of de-culturalization among the people of India. The prevailing view was that Christianization meant Europeanization, in terms of both faith and culture. However, village Christians have resisted this pressure in many ways. Indian Christian peoples have, to a great extent, sustained their cultural autonomy. Despite the fact that Christianity came to India through the medium of Middle Eastern or Western missionary agencies or institutions, as part of either commercial or colonial structures, Christianity has carved out an authentic indigenous space for itself. This is also despite the fact that in various ways, Western lifestyles, ecclesiology and doctrines have been transplanted into Indian soil, and that so many churches still outwardly look like symbols of a Western or foreign religion. The soul of Indian Christianity, we can see, is Indian in many ways. The singing, the simple belief systems, the 'jatras' (festivals at the grassroots level), have all been shaped by common people rejecting the official and formal dimensions of Christianity in their own subtle ways. It is in these aspects that Christianity is seen to be a living faith in India.

Political nationalism and Christians

The Indian Christian response to the struggle for national independence from British imperialism is significant, considering the fact that the Christian community in general was either indifferent to nationalistic movements or supportive of the continuance of British rule. The rising national consciousness and the struggles for political freedom had an impact on several Christians, particularly the highly educated. In the early history of the Indian National Congress (the leading nationalist movement), and in its organization, the contribution and active participation of Indian Christians was indeed significant. Some of the prominent Christian leaders in the Congress movement included R. S. N. Subramania (*fl.* 1880s), Kali Charan Banerji (1847–1907), Madhusudan Das (1848–1934), Charles Golak Nath (*fl.* 1880s), Peter Paul Pillai (*fl.* 1880s–1890s) and Pandita Ramabai. However, by the early 1900s as the Congress began to agitate for complete political independence (in a way that made Western missionaries in India quite nervous), Indian Christian participation in the Congress movement began to notably decline. Moreover, the National Christian Council of India, the apex body of the Protestant churches at the national level, did not take a definite stand with regard to the question of Indian independence.

However, defying the norms and general expectations of the time, Christian leaders and theologians such as Susil Rudra (1861–1925), S. K. Dutta (1878–1948), K. T. Paul (1876–1931), V. S. Azariah (1874–1945) and S. K. George (1900–60) supported the Indian national struggle and some of the Gandhian initiatives in particular. Some of them were at the forefront of the movement and close associates of Gandhi – at a time when fear of Hindu domination had begun to creep into the minds of the Indian Christian community. Efforts by these Christian leaders to bring the Christian community into the mainstream of the Indian independence movement seem to have succeeded to a great degree. By the 1930s and 1940s many were actively supporting and involved in the Indian National Congress. The Indian Christian Association and the Patriotic Group of Madras were some of the Christian organizations that emerged during this time.

In the early part of the twentieth century, within Protestant circles and as a direct response to nationalism, both Western missionaries and some Indian Christians began to search for an Indian Christianity that was in tune with the Hindu way of thinking and culture. Among Western missionaries, H. G. Hogg (1875–1954) and William Miller (1838–1923) were in favour of developing a form of Christianity that did not demand severance from cultural affiliations but was simply a commitment to Christ. One such Hindu-Christian believer in Madras was O. Kandaswamy Chetti (1867–1943). He believed in Jesus Christ as the only saviour but declined baptism as a symbol of his rejection of the Western type of Christianity, which demanded complete severance from one's own community and kinship relationships. He founded the Fellowship of the Followers of Jesus to express this aspiration. However, this was not a movement which found favour among many Indian Christians.

Indian Christian theology

The development of an Indian Christian theological movement among Protestant Indian theologians also reflected the impact of Indian nationalism. The Madras Rethinking Group, which met in the 1930s and 1940s to develop an Indian Christian theology, needs particular mention in this regard. This group and other theologians articulated a Christian theology on the basis of Indian philosophical traditions during this time. Prominent figures in this movement included A. S. Appaswamy (1848–1926), P. Chenchiah (1886–1959), V. Chakkarai (1880–1956), K. T. Paul (1876–1931), R. C. Das (1887–1976) and A. J. Appaswamy (1891–1975). Their theology was shaped by the growing national and cultural consciousness of the time, and some of them were active participants in the political movement. The positive aspects of pre-Christian traditions and belief systems found theological expression in their writings. Geoffrey A. Oddie observes that, in this movement, there was a clear-cut rejection of Europeanized faith and interpretations, and a meaningful Indian version of the gospel was being articulated. He writes:

One important characteristic of Indian Christian theology up to the period of independence was the growing recognition that for Christians the main issue was not so much the domestication of the pre-packaged European faith, but a new, dynamic and living version of a gospel which would reflect Indian insights and experience and be somewhat different from the foreign missionary models. In the view of Chakkarai, and others as well, what was important was not the repetition of understandings derived from European experience, but an openness to what God appeared to have been doing and saying in Indian traditions. Indian Christian theology was, therefore, for them, largely a two-way process of listening to what they believed was the voice of God in India's history and culture, and of reinterpreting and making known the Christian Gospel – a message which, far from being European, would be appropriate and relevant in the Indian situation.

(Geoffrey A. Oddie, 'Indigenization and nationalism', *Archives de Sciences Sociales des Religions*, no. 103 (1998), p. 149)

This conscious process of indigenizing Christian theology was part of a radicalizing approach in which Christianity in India became Indian Christianity.

Indian church union movements were another expression of nationalism. By rejecting forms of Western denominational ecclesiology, Indian Christians, along with some Western missionaries, asserted the need for church union in India. This led to the formation of the Church of South India (CSI), which brought together various confessional groups such as those from the Congregational, Presbyterian, Methodist and Anglican traditions. This organic union of churches was historically unprecedented. The deep division between the episcopal churches and non-episcopal churches created during the Reformation was healed by their union. Thus, four major post-Reformation traditions were integrated into one organic union as the Church of South India in September 1947, the year that India achieved its freedom from the colonial domination of British imperialism.

In 1970 a similar but wider union of various ecclesial traditions, including the Baptists, Church of the Brethren and Disciples of Christ, emerged in North India under the Church of North India as part of the continuing search of Indian Christians to come to terms with their Indianness. This was clearly related to the process of the Church in India becoming a people's church. These developments would have repercussions in the West where denominationalist barriers prevailed strongly. Most recently, the Communion of Churches in India has emerged as a result of the ecumenical affinity among the Church of South India, the Church of North India and the Mar Thoma Church, a denomination emerging out of the Orthodox group of churches in the nineteenth century.

Post-Independence

The history of Christianity in India in the post-Independence period (after 1947) has been characterized by winds of change and direction-altering developments. The Christian community, particularly its theological leadership, began to find meaningful expressions of participation in nation-building and reversed the tradition of shunning socio-political involvement. Protestant theologians such as P. D. Devanandan (1901–62) and M. M. Thomas (1916–96) began to challenge the whole Christian community to be a part of a prophetic movement within the independent nation. Issues of justice and interreligious dialogue were at the forefront of this theological movement. The founding of the Christian Institute for the Study of Religion and Society, Bangalore, an offshoot of the theological leadership of the United Theological College, Bangalore, was a definite manifestation of such an effort by Christians. These movements valued the secular socio-political fabric that was emerging in India, where religious freedom and identity were recognized as inalienable human rights. S. Kappen (1924–93), a prominent Jesuit, constructed a distinct theology of political action and liberation in the 1970s.

The postcolonial period also ushered in an era of interreligious dialogue. The World Council of Churches Assembly of 1961 in New Delhi and the Second Vatican Council (1962–5) gave added impetus to a new willingness to engage with the religiously pluralistic context of the subcontinent. Mutual enrichment and a reduction in religious conflicts became the focus among many mainline churches. The Christian–Hindu relationship shaped pioneering efforts that were then taken to the global ecumenical level by the leadership and theology of Indian theologians such as S. J. Samartha (1920–2001), who authored books such as *The Hindu Response to the Unbound Christ* (Madras: CLS, 1974) and *One Christ – Many Religions* (Bangalore: SATHRI, 2000). The National Biblical Catechetical and Liturgical Centre in Bangalore experimented with expressions of inculturation, pioneering a movement in the Roman Catholic community. D. S. Amalorpavadass (1932–90), a Roman Catholic theologian, was at the forefront of the movement. Jyothi Sahi (b. 1944), a Roman Catholic painter and theologian, used painting to depict the Hindu–Christian dialogue and more recently began to incorporate tribal–Dalit motifs in his art. Frank Wesley (1923–2002), a Methodist from Uttar Pradesh, articulated a creative indigenous search in his paintings by incorporating Hindu and Asian perspectives.

Dalit theology

Since Dalit and tribal Christians comprise a substantial majority of the Christian community in India, they are in a strong position to shape the new or emerging theological discussions. The emergence of Dalit Christian theology in India is intrinsically linked to more recent and significant developments within the Dalit movement in India dating from the 1970s. Many Dalit Christian leaders refer to the thrice-alienated situation of the Dalit Christians in India based on: 1) discrimination within the Church;

2) discrimination by Hindu culture; and 3) discrimination by the state (since they are denied 'Scheduled Caste' status in the Constitution and the related privileges which come with that status). Additionally, the historical experience of the Dalits and their pre-existing belief systems greatly influence the way they look at their faith and interpret it.

Although Dalit Christians constituted approximately 70 per cent of the Indian Christian population, they were marginalized and ignored until recently. At the Catholic Bishops' Conference of India in 1991, Archbishop George Zur (1930–2019), Apostolic Pro-Nuncio to India, observed:

> Though Catholics of the lower caste and tribes form 60 per cent of Church membership they have no place in decision-making. Scheduled caste converts are treated as lower caste not only by high caste Hindus but by high caste Christians too. In rural areas they cannot own or rent houses, however well-placed they may be. Separate places are marked out for them in the parish churches and burial grounds. Inter-caste marriages are frowned upon and caste tags are still appended to the Christian names of high caste people. Casteism is rampant among the clergy and the religious. Though Dalit Christians make 65 per cent of the 10 million Christians in the South, less than 4 per cent of the parishes are entrusted to Dalit priests. There are no Dalits among 13 Catholic Bishops of Tamilnadu or among the Vicars-general and rectors of seminaries and directors of social assistance centres.
>
> (Quoted in James Massey, *Dalits in India: Religion as source of bondage or liberation with special reference to Christians* (New Delhi: Manohar, 1995), p. 82)

The situation in the Protestant Church is no different except that some Dalits have recently been elevated to the bishopric and other positions of power.

From the early 1980s efforts have been made to systematically articulate the newly emerging Dalit aspiration for liberation. A. P. Nirmal (1936–95), James Massey (1943–2015), M. Azariah (1934–2012), Kothapalli Wilson (*fl.* 1982) and V. Devasahayam (b. 1949) are among prominent leaders of this theological movement. Since Indian Christian theology has long served elite interests and marginalized the Dalit experience, Dalit theology manifests itself as a counter-theology movement by articulating its concerns exclusively. This is to say that re-formulation and re-visioning are the main objectives rather than reconstruction and deconstruction. Both the European missionary movement and the traditional Indian Christian theology of the early twentieth century are rejected as metaphysical speculations with little relevance to the history and existence of the marginalized majority within the Indian Church.

Pentecostal and Charismatic movements

The unprecedented expansion of Pentecostal and Charismatic movements since the 1950s and their impact on and interactions with the mainline churches mark a recent shift in Indian Christianity. These movements can be divided into three strands.

1 *Classical pentecostalism*. This incorporates groups that trace their origins to the early twentieth-century Pentecostal revivals in the USA, including the Assemblies of God, the Indian Pentecostal Church and the Church of God (Full Gospel) India. These groups are comparatively more pan-Indian in their presence.

2 *Charismatic movements that emerged in the 1970s and 1980s within the mainline churches*. These are mainly indigenous in character. The Catholic Charismatic Renewal ministry of Divine Retreat Centre in Muringoor (Potta), Kerala, is a typical example of this kind of development.

3 *Independent pentecostal–charismatic churches*. These largely arise around a charismatic prophet or pastor, mainly imitating Western forms. They are mostly congregational or house-based, but may also be part of an organized grouping or a megachurch. Examples include New Life Fellowship in Bombay and the Sharon Fellowship Church.

The growth of the Pentecostal–Charismatic movements in India over the final two decades of the twentieth century was phenomenal. This extraordinary expansion has transformed the Christian landscape in India in an unparalleled way. Statistical indicators of religious expansion are always open to debate, but they provide a useful picture. The *World Christian Encyclopedia* (2001) states that the Indian Pentecostal Church of God grew from 500,000 adherents in 1970 to 900,000 by the year 1995. Church of God (Full Gospel) India had increased from 30,000 to 148,000 during the same period. Charismatic groups demonstrate similar trends. Catholic Charismatic Renewal weekly meetings are attended by 150,000 people, and as many as 150,000 people attend five-day annual summer conventions held by Divine Retreat Centre at Potta in Kerala. The recently emerged Independent Pentecostal groups have also grown in amazing proportions. The New Apostolic Church founded in 1969 has 1,448,209 members and the New Life Fellowship claims 480,000 followers. Sharon Fellowship, which was founded by an individual in 1975, has 90,000 members, including Arabian Gulf Indian immigrants. According to some sources, Pentecostalism in India ranks as the fifth-largest group of Pentecostals in the world.

Historical accounts of Pentecostal–Charismatic movements in India typically link their origins to the emergence of Pentecostalism in the USA in the early twentieth century. However, more recent assessments have emphasized the indigenous genesis of the movement in India. These point to the revival in Tinnevelly in 1860, associated with the ministry of Karl Rhenius (1790–1838, an Anglican missionary) and Anthony Norris Groves (1795–1853, an independent missionary with the Plymouth Brethren), which spread to southern parts of Kerala. John Christian Aroolappen (1810–67), an Anglican catechist trained by Rhenius and Groves, was the leader of the movement, in which 'unknown tongues', healing and visions were the basic features. Kudarapallil Thommen (*fl.* 1870s) and the Brahmin convert Justus Joseph (1835–87) also figure in these histories. Out of this arose the Revival

Church or 'Six Years Party' in 1875, which held that Christ would return in 1881. However, it should be noted that Classical Pentecostal churches were the main manifestation of the Pentecostal movement in India before the 1950s.

A strong counter-cultural dynamic can be perceived in the emergence and expansion of Pentecostal and Charismatic movements. This is mainly in response to the mainline churches' institutional and ritual emphases. Thus, what we see in Indian Pentecostal–Charismatic movements is a hybridization of mainline and Pentecostal features, a phenomenon that was at the margins of Christianity until the middle of the twentieth century.

The membership of these churches in urban and rural areas comprises both the socio-economically poor and the upwardly mobile middle classes. However, it was the poor and socially disadvantaged who responded positively to Pentecostalism during its beginning stages in India, though this was generally true of any Christianization process. In the Kerala region, the first recruits for all Classical Pentecostal groups were the economically marginalized St Thomas Christians and Dalit Christians. There was an element of protest as well as a desire for respectability in these responses. The subversive element in the initial spread of Pentecostalism among the poor was strongly evident. In particular, such disadvantaged people are attracted to an alternative vision of society in which socio-cultural barriers are transcended by the power of the Holy Spirit. In this sense, the spread of Pentecostalism in India is linked to the continuing struggle of the marginalized to come to terms with their dignity and humanness.

That said, Pentecostalism is no longer a movement of the socially deprived alone. After the 1960s urban poor and upper-middle-class Roman Catholics and Protestants embraced the movement in an unprecedented manner. The massive social changes occurring through urbanization, modernization and economic transitions in India caused a great sense of disconnection from traditional contexts for urbanized Christians. Since Christians are one of the most urbanized religious groups in India, the linkages between modernization and 'Pentecostalization' are easily explained. This could also be a result of their search for valid explanations for the newfound upward economic mobility and accessibility to luxuries which were denied to many middle-class families in their rural contexts. The fact that Chennai, Bangalore and Mumbai are some of the most successful centres of the Charismatic movement is thus not surprising.

The expansion of Pentecostal–Charismatic churches into the North Indian regions is also part of the story. Pentecostal–Charismatic ministries operating through schools, orphanages, medical and other charitable organizations have won growing numbers of new converts. The Church of God has a feeding programme for over 20,000 per day in Calcutta. It also runs hospitals, nursing schools, junior colleges, vocational schools, village clinics, homes for the destitute, drug prevention programmes, and schools for about 6,000 children. These types of ministries are increasing substantially.

Due to the growth of militant Hinduism and fervent opposition to religious proselytization, many Pentecostal–Charismatic groups in the North depict their missional efforts in terms of humanitarian aid. However, it seems that increasing numbers of North Indians are ready to affiliate themselves with Christianity through these movements.

Pentecostalism in India is characterized by separateness and limited interaction with other religions, particularly with Hinduism. This is because it is believed that sustained contact would corrupt beliefs and could be sinful. This attitude of separation is even applied to other Christians in some cases. For many Pentecostals, contact with people of other faiths is solely for purposes of evangelism.

Christian identity in South Asia

In recent times, Christians in South Asia have begun to wrestle with the question of identity in a context of religious fundamentalism. Christian minorities in India face issues of nationhood and religio-cultural resurgence. In India, Pakistan, Bangladesh and Sri Lanka, radical neo-nationalism based on religio-cultural consciousness is emerging in an unprecedented way. This is taking shape in the context of globalization and the general contestation over modernity and Westernization. Nation states are trying to assert themselves against the 'Christian' West and the forces of globalization. In an effort to impress upon others that they are embracing modernity without sacrificing their indigenous moorings, the rhetoric of the right-wingers in these situations always turns against the Christian minority. This has repercussions for the majority of Christians in South Asia, especially because they do not traditionally truly belong to the mainstream of anything, whether religions or cultural settings – and this is by conscious design. As a result, they are vulnerable and fragile.

To put it more specifically, there is an effort by the citizens of various countries to define their nationhood in relation to a major religion as well as a culture that has been evolving on the basis of that dominant religion. In India, for instance, Hindu nationalists question the loyalty of Indian Christians to the nation, implying that their loyalties are foreign in nature. This poses a major challenge to Indian Christians because it creates an enormous tension between being Indian and being Christian. How to deal with competing religious and ethnic–national identities is a major question for Christians in the region.

This is not to suggest that there is a monolithic Christian identity in South Asia, but rather that believers are confronted by similar challenges. Christians in South Asia have to deal on a daily basis with world religions such as Hinduism and Islam and other dominant faiths. The fact that many of these religions are experiencing a resurgence makes these interactions highly sensitive. In Pakistan and Bangladesh where Muslims are a majority, in India where Hindus constitute a majority and in Sri Lanka where

Buddhists are the largest community, Christians face numerous predicaments. Violent clashes and conflicts are increasing significantly. The crusading and apocalyptic value system of many fundamentalist Christian groups further aggravates these situations. There is intense hostility to evangelism and conversion within the general society. As members of minority and often marginalized groups, Christians are aware that the opposition to their very existence increases the already intense pressure on them regarding issues of identity and conformity.

The situation of Christian believers in the rural areas of India, Pakistan, Bangladesh and Sri Lanka demonstrates that they have, in their own way, evolved systems of existing with multiple identities in their socio-religious milieu. There are many limitations and shortcomings within these processes. But these are genuine efforts on the part of the Christian peoples in the subcontinent to come to terms with their religio-cultural context. We observe a plurality of experiences in Indian Christianity.

Despite the fact that the Christian community constitutes a mere 2.4 per cent (approximately 25 million) of the Indian population, it has remained an influential religious community. In the recent past, however, anti-Christian violence, mainly perpetrated by Hindu extremist groups, has been gradually affecting the religiously tolerant and secular fabric of Indian society and the confidence of Christians. A series of attacks on Christian worship centres and believers in the state of Orissa, and the gradual spread of violence against Christians to other regions in 2008, demonstrated the stark assault on the fundamental character of Indian religious tolerance. One can only hope that such happenings are only an anomaly in the otherwise bright and influential place that Christianity and Christians maintain in Indian society.

Pakistan and Bangladesh

What has been said about Christianity in India is generally applicable to the whole region, including Pakistan and Bangladesh, which were part of India prior to the partition in 1947. Bangladesh was part of Pakistan until it liberated itself in 1971. These regions deserve some additional comments.

Christians in Pakistan accounted for only 1 per cent of the population at the time of the partition. In the late 1950s there were over 500,000 Christians in West Pakistan and the majority belonged to the Punjab province. Roman Catholic and United Presbyterian churches constituted the largest components. A strong indigenous leadership emerged during this period, although the colonial legacy and foreign missionary leadership and interventions continued in certain denominations, for example the Lutheran churches, where Western missionaries such as Bishop Jens Christensen (1899–1966) continued to exercise great power over the local peoples. The Anglican Church received Bishop Chandu Ray (1915–83) as its first Pakistani assistant bishop in 1957. The Pakistan Christian Council's leadership in ecumenical processes was commendable during this period. At the forefront of the ecumenical thinking was a church union modelled after the Church of South India. The Anglican Church, the Methodist Church of Southern Asia, the United Presbyterian Church and the Lutherans were involved in the negotiations. In the Bangladesh region, additionally, Baptist churches were a prominent partner in the negotiations, among others. Following these efforts, the Church of Pakistan was founded in 1970.

Pakistan's adherence to an Islamic ethos from the moment of partition, and the establishment of Islam as its state religion in 1973, effectively sidelined Christians as a powerless minority. Since 1988 the increasing Islamization of the nation has placed further pressure on Christians, who make up roughly 2.5 per cent of the total population according to the government census of 1999. The marginalization of Christianity by the government was obvious, although freedom of religion is assured in the Pakistani constitution. Christian missionary work and conversion has been greatly restricted as a result. Attacks against Christians and their places of worship are increasing in frequency due to Muslim militancy and disharmonious relationships.

The influence of Christianity through educational institutions remains considerable, and Roman Catholics, who constitute 51 per cent of the Christian population, led in the endeavour by managing 552 institutions by 1982. The presence of Christian non-governmental organizations such as CARITAS, which works among Muslim women, has helped to create a new Christian identity. Christian Hospitals Association of Pakistan is responsible for more than 60 hospitals in the country.

When Bangladesh was carved out of Pakistani territory in the East Bengal region in 1971, the proportion of Christians there was less than 1 per cent of the population. The lack of power and the rural character of the Christian community contributed to its marginalization. Approximately half of the Christians have a tribal ethnic background. The continual political upheavals and coups in the recent past have exacerbated the vulnerability of Christians.

While the Bangladeshi constitution declares that Islam is the state religion, it assures religious freedom. Christians are only 0.5 per cent of the highly dense population of 120 million; 86 per cent are Muslims. The National Christian Council of Bangladesh works very closely with the government in initiating community-based programmes and projects for their poor constituents. Pentecostals and Korean Christians were actively seeking to establish churches during the last decades of the twentieth century, and Christians continue to grow in numbers.

✳ Sri Lanka

Sri Lanka, which is predominantly a Buddhist country, has a much larger proportion of Christians (8 per cent) than any other South Asian country.

A substantial majority of the Christians are the descendants of people who converted to Roman Catholicism in the sixteenth century during the height of Portuguese colonial power. By the turn of the nineteenth century Catholic missionary endeavours were in disarray. This was not only due to the interruptions created by Dutch colonial rule in the seventeenth and eighteenth centuries but also to internal disorganization within the Roman Catholic Church. Roman Catholic influence was restored by the establishment of the Vicariate Apostolic of Ceylon in 1834.

When Protestant missionary work expanded in Sri Lanka at the beginning of the nineteenth century, British colonial power was ascendant and its support for missionary involvement was unreserved. Further, Protestant missionaries built on the strong foundation laid by the Dutch Reformed Church's focus on education as the chief means of propagating Christianity. Protestant missionary work mainly concentrated on the Tamil population and, consequently, their culture and language. Revd Dr Peter Percival (1803–82), a Methodist missionary, was one of the greatest scholars of the Tamil language. A strong educational system was in place during the first half of the nineteenth century due to the leadership of the Protestant missionary movement. Every Tamil village had a school, and a quarter of the pupils were female. American missions calculated that over 90,000 pupils had gone through their schools by 1850. From the Batticotta Seminary emerged the giants of Tamil literature of the nineteenth century: C. W. Thamotharampillai (1832–1901) and A. Sathasivampillai (1820–95). Christians are almost equally divided among the two major ethnic groups, Sinhalese and Tamil.

As was the case in India, Christian educational involvement eventually generated counter-movements and a religious resurgence by the majority. Arumuka Navalar (1822–79) initiated a Sanskritic Hindu revivalist and reform movement. Buddhist revival and restoration was another similar response during the early twentieth century. Sri Lanka's independence in 1948 and Buddhist dominance in the political arena eroded the influence of Christianity. The nationalization of educational institutions in 1960 additionally supplanted this area of Christian hegemony. In the 1970s the Sri Lankan constitution was amended to give dominance to Buddhism as the preferred religion of the state, although other religions could function in freedom. However, people from various faith persuasions continued to convert to Christianity.

In the face of the new challenges, there was an emerging theological culture of indigenization and localization. The ecumenical movement and the Ashram movement were some of the visible expressions of this process. Bishop Sabapathy Kulundran (1900–92) and D. T. Niles (1908–70) were symbols of creative vigour and leadership. Niles became the first General Secretary of the Christian Conference of Asia and was an influential ecumenical thinker and writer. Interfaith dialogue movements, which were pioneered by such leaders, have continued through the work of recent thinkers and ecumenical leaders, for example S. Wesley Ariarajah (b. 1941). Christians have also had an influential role in the peace initiatives in the midst of the Tamil–Sinhalese conflict which ensued from Sinhala-Buddhist linguistic and theocratic nationalism. The Centre for Society and Religion, founded in 1970 in Colombo under the leadership of Father Tissa Balasuriya (1924–2013), worked at the grassroots level to achieve peace and harmony.

Pentecostal–Charismatic growth since the 1980s has been phenomenal in Sri Lanka, as is the case elsewhere in South Asia. The Ceylon Pentecostal Mission, which was established in 1924, has spread to many other parts of the globe, especially India.

✳ Nepal

The Hindu kingdom of Nepal restored King Thribhuvan (1906–55) to his throne in 1951 and at the same time opened its doors to the outside world. During the early part of the seventeenth century Jesuits and Capuchins had established Christianity in the kingdom. However, in 1769 Christians were exiled and Christianity was forbidden for the next 180 years. The oppressive rule of Ranas in the nineteenth century brought many migrants to India and thus into contact with Christianity and with Protestant Christian missions, paving the way for the entry of Christianity into Nepal. The Bible was translated into Nepali. Further, many Nepalis who were converted in India began to return, eventually making a Christian impact on their homeland.

The first meeting of the Nepal Christian Fellowship in 1959 marked a new beginning for Christians, which helped in the formation of various churches and the gathering of scattered believers. By the 1970s it was reported that there was a tiny group of 500 Christians belonging to about 30 congregations. Despite the government's complete prohibition of conversion from Hinduism, biblical teaching, training and evangelism continues to takes place in Nepal. The Bible Society continues to be active, especially after the 1980 national referendum and the easing of restrictions on Christianity. It was estimated that there were over 25,000 Christians in Nepal by 1985. The victory for the democratic movement in 1990 brought greater religious freedom, and conversion to Christianity continues to take place. Many Christians who were imprisoned were released. The 1991 census recognized that there were over 30,000 Christians in the kingdom. However, Christian sources put the numbers much higher, and according to these organizations there are about 1,500 churches or fellowship groups existing in Nepal.

In 2008 Nepal made headlines through the overthrow of its monarchy and the takeover of the government by people's democratic movements and the Maoist Party. The ramifications of this for Christians in the country are not yet clear.

❓ DISCUSSION QUESTIONS

1 Describe briefly the major contribution made to Christianity in the Indian subcontinent by each of the following:

(a) William Carey;

(b) Alexander Duff;

(c) V. Chakkarai;

(d) D. T. Niles;

(e) Tissa Balasuriya.

2 What is Hindu revivalism and what are some of its features? What was the Hindu response to Christianity and Christian conversion during the nineteenth century?

3 Why did the majority of the Christians come from the marginalized sections of South Asian society?

4 Who are Dalits? How and why did the Dalit theological movement emerge during the second half of the twentieth century? Describe the major features of the movement, and name three of its theologians.

5 Who is Panditha Ramabai, and what were some of her contributions to the feminist movement in India and to the identity of women in relation to Christian conversion?

6 Discuss the major commonalities and differences between the experiences of Christians in Pakistan and Bangladesh after 1947. Why are there differences, if any?

7 What is interreligious dialogue? Describe and discuss its significance in the light of the experience of Christians in Nepal and India. What are the major contributions of S. J. Samartha to the religious dialogue movement?

8 The fact that Christianity is a minority religion in the subcontinent seems to affect the way Christians function in the region. How has it shaped the presence and the influence of Christianity in the region? Use recent developments to illustrate your assessment.

🏛 Further reading

Boyd, Robin. *An Introduction to Indian Christian Theology*. New Delhi: CLS, 1975.

Collins, Paul M. *Christian Inculturation in India.* Aldershot: Ashgate, 2007.

Downs, Frederick S. *History of Christianity in India,* Vol. V, Part 5, *North East India in the Nineteenth and Twentieth Centuries.* Bangalore: CHAI, 1992.

Kent, Eliza F. *Converting Women: Gender and Protestant Christianity in colonial south India.* Oxford: Oxford University Press, 2004.

Luke, P. Y. and Carman, John B. *Village Christians and Hindu Culture: Study of a rural church in Andhra Pradesh, south India.* Geneva: WCC, 1968.

Massey, James. *Dalits in India: Religion as source of bondage or liberation with special reference to Christians.* New Delhi: Manohar, 1995.

Oddie, Geoffrey A. (ed.). *Religion in South Asia: Religious conversion and revival movements in South Asia in medieval and modern times.* New Delhi: Manohar, 1991.

Oddie, Geoffrey A. 'Indigenization and nationalism', *Archives de Sciences Sociales des Religions,* no. 103 (1998), pp. 129–52.

Oommen, George. 'The emerging Dalit theology: a historical appraisal', *Indian Church History Review,* no. 1 (2000), pp. 19–38.

Oommen, George. 'Pentecostal–Charismatic movements in post-independent India: an appraisal', *Doon Theological Journal,* vol. 2, no. 2 (July 2005), pp. 142–63.

Paul, Rajaiah D. *The Cross over India.* London: SCM Press, 1952.

Ross, Kenneth R., Jeyaraj, Daniel and Johnson, Todd M. (eds). *Christianity in South and Central Asia.* Edinburgh: Edinburgh University Press, 2019.

Studdert-Kennedy, Gerald. *British Christians, Indian Nationalists and the Raj.* Oxford: Oxford University Press, 1991.

Webster, John. C. B. *The Dalit Christians: A history.* Delhi: ISPCK, 1992.

6

South-East Asia

Chansamone Saiyasak

South-East Asia is now comprised of Myanmar, Thailand, Vietnam, Laos, Cambodia, the Philippines, Malaysia, Brunei, Singapore, Indonesia and East Timor. With the exception of East Timor and the Philippines, Christianity is largely viewed as a recent phenomenon with the status of a minority religion. Major 'Christian' events in South-East Asia have occurred only since the late nineteenth century. Nevertheless, the contributions of Christianity in shaping the modernization of the nations of South-East Asia through the provision of education, medical care and social work are of paramount importance.

Although it appeared in South-East Asia in the seventh century, the Christian faith made a lasting impact only from the sixteenth century when, together with trade, conquest and migration, it spread formally in connection with European colonial powers. It was not until the latter part of the twentieth century, after most of the nations of South-East Asia had gained independence, that churches transitioned from European colonial control to a new Asian identity under indigenous leadership, discovering their own mission among other religions and cultures. Towards the end of the twentieth century and the beginning of the twenty-first, major trends in South-East Asian Christianity have emerged, including independent Asian church movements, a changing relationship with other religions, and a growing awareness within the Asian Church of its missionary responsibility as well as its continuing impact on the societies and cultures of the region.

The ability of Christianity to adapt its social and cultural context and address the religious needs of its people will be the key determining factor for its future course. Currently in some parts of South-East Asia, the impact of Christianity has created social tensions; these have resulted in a period of persecution of Christians which is expected to continue.

✳ Thailand

Thailand (formerly Siam), never colonized by the West, has the lowest percentage of Christians of all the nations of South-East Asia. In 2008

Christians represented 0.98 per cent of the country's population of 65 million (0.52 per cent Protestants and 0.46 per cent Catholics).

Christianity formally reached Thailand in the sixteenth century (1567) through the Roman Catholics. External political situations and internal divisions among Catholic missionaries characterized early missionary work. Yet, in the seventeenth century, the Catholics wielded considerable influence in the Thai court and flourished under the control of King Narai (1632–88). Nevertheless, their early lack of success in converting the Thais resulted in periods of repression and in the stagnation of Christianity in Thailand for a century and a half.

Protestantism first entered Thailand in the nineteenth century (1828) through the London Missionary Society. Yet permanent Protestant work did not begin until the later arrival of American Baptists (1833) and American Presbyterians (1834). Both the Catholic Vicar-Apostolic, Bishop Jean-Baptiste Pallegoix (1805–62), and the Protestant missionary Dr Dan B. Bradley (1804–73) developed close relationships with Prince Mongkut (1804–68), who later became King Rama IV. Bradley's medical work and Pallegoix's Thai–Latin–French–English dictionary confirmed Christianity's significant role in Thai society. While the Thais readily recognized the contributions made by Christians to the modernization of Thailand through education and modern medicine, they merely tolerated the message of Christianity. Early converts were made among the Chinese and other ethnic minorities. Only in 1840, more than ten years after the arrival of Protestantism in Thailand, did its missionaries succeed in gaining their first Thai convert, Nai Suk (*fl.* 1840s).

The growing movement to found a national, ecumenical church began in 1920 with two Presbyterian missions united under the American Presbyterian Mission in Siam (APM). In 1930 the National Christian Council of Siam was established and the Church of Christ in Thailand (CCT) followed in 1934. In 1945 new missionary agencies began to enter Thailand. The rapid increase in the number of missionary agencies not affiliated with the CCT led to the formation of the Evangelical Fellowship of Thailand (EFT) in 1969. Meanwhile, in 1957, the APM dissolved itself into the CCT, and church leadership has since come under the direction of Thai nationals. The period beginning in 1970 marked a phase of spiritual renewal for the Thai churches in which Thai church leaders and missionaries jointly organized their first national congress, which led to the formation of the Thailand Church Growth Committee in the following year. In 1971 the Baptist churches under the Southern Baptist Convention came together to start the Thailand Baptist Churches Association (TBCA). From 1978 onwards the Thai churches experienced rapid growth, following the arrival of Pentecostal and Charismatic movements.

Although Christianity has now been in Thailand for almost two centuries and has played a significant role in helping the country to establish trade with the West and transition into a modern state, Thailand has remained resistant to Christian conversion. Those who converted to Protestant Christianity were mostly members of tribal groups in northern Thailand or descendants of Chinese immigrants. The Isan of north-east Thailand, who had initially converted to Roman Catholicism, were predominantly slaves, social outcasts and impoverished families. A respected sociologist, Erik Cohen, at the Hebrew University of Jerusalem, has attributed Protestantism's failure in evangelism in Thailand to the following factors:

> The failure of Christianity to make a significant number of converts among the Thais could be partly explained by the fundamental differences in the basic worldviews of Christianity and Therevada (*sic*) Buddhism, partly by the salience of Buddhism in the Thai identity and way of life, and partly also by the often uncompromising attitudes of both Catholic and Protestant missionaries toward the 'heathen' beliefs and customs of the natives whom they have sought to convert.
>
> (Erik Cohen, 'Christianization and indigenization: contrasting processes of religious adaptation in Thailand', in Steve Kaplan (ed.), *Indigenous Responses to Western Christianity* (New York, NY: New York University Press, 1995), p. 36)

In 1988, with the exception of the Seventh-day Adventists, all three main denominations, namely the CCT, EFT and TBCA, united to establish an umbrella organization, the Thailand Protestant Churches Coordinating Committee, for collaborating on Protestant work with the goal of establishing a church in every district throughout Thailand by 2010. More cooperative efforts than ever before are currently under way among Protestants keen to evangelize Thailand, yet the response of the peoples of Thailand to Christian conversion is expected to continue in the same gradual upward movement that has characterized previous decades.

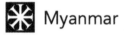 Myanmar

Myanmar (previously Burma), a former British colony, gained its independence in 1948. Christianity formally entered Myanmar in the sixteenth century (1554) through the Roman Catholics. Although Christianity received a favourable initial response, war and persecution later caused difficulty. Yet the Catholics had managed to establish mission work by the beginning of the nineteenth century (1806). Today, 90 per cent of Catholics in Myanmar, consisting of 1.3 per cent of the population, are found primarily among the hill tribes.

Protestants first arrived in Myanmar in the nineteenth century (1807) through the British Baptists in India, but later the work was taken over by American Baptists led by Adoniram Judson (1788–1850), who arrived in 1813. Although focusing on evangelism, Protestants were recognized for their educational and social work under British colonial rule. Six years after his arrival, Judson baptized his first convert, Maung Nau (b. *c.*1784). He focused on making Christianity relevant to the Burmese context while respecting the truth and integrity of the Christian faith. Protestants also established schools and hospitals.

While only a few converts responded from the Buddhist population, Protestants, like Catholics, found that the greatest growth in numbers occurred among the hill tribes. The oral traditions of the Karen people spoke of a creator, Y'wa, who would send a 'lost brother' back to them bearing a book and ushering in a new era of reconciliation with Y'wa, prosperity and literacy. In 1818 an unnamed Karen arrived in a village headed by a man named A-Pyah Thee (fl. 1810s); the visitor carried a book and instructed the villagers in a number of new religious practices before leaving. For A-Pyah Thee and his village, this was the 'lost brother' of the prophecy, and the encounter set him on a quest to find those who could read the book and instruct them further. The resulting conversion of the Karen to Christianity was led by Karen evangelists such as Ko Tha Byu (c.1778–1840), who explored the connections between Karen religion and the Christian faith, and also the fresh revelation brought by the latter. The three Anglo-Burmese wars of the nineteenth century weakened the grip of the Burmese state on tribal groups and so created an expectation among them of a new order, which some experienced through their new-found Christian faith. These people-groups included not only the Karen but also the Chins (1845) and Kachins (1876). Almost all of the initial expansion of Christianity occurred among the ancient tribes in British-ruled territory, instead of among the Buddhists in Burmese-controlled territory. Immigrants from India and China added to the growth of the Church.

In 1865 the Burma Baptist Convention was organized, and all regional and linguistic groups of Baptist churches in Myanmar now became affiliated to it. In 1914 a regional body known as the Christian Council for Burma, an ecumenical movement, was formed under the National Christian Council of India. However, after Burma gained independence from British rule in 1948, the Protestant groups formed the Myanmar Burma Christian Council, which became affiliated to the Christian Conference of Asia (CCA).

In 1965 all Christian schools, hospitals and training colleges were nationalized and all missionaries expelled by the Burmese government. Subsequently, instead of disintegrating, the Church not only survived and flourished but also birthed a vibrant missionary-sending movement.

As in Thailand, the Burmese identify Buddhism with nationality. Christians in Myanmar struggle for the right to freedom of religion and worship. Consequently, the future of the Church in Burma is contingent on their ability to use their own resources in order to deepen the roots of Christianity in the cultural soil of Myanmar as well as establish and strengthen their connection with Christians globally. Today, Christians account for 8.7 per cent of the population, with Protestants representing 7.38 per cent.

 Vietnam

Vietnam, a former French colony, achieved its independence in 1975. Although Roman Catholic Christianity arrived in Vietnam from other

Asian countries starting in the sixteenth century, the beginning of Roman Catholicism in Vietnam is often credited to the arrival of a French Jesuit missionary, Alexandre de Rhodes (1591–1660), in 1624. Rhodes gained 121,000 converts after only 16 years of mission work. He recruited a sizeable number of catechists, built a seminary for the training of local clergy, established the Roman Catholic hierarchy and romanized the Vietnamese script. The Paris Society for Foreign Mission (PSFM), influenced by Rhodes, entered Vietnam in 1662. The strength of the work done by both the Jesuits and PSFM lay in their commitment to indigenous leadership and its training.

From the seventeenth to the nineteenth centuries, Catholics in Vietnam faced serious difficulties caused by a number of factors. The first factor was the unstable political situation resulting from conflicts between two powerful clans, which eventually separated the country into North and South. Missionaries were often suspected of spying for the rival side. The second factor was the tensions between two separate ecclesiastical systems in the country. On the one hand, Vietnam fell under the jurisdiction of the Portuguese Crown as a result of the fifteenth-century *padroado* system. On the other hand, its two dioceses fell under the jurisdiction of the Congregatio de Propaganda Fide, with missionary orders from different European nations lining up behind these two different jurisdictions. The resulting tensions and disputes plagued the Church for several centuries.

The third factor related to controversial ancestral veneration rites. In the early eighteenth century, the papacy had banned ancestral veneration across East Asia. As a result, Bishop Alexandre de Alexandris (d. 1738) excommunicated Charles de Flory (d. 1733), the superior of French missionary priests in Vietnam, for allowing an ancestral veneration rite to take place. However, in 1964 the Catholic Church reinterpreted these rites and declared them to be expressions of devotion and respect, and therefore they were allowed in Vietnam. The final factor involved persecution by Vietnamese rulers. An estimated 130,000 Catholics were put to death for their faith from the seventeenth to the nineteenth century. The early period of persecution grew out of the hostility of Vietnamese rulers towards Christianity and their distrust of Christians. They were concerned about the decline in devotion to ancestors and the neglect of filial piety, and feared that Christianity might be a pretext for a European takeover of Vietnam. The subsequent period of persecution, however, was largely a protest against the growing power of the French.

The French gained full control of Cochin-China (South Vietnam) in the second half of the nineteenth century and granted religious freedom to the people. Thereafter, new Catholic missions entered the country and the Church grew rapidly. Nevertheless, Christianity was viewed as a French religion aiding the French in their achievement of political dominance in the region. In 1945 Vietnam declared its independence. However, the conflict continued between the two sides, namely the French and the communist regime, resulting in the country's division once again into North Vietnam (communist) and South Vietnam (pro-Western) in 1954. Consequently, almost 46 per cent of the Catholic laity and clergy (amounting to 700,000 people) fled the North to reach safety in the South.

The USA became involved in the war from 1964 to 1975. After the communist regime seized control in 1975 Catholics in South Vietnam faced serious challenges. All Christian educational and social institutions were taken over, religious organizations dissolved, leaders sent to re-education camps, and religious activities restricted. Since 1988 however, government policies towards Christianity have relaxed.

Regarding Protestant influence in Vietnam, after their second attempt, Protestants managed to enter Vietnam and start work in central Vietnam in 1911 through the Christian and Missionary Alliance (C&MA). Sixteen years later, in 1927, the organization had over 4,000 members and had established a Bible training centre and the Evangelical Church of Vietnam (ECVN). As the sole Protestant mission operating in Vietnam, the C&MA implemented self-support policies from the onset of its work, and this led all Protestant churches to become self-supporting by the end of the Second World War.

In 1954 Protestant refugees who had fled the communist North were admitted into the ECVN in South Vietnam. The identification and cooperation of the C&MA and the ECVN with the US–Vietnamese government of South Vietnam thereby created opportunities to broaden their work. As the war intensified, new Protestant groups began arriving in South Vietnam, responding to the people's social and physical needs. Even the ECVN, initially focused solely on spiritual need, started to run social projects. These groups also collaborated in educational work. In the midst of much suffering, the Church nonetheless continued to flourish. One Protestant organization in Vietnam reported 150,000 Protestants in 1975. This number had grown to an estimated 2.1 million by 2002.

In 1975 all missionaries and numerous Christians were forced out of the country, while at least 500 indigenous church leaders remained and faced either execution or 're-education' in prison camps. Ninety per cent of the tribal churches and 100 Vietnamese churches were shut down. In spite of such adversity, the Church experienced revival and rapidly increased. With the government today remaining practically in full control of all religious activities, persecution continues to be severe for unregistered and ethnic minority churches. But the growing trend of Christianity, particularly among the tribal groups, is evident; and churches are vibrant and thriving, with 8.16 per cent of the population being Christians, of which 1.7 per cent are Protestants and 6.46 per cent Catholics.

 # Laos

Laos, a former French protectorate, declared its independence in 1953. The first Catholic missionary arrived in Vientiane in 1642 but only stayed until 1647 due to stiff opposition from Buddhist clergy. In 1885 the PSFM entered

Laos, achieved some initial conversion success, and had established a mission by 1899. The first Lao priest was ordained in 1963 and the first Lao bishop, Thomas Nantha (1909–84), was consecrated in 1974. The Catholic Church, officially recognized by the government, is comprised of 45,000 members (0.7 per cent of the population), many of whom are Vietnamese.

Protestants first arrived in northern Laos (Luang Prabang) from northern Thailand (Chiang Mai) when a non-residential American Presbyterian missionary, Daniel McGilvary (1828–1911), entered the country in 1872. His work resulted in 500 baptized Khmu converts. Two members of the Swiss Brethren, Gabriel Contesse (1878–1908) and Maurice Willy (*fl.* 1900s), became the first residential Protestant missionaries, reaching Laos in 1902 through the Missionaire Évangélique from Switzerland. Their work involved Bible translation and distribution of the Scriptures among the Lowland Lao in southern Laos (Savannakhet). By 1932 another Swiss Brethren missionary, Fritz Audétat (*fl.* 1908–1930s), had completed the translation of the entire Old Testament into Lao.

Residential Protestant missions in northern Laos only began in 1929 when G. Edward Roffe (1905–2000) of the C&MA embarked on a campaign among tribal groups. Roffe worked with the Lowland Lao and maintained contact with the Khmu believers from the Presbyterian mission, which later was turned over to the C&MA. In spite of the hostility shown towards them by the French colonial government and Roman Catholics, Protestant missions experienced a surge in successful mass conversions in 1950, when a C&MA missionary couple, Ted (1920–69) and Ruth (1919–2004) Andrianoff, converted a Hmong shaman, Boua Ya Thao (d. *c.*1963). Boua Ya Thao had watched a Khmu Bible-school student, Nai Kheng (*fl.* 1950), and his family move into a neighbouring house where spirits resided. The spiritual protection provided to Nai Kheng, coupled with his own failure to heal a relative, led Boua Ya Thao to enquire about the Christian faith from Nai Kheng and the visiting Andrianoffs. Two months later, Boua Ya Thao and Nai Kheng led the conversion of over 1,000 people, mostly Hmong. Three years later, in 1953, the C&MA had gained a community of 5,000 converts in northern Laos. The Swiss mission in southern Laos, however, gained only 452 baptized members after a half-century of work.

After the First World War, new missionary organizations entered Laos. In 1956 the C&MA formed the Lao Evangelical Church (LEC), the first national church in Laos, exclusively representing the churches in northern Laos. Because of their different ecclesiology, the Swiss-affiliated churches did not participate in the LEC until the late 1980s. The LEC was granted corporate status by the Lao government in 1960, and afterwards joined the CCA in 1967.

The C&MA and the Swiss Brethren withdrew from Laos prior to the communist takeover in 1975. Following the takeover, approximately 5,000 Lao Christians and 90 per cent of the Lao church leaders also fled to Thailand. Church properties were seized and religious education eliminated by the government. Between 1975 and 1990 the Church had hardly any contact with the outside world. Religious activities were restricted and Christians were singled out for harassment. All known Protestant and Catholic churches in the three northern provinces were closed and Christians were coerced into renouncing their faith, with the result that many believers began to worship in secret.

In 1983 World Concern and Laos Christian Service began working in Laos. The period from 1990 saw the easing of government policy towards religion, allowing Protestants to link up with overseas Christian organizations, including the CCA. While the constitution of 1991 guarantees the right to freedom of religion, and Decree 92 (2002) legitimizes proselytizing by Lao nationals, all these rights are conditional on the government's approval. In 1993 the LEC started to improve its relationship with the government, but at the end of 1994 the relationship was marred by the government's effort to close churches in a number of provinces as well as to pressure Christians to renounce their Christian faith. At least 40 LEC churches were destroyed or converted into schools or government offices. Since 1975 no expatriate missionaries have been allowed back to work within Laos.

Except for Seventh-day Adventists, the LEC is the only officially recognized Protestant denomination in Laos and now has an estimated 100,000 members (1.6 per cent of the population) in 400 LEC congregations throughout the country. Protestant groups with adherents not officially recognized by the government include the Methodist, Church of Christ, Assembly of God, Lutheran and Baptist churches. To restrict the religious freedom of the non-recognized Protestant groups, the government, through Order Number 1 of March 2004 (of the Lao National Front for Construction), obliged all Protestant groups to become part of the LEC or the Seventh-day Adventist Church.

The LEC joined the Evangelical Fellowship of Asia (EFA) and in 2008 became a member of the World Council of Churches (WCC). In the midst of hardship and persecution, the Church is currently experiencing considerable growth throughout Laos. Today, Roman Catholics and Protestants constitute approximately 2.3 per cent of the population.

 Cambodia

Cambodia, or Kampuchea, declared its independence from the French in 1953. Christianity initially entered Cambodia with the arrival of a Roman Catholic missionary from Malacca, Malaysia, in the sixteenth century (1555), yet it received very little response from the Cambodians due to strong opposition from the Buddhist clergy. Catholicism's permanent work only began in the seventeenth century. Japanese Catholics from Japan and Eurasian Catholics from Indonesia, escaping persecution, as well as Vietnamese Catholic immigrants, resettled in Phnom Penh. Foreign Christians comprised nearly all of the membership of the Catholic Church due to the Cambodians' indifference towards Christianity.

The second half of the eighteenth century saw the first missionary efforts to work with the Khmer. In 1770 a plan for evangelization was drawn up by the French missionary Father Gervais Levavasseur (1730–77), who had also translated the catechism into the Khmer language. However, the French colonial government discouraged any evangelization of the Khmer. Thus, by 1842, after almost three centuries since its first arrival in Vietnam and following almost 200 years of work by the PSFM, Catholic Christianity could claim only 222 members in four churches, comprised primarily of foreigners – Vietnamese, Chinese, French and others.

In 1863 France established Cambodia as its protectorate, subsequently allowing Vietnamese immigrants, mostly Catholics, to settle in Cambodia, and thereby hindering the evangelization of the Khmer because of the increasing perception of Christianity as a foreign religion. In 1957 Simon Chhem Yen (b. 1928) was the first Cambodian ordained to the priesthood, and in 1975 Joseph Chhmar Salas (1940–77) became the first Cambodian consecrated bishop coadjutor.

Despite French antagonism, which hindered their admission into the country, Protestants finally managed to enter Cambodia through the C&MA in 1922. Like the Roman Catholics, they discovered that their message was generally received with disdain. Nevertheless, their work expanded more extensively than was the case with the Catholics. The first Bible school was started in 1925, the New Testament translated and published by 1934 and the entire Bible published in 1954. However, in 1965 Protestant work was terminated when the government's anti-American sentiments under the rule of Prince Sihanouk (1922–2012) caused the withdrawal of all missionaries, leaving behind fewer than a thousand Protestants.

In 1970, after the establishment of a pro-American government, and at the beginning of the war with the Khmer Rouge (the popular name for the Communist Party of Kampuchea or CPK), missionaries returned and the Church rapidly increased. Because of revival, Protestant churches multiplied at least ten times in five years. In 1975, when the Khmer Rouge led by Pol Pot (1925–88) seized power, all missionaries were again driven out of the country. Numerous churches were destroyed as part of a brutal persecution of Christians. Around 90 per cent of believers and church leaders were either martyred or escaped into Thailand. A significant percentage of the non-Christians who escaped to refugee camps converted to the Protestant faith and took up residence primarily in the USA, France, Australia and New Zealand. Only 10,000 Christians and 14 indigenous Protestant leaders stayed behind in Cambodia. The Khmer Rouge executed and starved an estimated 2.5 million Cambodians. In 1979 the Vietnamese invaded and occupied Cambodia, after which only 1,000 Evangelical Christians and three indigenous Protestant leaders remained in the country, meeting for worship in secret because of persecution.

In 1990 the Vietnamese ceded control to the Cambodians, and a free election was held in 1993. Religious freedom was reinstated and churches were reopened. In 1991 mission organizations re-entered Cambodia and re-established their work. From 1996 onwards Protestant Christianity was reported to be experiencing a surge, so that by 2004 the number of Evangelical Protestant Christians was as high as 200,000 people, worshipping in no fewer than 2,000 congregations of the Evangelical Church of Cambodia. However, the Roman Catholics maintained only 20,000 members, comprising 0.15 per cent of the population, most of whom were Catholics of Vietnamese descent.

In 1994 the Cambodian Christian Evangelical Alliance was formed and recognized by the government, serving mostly independent Khmer Protestant churches throughout Cambodia along with several major denominations from abroad. Later, a formal Christian body, the Evangelical Fellowship of Cambodia, was set up for expatriate Protestant churches. The Khmer Baptist Convention was organized in 1995 and a regional ecumenical movement, Kampuchea Christian Council (KCC), was founded by churches and Christian organizations in 1998. KCC later became a member of CCA.

The Philippines

The Philippines boasts the second-largest Christian majority in South-East Asia (East Timor being the first). Christianity was first introduced in the sixteenth century by Spanish explorers, followed by Catholic religious orders. Although Filipino Muslims and some tribal groups strongly resisted conversion, almost half of all Filipinos had converted to Catholic Christianity by the early seventeenth century. All those residing in the coastal and lowland territories, with the exception of the southern region under the influence of Islam, had converted by the beginning of the eighteenth century.

In the latter half of the nineteenth century, Filipino Christians revolted against the Catholic monastic orders, predominantly as a reaction to the friars' refusal to recognize the leadership of the Filipino clergy and the monopoly of power and property enjoyed by the religious orders; there was also resentment about the denial of the Filipinos' equality with citizens of Spain. The Catholic orders were expelled and their properties confiscated. All this took place as part of wider Filipino movements towards political independence from Spain, which, although achieved in 1898, resulted in the transfer of the Philippines to the United States. Independence from that country was finally gained only in 1946. Subsequently, the nationalist and Unitarian Philippine Independent Church (PIC) was organized in 1902 by Gregorio Aglipay (1860–1940), attracting large numbers of Roman Catholics. However, properties of the Catholic Church seized by PIC were eventually returned to the Catholic hierarchy, and PIC later adopted more orthodox teaching. In 1905 Jorge Imperial Barlin (1852–1909) was the first Filipino to be made a bishop.

After the Spanish–American War in 1898 Protestants began flooding into the Philippines. The first groups to arrive were American Presbyterians and Methodists (1898), followed by Baptists and members of the Christian and Missionary Alliance (1900); Episcopalians, United Brethren and Disciples of Christ (1901); Congregationalists (1902); and Seventh-day Adventists (1906). Being mostly Evangelical and identifying with the USA as the ruling power, early Protestant missions drew their initial converts from the educated classes and upper middle classes.

Nationalistic sentiment and reaction against Western power affected Protestant churches during the US control of the Philippines. Protestant churches with a dominant American missionary presence were faced with a rift due to the intense nationalistic feeling among the people. An indigenous, independent Evangelical movement imbued with a strong sense of Filipino nationalism was organized in 1913 and culminated in the founding of the Iglesia ni Christo (Church of Christ (INC)) by Felix Manalo (1886–1963). The INC attracted people from the lower socio-economic classes and objected to the stance of the Western-governed Catholic and Protestant churches.

Despite the apparent division on nationalistic grounds, Protestant mission work shifted its emphasis from foreign control to local leadership while maintaining a degree of collaboration. The Evangelical Union of the Philippine Islands (1901) promoted cooperation among Protestant groups and sought to organize Protestant churches throughout the entire country. This led to the establishment of the first unified Protestant church, the United Evangelical Church, which brought together the Presbyterians, Congregationalists and United Brethren. From this union other cooperative efforts were birthed, including the formation of the National Christian Council (1929), the Philippine Federation of Evangelical Churches (1938), the Philippine Federation of Christian Churches (1948) and an ecumenical body, the National Council of Churches in the Philippines (1963). In 1948 the United Evangelical Church itself merged with the Philippine Methodist Church and the Evangelical Church in the Philippines to form the United Church of Christ in the Philippines, which has become the largest Protestant denomination in the country.

The period following the Second World War saw the arrival of new Protestant missionary organizations, most of which were generally conservative and evangelical. Because of their evangelistic passion, these groups transformed the characteristics of Protestantism in the Philippines, resulting in a split. A number of these missionaries established the Philippine Council of Fundamentalists, whereas others, who were non-fundamentalists, organized the Philippine Council of Evangelical Churches in 1956.

Ecumenical and Charismatic movements had a positive impact on Filipino Christianity. Ecumenism, initiated by both Catholic and Protestant leaders, ensured the support of their members and amiable relationships between the two groups. The rise of a Charismatic movement involved Catholic, Protestant and independent churches, resulting in understanding and cooperation as well as a softening of denominational distinctions. Although initially giving prominence to evangelism, education and medical work, both Protestant and Catholic churches became less dependent on providing medical services and placed greater emphasis on social justice as health care improved in the country. Today, the Christian Church in the Philippines consists of 81 per cent Roman Catholics and 8 per cent Protestants.

 Malaysia

Malaysia, a former British colony which achieved its independence in 1957, had contact with the Church of the East in the seventh century, yet the impact of Christianity was not fully felt until the advent of colonizers from Portugal, the Netherlands and Britain. Christianity was first established in Malaysia through Roman Catholicism when Portugal took control of Malacca in the early sixteenth century. Protestants first entered Malaysia in the mid seventeenth century (1641) after the Dutch had gained control from the Portuguese. The mission work among the Malays commenced only after the British came to power in 1795. Unable to gain entry into China, the London Missionary Society (LMS) entered Malaysia in 1814, labouring predominantly among the Malay-speaking Chinese, and established the Anglo-Chinese College in 1815 in order to train missionaries for China.

The propagation of Christianity was limited by the treaty between the British and the Malay sultans in 1874, in which Malays were defined as Muslims. Consequently, the British did not authorize the evangelization of the Malays except in Penang and Singapore. Even in today's Malay-speaking congregations, nearly all members are descendants of Chinese, Indians and Eurasians. Nevertheless, Christianity made some advances among the tribal groups in Sarawak, where the Anglicans, endorsed by James Brooke (1803–68), the ruler of the self-governing state of Sarawak (from 1841 to the 1940s), were involved in active missionary outreach for 40 years. In other parts of Malaysia, the Methodists carried out effective and notable work in schools. Yet the faith as a whole was still limited to the foreign community and very little effort was made to train local Christians for the work of the Church.

Following the Second World War (1941–5) and the withdrawal of Japan, the Church placed a high priority on enhancing its Asian identity and its ecumenical goals. Although Presbyterians and Anglicans had cooperated in the past, their differences forced them to choose one of two camps: those in favour of ecumenism and those opposed to it. In 1975 the National Council of Churches of Malaysia (NCCM) was formed. Also, broader cooperative efforts led to the formation of the Christian Federation of Malaysia (CFM) in

1985, comprising the Roman Catholic Church, the NCCM and the National Evangelical Church Fellowship. Because of its official recognition and registration, the CFM was in a good position to mediate on behalf of Christians with the government.

The Charismatic renewal movement in the 1990s had a great impact on the Church in Malaysia and resulted in increased evangelistic activities. Mission and evangelism became important priorities and collaborative evangelistic efforts were seen among Catholic and Protestant denominations. In addition, the tribal churches in Sarawak and Sabah assumed a more active role in the overall leadership of the Church. Today, Malaysian Christians, consisting primarily of Chinese and a small number of Indians, are estimated to make up 8.6 per cent of the population. Of these, slightly less than 50 per cent are Catholics and 50 per cent are Protestants; most of the latter are concentrated in Sarawak and Sabah.

Brunei

Brunei, an Islamic state, makes Islam obligatory for all Malays. It achieved its independence from the British in 1984. Although Christianity first came to Brunei in the sixteenth century (1521) through Magellan's expedition, Roman Catholicism did not become established until several centuries later. Yet in 1991 most of the Catholic priests and nuns were expelled. Presently, the majority of Catholics in Brunei are Chinese, Indian and European expatriates, with only a handful of Catholic Christian Malays, who face severe persecution. The first Protestant missionaries were Anglicans and entered Brunei in 1846. Several registered Anglican churches and an increasing number of independent churches now exist in Brunei. Many Christians meet secretly for worship. No Protestant or Catholic missionaries are currently reported to be working in the country.

The government requires that Islam be taught in public schools and prohibits the proclamation of any religion other than Islam. It outlaws the importation of religious teaching materials or Bibles, and forbids the celebration of Christmas. Today, 8 per cent of the population are Christians, with half Catholic and half Protestant, comprised mostly of Chinese immigrants.

 Singapore

Singapore, run by a secular government, became independent from British rule in 1959 and then from Malaysia in 1965. Catholics built their first chapel in the country in 1831, followed by the Armenians in 1835. The earliest Protestant missionaries entered Singapore shortly after British colonization in 1819. The London Missionary Society, the Board of Commissioners and the Church Missionary Society were among the early pioneer missionary societies. Early Anglican settlers from the British East India Company also arrived in Singapore in 1819, yet it was 18 years before the first church building was erected in 1837.

Initially, Protestants worked primarily among Europeans and only later planted churches among Asians. By the end of the nineteenth century, Anglican, Presbyterian, Christian Brethren and Methodist denominations had been established. These Protestant denominations, and also the Roman Catholics, set up schools to train Christian leaders for both the Church and the state.

At the beginning of the twentieth century, a number of other Protestant groups entered Singapore and started work in different parts of the country. By the second half of the twentieth century, sizeable indigenous denominations and parachurch organizations emerged and initiated significant mission work. Protestant groups from both mainline and Evangelical churches also founded theological colleges and Bible schools.

In 1974 the National Council of Churches of Singapore was constituted, bringing together the majority of non-Catholic churches. The period between 1970 and 1980 saw Charismatic renewal among older Protestant denominations and the emergence of independent Charismatic churches. As mainline Protestant groups and Catholics maintained steady growth, the younger churches, consisting primarily of independent, non-denominational megachurches, experienced rapid growth. In 1980 the Evangelical Fellowship of Singapore, made up of churches and parachurch organizations, was formed, and the Singapore Center for Evangelism and Missions was created in response to considerable interest in evangelism and overseas missions.

By 1990 over 30 per cent of Singaporeans with a tertiary education were Christians, indicating the high level of Christian influence over the years. A large number of Singaporean professionals are Christians. Moreover, the Singaporean parliament has a higher percentage of Christians than their proportion in the population. Today, Christians account for 15 per cent of the population, and are mostly of ethnic Chinese background. Of this total, 33 per cent are Catholic and 67 per cent Protestant.

Indonesia

Indonesia, the largest Muslim country in the world, declared its independence from Dutch colonial rule in 1945 and held parliamentary elections in 1999. Although Christians belonging to the Church of the East settled in the Indonesian islands of Sumatra and Java from the seventh to the fifteenth century, the subsequent rise of Islam obliterated them. The Portuguese introduced Roman Catholicism to Indonesia in the sixteenth century, but their work soon faded after the Dutch came to power in the early seventeenth century (1605). The Dutch suppressed Catholicism and advanced Protestant Christianity.

The Dutch East India Company initially established a Protestant church to serve its officials and employees. As the Dutch failed in their early efforts to spread Christianity, they also prohibited the work of other Protestant groups in the islands. Other mission organizations entered Indonesia only after the British took control in 1811, after which evangelism increased and church growth occurred. Conversion to Christianity in East Java resulted predominantly from the labours of several zealous laymen, including Coenraad. L. Coolen (1775–1873) and Johannes Emde (1774–1859). Coolen's advocacy for the development of Javanese Christianity was later made a reality by Ludwig Ingwer Nommensen (1834–1918) of the Rhenish Missionary Society, the first missionary to establish an indigenous church – and one that is still identified with local society and customs. As the support for indigenous forms of Christianity grew, however, the European dominance of the Indonesian Church became increasingly questionable, particularly from 1927 onwards. Based on his experience in Indonesia, the well-known missiologist Hendrik Kraemer (1888–1965), along with other prominent thinkers, argued against Western dominance in the Church.

The achievement of independence from the Dutch in 1945 brought new changes. Protestants, who had supported and fought for the country's freedom, successfully formed the National Council of Churches in Indonesia in 1950. Since its independence, Indonesia has required by law that its citizens must choose to be adherents of one of four faiths: Islam, Protestantism, Roman Catholicism or Hindu-Buddhism.

Major barriers for propagating Christianity in Indonesia included the inaccessibility of parts of the islands, the broad linguistic diversity, Islamic dominance in most regions and the association of Christianity with the foreign colonial rule of the Dutch. With the rise of nationalism and the struggle for independence, the Christian minority found itself viewed as the enemy by many Indonesians. In spite of these difficulties, the Church continued to grow, particularly among the non-Javanese minorities in the areas where indigenous religions had not been touched by Islam. The period between 1965 and 1970 saw 2.5 million mass conversions to Christianity, and many of these came as a result of the evangelistic work of Indonesian Christians. Protestant Christianity accounts for 11.3 per cent of the population while Roman Catholicism constitutes only 2.7 per cent.

The continual spread of Christianity in Indonesia is largely restricted by the dominance of Islam, which in this context is hostile to other religions. From the 1960s to the 1990s there was extensive persecution of Christians by Muslims, and many attacks were carried out on churches, resulting in the destruction of approximately 500 sacred buildings. Notwithstanding the persecution, Christians of various denominations have maintained their presence due to links with sister churches in the same denominations overseas. Yet challenging factors remain, such as socio-economic problems, Islamic hostility towards Christianity, the question of how Christians relate to other religions and the state, as well as geographical isolation and linguistic diversity.

✳ East Timor

East Timor, a former Portuguese colony that was also invaded by Indonesia at one time, became internationally recognized as a sovereign nation in 2002. Although Roman Catholicism first made sporadic contact with East Timor from the early sixteenth century through Portuguese traders, Christianity's permanent influence only began in 1642 when Portugal colonized East Timor.

The year 1975 marked the end of Portuguese control and the beginning of Indonesian military rule, at which time 30 per cent of the population were baptized Catholics. By the end of 1999, approximately 95 per cent of East Timorese had converted to Catholicism as a result of a law passed by Indonesian authorities requiring all followers of indigenous religions to embrace a world religion.

During the Indonesian occupation East Timor was closed off to the outside world, and in this period approximately 200,000 people were killed. The Catholic Church, exerting immense influence in society, was the only independent body that spoke out against the brutal actions of the Indonesian army. The continual involvement of the Catholic Church in politics was evident even after East Timor's independence from Indonesia, particularly when it confronted the government in 2005 regarding the issue of religious education in schools as well as the forgoing of war crime trials against Indonesia for atrocities committed against the East Timorese.

The first Protestant missionary to reach East Timor was Matthias van den Broecke (b. 1583/4), a chaplain for the Dutch military, who arrived in 1611. After the Portuguese regained control (eventually ruling until 1975), Protestants made little headway. Protestantism did not manage to establish its presence until the mid 1940s, and then only as the church of the colonialists. The Protestant Church in East Timor (PCET) was formed in 1979 and became the first coordinating body for Timorese Christians.

The Indonesian military and officials were associated with PCET during their occupation of East Timor. However, after the country's independence from Indonesia in 1999, most of the clergy were put to death or expelled; many fled to West Timor, and church members too were driven out of the country and their homes burned. Moreover, numerous churches were destroyed. Subsequently, Protestant numbers declined significantly, since at least half of the congregations, formerly comprised of military personnel and civil servants, had evacuated the country.

The Protestant Church in East Timor joined the WCC in 1991 as well as the CCA and the World Alliance of Reformed Churches. Membership in Protestant churches has increased since East Timor's international recognition as a sovereign state in 2002. The 2005 World Bank report indicated that the population of East Timor was 98 per cent Catholic, 1 per cent Protestant and less than 1 per cent Muslim.

 Conclusion

The churches in South-East Asia vary greatly in their current size and make-up. At one end, the Church in the Philippines enjoys widespread support from the majority of the population; at the other, the Church in Brunei barely registers in its underground existence. As in other parts of the world, the planting of these churches was both facilitated and hindered by European and US colonial rule in the region. In Vietnam, the Philippines, Singapore and Indonesia, traders and rulers from the West advanced missionary endeavour; while in Cambodia and Malaysia, colonial rule restricted the Christianization of some groups. In some instances (Thailand, Myanmar) the provision of Western educational and social services was seen as the route to modernization, without widespread conversion; in others (Vietnam, Laos, Cambodia) the Church's close association with imperial power and the West resulted in vicious persecution as the tide of nationalism rose. Yet as persecution receded, the churches grew. The Church's closeness to political and economic power has left an ambiguous legacy, at best, in Christian history.

However, the churches in South-East Asia cannot be understood solely in relation to agents from and associations with the West. In a number of countries, while Christianity has had less impact among the majority of the population, it has been embraced with enthusiasm by more marginal people-groups and to a lesser extent by immigrant populations. Particularly among tribal peoples, the Christian faith is the response to an indigenous religious quest, with Karen or Hmong individuals playing a central role. In a similar way, the churches of South-East Asia have by and large rejected the divisions introduced by Western Christianity, choosing instead to forge a wide range of confessional and ecumenical organizations. Pentecostal and Charismatic expressions have opened up spaces to address regional concerns for well-being and empowerment in the present. As elsewhere, it is this trajectory of adapting to the social and cultural context and to the religious needs of its people that will determine the future of Christianity in South-East Asia.

DISCUSSION QUESTIONS

1 Christianity made a lasting impact on South-East Asian nations in the sixteenth century and began transitioning from Western colonial control into a new Asian identity in the twentieth century. List some important events that marked both the 'lasting impact' in the sixteenth century and the transition in the twentieth century.

(a) What caused those events?

(b) Who were the initiators of each of those events?

2 With the exception of Thailand, which was never colonized, what colonial power dominated in each of the South-East Asian nations and how did colonial rule affect the spread of Christianity in each country?

3 Who were the initial groups that responded to the spread of Christianity in South-East Asia? Give reasons why they were responsive.

4 Religious restrictions and/or persecution have at one time or another characterized the spread of Christianity in most South-East Asian countries.

(a) What caused those restrictions and/or periods of persecution?

(b) What impact did religious restrictions and/or persecution have on the spread of Christianity?

(c) What should constitute the strategies of Christian missionary agencies and indigenous churches for the spread of Christianity in countries where religious restrictions and persecution exist?

5 Since the onset of its expansion, Christianity has experienced rapid growth in some parts of South-East Asia, while other parts have seen very little impact.

(a) Explain the reasons for both the receptivity and the resistance to the Christian faith.

(b) How should Christian missions and indigenous churches form strategies for the expansion of Christianity in each of the countries of South-East Asia in view of its receptivity as well as its resistance to the Christian faith?

6 Anti-colonial movements, independent church movements and Charismatic renewal movements all had an impact on the spread of Christianity in South-East Asia.

(a) What are the similarities and differences in the three movements?

(b) Discuss the negative and positive effects of these movements on the spread of Christianity in South-East Asia.

Further reading

Anderson, Gerald H. (ed.). *Christ and Crisis in Southeast Asia*. New York, NY: Friendship Press, 1968.

Anderson, Gerald H. (ed.). *Christianity in Southeast Asia: An annotated bibliography of selected references in Western languages*. New York, NY: Missionary Research Library, 1966.

Camps, Arnulf. *Studies in Asian Mission History, 1956–1998*. Boston: Brill, 2000.

Evers, George. *The Churches in Asia*. Delhi: ISPCK, 2005.

Goh, Robbie B. H. *Christianity in Southeast Asia*. Singapore: Institute of Southeast Asian Studies, 2005.

Kaplan, Steven (ed). *Indigenous Responses to Western Christianity*. New York, NY: New York University Press, 1995.

Moffett, Samuel Hugh. *A History of Christianity in Asia*, Vol. II, *1500–1900*. New York, NY: Orbis, 2005.

Saphir, Athyal (ed.). *Church in Asia Today: Challenges and opportunities*. Singapore: Asia Lausanne Committee for World Evangelization, 1996.

Sunquist, Scott W. (ed.). *A Dictionary of Asian Christianity*. Grand Rapids, MI: Eerdmans, 2001.

Thomas, Winburn T. and Manikam, Rajah B. *The Church in Southeast Asia*. New York, NY: Friendship Press, 1956.

7

Latin America and the Caribbean

Pablo Dieros and Jehu J. Hanciles

✳ Colonialism versus liberalism: 1800–1929

During the eighteenth century, Spanish influence in Latin America rapidly declined, even as weak Spanish monarchs increased their financial demands on the colonies to support the excessive expenditures of royal bureaucracy.

South America

Most of the burden fell on the shoulders of the Creole oligarchy, the descendants of European settlers born in the Americas. They were heavily taxed, but they had little power in the colonial system. As resentment grew, so did a sense of national identity that was centred on local values and interests.

The occupation of Spain by Napoleon's armies in 1808 marked the beginning of the period of national liberation of the Latin American colonies of Spain and Portugal. After wars of independence all these colonies attained their liberty and declared themselves republics in the 1820s, though the fight continued up until 1898 in the Caribbean. But political independence in Latin America was more a consequence of the efforts of the Creole oligarchy to free itself from exploitative Spanish control than the result of a search by the whole people for their own identity and freedom.

✳ Political independence and ecclesiastical crises

The years from 1808 to 1825 represent a period of major crisis for the Roman Catholic Church in Latin America. As the colonial church, it was strongly tied to the old structures of foreign domination, and the rise of the independence movements threatened its existence. Opposition to Spanish political rule also had religious implications, since it was also a revolt against the Spanish-controlled church. Furthermore, the movement towards independence was partly inspired by Enlightenment ideas (from Europe and the United States) that stressed reason, scientific progress and individual freedom as guiding principles. Since these ideas downplayed, even rejected, the importance of religion, the leaders of the new Latin American states did not hold Catholicism in the same esteem as the former colonial masters. Indeed, one of the issues at stake at that time was the separation of church and state, which had strong supporters in patriots such as Símon Bolivar (1783–1830), one of the greatest leaders of the independence movement.

But the Catholic Church had a number of factors in its favour. Religion was integral to the way of life of Latin American peoples, and the church enjoyed a complete monopoly over institutional religion. Other than the indigenous religious systems and spirituality, sometimes called 'folk religion', the Catholic faith had no competitors. In truth, the leaders within the church were divided in their attitude towards the independence movement. The mainly Creole priests backed the revolt, while the majority of bishops, who were mainly Spanish and whose primary loyalty was to the Spanish ruling authorities, opposed the wars of independence. Most crucial was the fact that the Vatican, which had deep ties with the Spanish Crown through historic treaties and agreements, also opposed the independence movements.

From the perspective of Rome, the Latin American independence movement bore a strong similarity to the 1789 French Revolution in its anti-religion stance. Certainly, a strong anti-clerical feeling – hostility to the power and influence of priests – had grown within the Creole population. In 1816 a papal encyclical urged the bishops and clergy in Spanish America to win back their flocks to obedience to the King of Spain. In 1824 the Pope issued another anti-revolutionary encyclical urging the clergy in Latin America to support the royal cause.

Once the revolutionary movement all over Latin America succeeded in overthrowing Spanish rule, the position of the Catholic Church became very complicated. A major reason for this was the *patronato* (Portuguese, *padroado*): a fifteenth-century agreement, sanctioned by papal decree, whereby the Spanish monarchy was granted complete control of all ecclesiastical matters in its colonies. Ending Spanish rule meant that the Catholic leadership now lacked an appropriate authority to regulate the offices of the church, such as the appointment of bishops.

This left the Catholic Church within the new republics in a state of crisis. Once the Spanish hierarchy of the church had fled to Spain, the church in Latin America was leaderless. The exodus of Spanish priests and bishops, who were the best-trained clergy, also left the Latin American Church with a serious deficit in pastoral care. Lack of doctrine, poor discipline and inadequate evangelization became common characteristics of Latin American Catholicism. Meanwhile, even though the principle of separation of church and state was strongly cherished by some of the new Latin American leaders, they also saw in the Roman Church an appropriate tool to fulfil the important function of social control. In rural areas more so than in the cities, the support of priests guaranteed the peasantry's acceptance of the new order; thus patriotic ideals and popular religiosity were linked.

The Vatican found itself in a serious dilemma. It felt bound to honour the *patronato*, yet the lack of episcopal supervision could quite easily open the way for forces opposed to Roman authority to gain the upper hand in the new republics. In any case, the issue of the *patronato* became a major source of conflict between the church and the state.

During the colonial period, the *patronato* had been the means and symbol of the state's supremacy over the Catholic Church. The new revolutionary governments claimed to have inherited the powers of the Spanish colonial rulers and sought to assert their authority over the church – including the right to appoint ecclesiastical officials. Naturally, the Vatican rejected this argument. It insisted that the *patronato* was originally an authorization specific to the Spanish monarchy and therefore not applicable or transferable to the leaders of the new republics. Furthermore, it claimed that since the revolutionary movement had ended Spanish rule, the right to *patronato* reverted to the papacy, its original source.

For several years this controversy remained unsolved. The papacy eventually relented when it became obvious that the political process in the emerging republics was irreversible and that the long-term impact of continued conflict with the new governments would be disastrous for the Catholic

Church. In 1831 Pope Gregory XVI (1765–1864) passed the bull *Sollicitudo ecclesiarum*, which recognized the political legitimacy of the new republics and allowed the traditional rights of the Spanish Crown over patronage to be continued by them. However, this concession was made grudgingly and tensions remained between church and state. Worse still, the declining authority of the Roman Catholic Church in society opened the way for other religious groups, including Protestants, to spread on the continent.

The growth of Protestantism

The presence of Protestants in Latin America came in the wake of the sixteenth-century Protestant Reformation in Europe. Many arrived as sailors and merchants. But the Roman Catholic authorities in the colonies barred Protestant settlement and used the Inquisition to root out Protestant believers. However, as Protestant nations in Europe also expanded their influence in the region from the seventeenth century and established colonies of their own, especially in the Caribbean, the Protestant presence increased. For instance, Calvinist congregations emerged when the Dutch established a colony in Suriname (north-east of Brazil); and Anglican churches followed the British colonization of Jamaica, Barbados and other islands. But Protestantism in Latin America was mainly confined to immigrants.

Once they gained self-rule, many of the new nations in Latin America became more open to Protestant settlement, in large measure because they needed international trade. Port towns, in particular, were opened to foreign residents, and churches sprang up to serve them. Some countries also signed treaties of 'commerce and friendship' with Protestant countries, in which a clause secured religious tolerance for the citizens of the designated nations. In 1810 Portugal signed a treaty with Britain that allowed the establishment of Protestantism in its Brazil colony. Small congregations of English-speaking and German immigrants quickly came together.

Perhaps most importantly, the constitutions of some of the newly independent Latin American countries also included new clauses or laws that affirmed religious diversity. In Brazil, for instance, the new 1824 constitution granted permission for other religions to exist as long as their followers kept to their own homes or worship places and the latter did not look like churches. Some of the leaders of the new Latin American republics, it must be said, encouraged immigration (specifically European immigration) out of the belief that it would help to bolster and preserve the European culture against that of the indigenous population. In the event, the arrival of non-Catholic European immigrants allowed Protestantism to be established on a more secure footing in Latin America, with Brazil and Argentina home to the largest Protestant populations.

Across Latin America, Protestant Christians are described as '*evangélicos*'. Throughout the nineteenth century, these *evangélicos* were predominantly

English-speaking and largely confined to foreigners and immigrants. Seen against the backdrop of a predominant and pervasive Roman Catholicism, Protestants remained a tiny minority, but they maintained a distinctive religious identity despite this situation. Their growing presence also increased the religious options. Few members of this relatively small Protestant minority abandoned their faith in favour of the dominant religion, and many of them contributed considerably to the economic and cultural development of their adopted countries.

In addition to immigration, Protestantism was introduced into Latin America through the work of North American missionary agents and societies that made Latin America the focus of evangelistic efforts. The first sustained Protestant missionary effort to Mexico was organized by Melinda Rankin (1811–88), an American schoolteacher in Texas, who began distributing Spanish-language Bibles and other religious material, supplied by the American Bible Society, across the US–Mexico border. Between 1804 and 1807 the British and Foreign Bible Society (BFBS) published 20,000 copies of the New Testament in Portuguese. James Thomson (1788–1854), a Scottish Baptist pastor, arrived in Buenos Aires in 1818 and used the New Testament as a reading book in his efforts to promote public education. Over the course of a few years he travelled through the continent and the Caribbean selling Bibles, opening schools and sharing a Protestant message. Several other itinerant workers distributing Bibles and religious books followed him as agents of the BFBS and the American Bible Society. In many places, these *colporteurs* (sellers of religious books) represented the first encounter that indigenous peoples had with Protestantism. It is important to note that, in Latin America, the Bible arrived first and then the foreign missionaries.

The Protestant element grew rapidly from around the mid nineteenth century. By 1930 Protestants numbered just over half a million or less than 1 per cent of the entire Latin American population. It is an indication of their rapid growth that in 1950 Protestant numbers were approaching five million (with about half of them in Brazil), and by 1990 the number of *evangélicos* throughout the region was estimated at more than 40 million (or one in ten of the Latin American population). This remarkable growth, as indicated elsewhere in this book, was powered mainly by extraordinarily dynamic Pentecostal movements.

The impact of liberalism

The emergence of nation states in Latin America also produced a period of political instability. As mentioned earlier, the revolutionary wars that ended colonialism had been spearheaded by the Creole elites. The masses of the population were little more than bystanders. Since the socio-economic structures inherited from the colonial period remained untouched, the masses remained downtrodden and marginalized while the Europeanized elite in the cities constituted the ruling class. The old colonial structures had been revamped but not changed, leaving the long-standing economic and social divisions intact. This made it very difficult to forge a new national identity within the fledgling Latin American republics. In fact, the resistance of local *caudillos* (military commanders) to the claims of the metropolitan elite led to bloody civil wars.

The new order and the Catholic Church

By the middle of the nineteenth century the political turmoil was almost over. From 1850 onwards more stable political structures were formed according to liberal ideals. Liberalism was an ideology that covered a wide array of beliefs, including political and civil liberties, democratic government, a free market, equal rights, intellectual and individual (including religious) freedom and separation of church and state. This liberal mould was mainly represented by the national constitutions provided for the emerging nation states. Copying the constitution of the United States and following some of the political theories that came from Europe, the ruling elites wrote the basic laws that gave shape to the Latin American nations.

The embrace of liberalism by the new republics represented a serious attack on the old order and ushered in a period of radical change and major ideological conflict (primarily between those who defended the old ways and the more progressive groups). Throughout Latin America the Catholic Church faced a growing crisis and worsened conditions. Not only did independence lead to the collapse of the long-standing *patronato* system, but also the number of clergy dwindled, the number of ordinations decreased, and the level of theological education dropped due to lack of teachers and books. Moreover, the basic tenets of liberalism espoused by the new governments directly challenged the long-standing and all-encompassing authority of the Roman Catholic Church in society. The intimate partnership between church and state that dated back to the original conquest and settlement in the early sixteenth century now unravelled.

The Catholic Church was deeply conservative, which is to say that it embodied the old ways, defended traditional institutions and generally resisted modern progress. As one of the most important landowners of the continent, it was strongly invested in preserving entrenched power-structures in which a tiny elite controlled all the wealth. This put it on a collision course with the liberal project of the newly independent governments. The latter wanted to preserve some of the old authority enjoyed by the state, but they associated the Catholic Church with colonial domination and the passing order. Moreover, the ideals they embraced demanded a progressive reduction of ecclesiastical influence as a necessary condition for the construction of the modern state. The conflict between the two sides intensified with time. The church appeared inflexibly conservative, hostile to foreigners and nationalistic (in the sense that it linked national identity with the Catholic religion), while the governments' commitment to freedom from foreign control and ecclesiastical domination was boosted by growing international relations.

It needs to be said that the emerging modern democracies in Latin America were anything but perfect. Among other things, political independence brought little change to the acute social and economic inequalities that had marked the colonial period. For instance, despite the embrace of liberalism, the practice of slavery remained legal in many of the new republics until well into the nineteenth century. Yet by resisting the new order, with its lofty claims of progress and freedom, the Roman Catholic Church found itself completely out of step with the transformative change on the continent. It remained trapped in a bygone age.

Meanwhile, political developments based on liberalism gathered pace under the control of a small group of elites who, in their own way, were just as conservative and elitist as the church authorities, and who, also like the church, looked to foreign lands (such as France) for their models and ideals. Throughout Latin America, specific legislative measures designed to reduce the influence and power of the Catholic Church in public life were implemented. Among the first republics to implement constitutional reform stipulating the separation of church and state were Colombia (1851) and Mexico (1859). Brazil did the same in 1890. These developments were accompanied by legislative measures that had far-reaching implications for the role and influence of the Catholic Church in society. The following were notable:

- *Civil registration.* The Roman Catholic Church lost its control over the statistics of births, deaths and marriages. In this way it was dispossessed of an important tool for social control.
- *Civil marriage.* The end of the monopoly of the church over marriage was the result of the increasing secular influence of liberals and of the new social conditions produced by the increase in population, the shortage of priests and the coming of immigrants, some of them Protestants and Jews.
- *Abolition of tithes.* The collection of tithes had been granted to the Spanish Crown by Pope Alexander VI in the bull of 1501. The colonial administration had collected them and returned them to the Roman Catholic Church. They were among the first of the church's privileges to fall before the liberals' militancy.
- *Expropriation of church lands.* The landed wealth of the Roman Church was considered an impediment for effective modern government because it preserved a domain of ecclesiastical influence that was detrimental to progress. The church lands should, as a matter of right, belong to the nation.
- *Abolition of the ecclesiastical* fuero *(grant of privileges).* The legal immunities of the clergy and the exercise of jurisdiction over the laity were restricted or abolished in all the Latin American republics.

- *Public education.* Education was in the hands of the Catholic Church during the colonial period. Liberal dislike of clerical influence in schools, and the insufficiency of the church's human and economic resources, led to an increasing participation of the state in education.

Thus, even as the growth of Protestantism and other faiths ended the virtual monopoly over formal religious life that Roman Catholicism had previously enjoyed, the governments of the new states took greater control of services such as education and registration of marriages that had once been the preserve of the Roman Catholic Church. Not all of these measures were enforced and some were implemented only half-heartedly. Yet members of the church hierarchy now lost many of their age-old privileges and benefits. A large number, especially bishops, responded by looking even more to Rome for support, which did little to improve the image of Catholicism in the region. Latin American Catholicism would never quite be the same again.

In the final analysis, however, church and state needed each other. The Vatican was particularly anxious to reassert its religious authority over the church in Latin America, while Latin American governments were mindful of the fact that the Roman Church was the only truly national institution in every country and still a powerful influence in everyday life. Eventually, the Vatican accepted the revolutionary change and even managed to regain some of its old influence and play a more active role in Latin America. Pope Leo XII (1760–1829) named the first six bishops for Colombia; and his successor, Pope Gregory XVI, named six bishops for Mexico. All the new bishops were Latin Americans, not Spaniards, and they were appointed directly by Rome – further confirmation, if needed, that the *patronato* had ceased to exist.

The reorganization of the church hierarchy in some parts of Latin America soon followed. But efforts to renew the Catholic Church and introduce major innovations in church life, in response to political developments, produced mixed results. Better provisions were made for the training of the clergy and the control of ecclesiastical affairs, but the main reinforcements to fill the vacant episcopal sees and the positions in the parishes came from Europe. Indeed, the overarching objective was to shape Latin American Catholicism in terms of European models.

By the end of the nineteenth century the new republics had begun to make significant strides in terms of economic development and political progress. But the new governments increasingly found themselves in the North American sphere of influence (which led to a spate of military interventions in the region by the United States) and part of a neocolonial relationship involving economic dependence on Western countries. In this new relationship the new nations functioned as producers of raw materials for the centres of industrial power and became consumers of the products manufactured by the dominant industrial powers. With economic dependence came new forms of cultural subordination. The new leaders and the Latin American elites were fascinated by European civilization and idealized

European models. Education followed European patterns and was seen as the main means of annihilating indigenous culture and traditional values. In other words, much had changed but much remained the same.

Political ferment and Protestant growth

Throughout Latin America the period from 1930 to 1960 was one of great social change. Rapid urbanization led to large-scale migration from the rural areas to the cities, creating massive *favelas* (shanty towns) and grinding poverty. The worldwide crisis of 1929 significantly weakened Latin American liberal states and allowed Catholicism to regroup its forces.

The renewal and resurgence of Roman Catholicism came primarily through a lay movement known as Acción Católica (Catholic Action). Founded by Pope Pius XI (1857–1939) in 1922, Catholic Action sought to deepen faith and to encourage lay people to take a more active part in the life of the church. First established in Argentina, it spread to most countries in Latin America. It also absorbed many smaller movements and attracted a large membership. Through this and similar initiatives, lay movements were organized and social action among the working classes was stimulated. Christian Democracy, a movement strongly allied with Roman Catholicism that sought to apply Christian principles to public life, also appeared on the political scene as a major counterweight to liberal ideologies. Christian Democratic parties emerged across Latin America from the 1940s to 1980s, becoming dominant in El Salvador, Venezuela and Chile.

The political and economic crisis of the 1930s also witnessed the rise of the military as a force in Latin American politics. The Roman Catholic Church's support for the new military governments allowed it to reassert its enormous influence in the political arena. With the exception of Mexico, the governments of Getulio Vargas (1882–1954) in Brazil, Juan D. Perón (1895–1974) in Argentina, Marcos Pérez Jiménez (1914–2001) in Venezuela, López Pinilla (1900–75) in Colombia, José María Velasco Ibarra (1893–1979) in Ecuador and even Víctor R. Haya de la Torre (1895–1979) in Peru, all had positive relations with the Catholic Church. The tide of post-independence liberalism was pushed back and the church regained economic dominance and control of education. Elements in society considered incompatible with the 'Catholic and Hispanic tradition' – including Jews, Protestants, communists or Marxists – came under severe attack.

In the 1950s Latin America experienced considerable instability and a series of upheavals, in large measure because it became a major theatre of the Cold War conflict between the United States and the Soviet Union. In the universities Christian thinkers began to respond to the challenges of Marxism, an ideology which opposed capitalism (in favour of public ownership of all production) and rejected religion. New theological and philosophical journals were founded in which Christian scholars could put forward their views and share ideas. All in all, the Roman Catholic Church attempted a process of renewal on the basis of a 'New Christendom' model that was developed in the intellectual field, in pastoral practice and through new national and international institutions. Examples included the first Conference of the Latin American Episcopate and Latin American Confederation of Religious, established in 1955 and 1958 respectively. These institutions were directed by Christians concerned for justice and freedom in society.

But the Catholic resurgence was short-lived. Christian Democracy came to power in several countries, but failed to achieve its ends. Acción Católica also gradually lost steam as a lay organization by the 1960s. Even more serious was the growing process of de-Christianization and secularization. Attendance at Mass and active participation in the religious programmes of the Catholic Church diminished as new movements, especially of the ideological or political kind, captivated the interest of the ever-growing Latin American youth.

The rise in Protestant missions and Pentecostalism

In different parts of Latin America, Protestant groups suffered serious restrictions during this period, but Protestantism continued its remarkable growth due to the massive influx of foreign missionaries and the rise of Pentecostalism. With the closing of China to Western missions, North American missionaries began to pour into Latin America in record numbers during the 1950s. The influx continued with the arrival of other missionaries who were no longer able to work freely in the Arab world. By the 1960s Latin America had some 7,000 Protestant missionaries, with 30,000 local pastors and lay workers, 45,000 places of worship and a total church membership of 12.5 million. Foreign missionaries were most numerous in north-eastern Brazil and Chile, and least numerous in the countries of north-western South America. The chief purpose of their work in this period was to build up and instruct Christian congregations, but the expansion in missionary numbers also produced a corresponding increase in the number of converts.

Pentecostal beginnings in Latin America date from the establishment of the Christian Congregation among Italian immigrants in São Paulo, Brazil, in 1910 by Luigi Francesco (1866–1964), an Italian layman from Chicago. But the Pentecostal movement emerged in its strongest form when two young Swedish immigrants, Daniel Berg (1884–1963) and Gunnar Vingren (1879–1933), also arrived in Brazil from Chicago in 1911. The ministry of these two men led to the establishment of Assembléias de Deus (Assemblies of God) – a name later used by another Pentecostal group in the USA. Starting with about 18 members in 1911, Assemblies of God (Brazil) grew to an estimated 12 million members by 2000, making it the largest Pentecostal movement in the world. The dramatic growth of Protestantism in Latin American from the mid twentieth century has been driven mainly by the extraordinary dynamism of Pentecostal movements.

It is also noteworthy that Latin American Catholicism has been directly influenced by Pentecostal impulses, most notably through the Charismatic Catholic Renewal (CCR) movement, which emphasizes speaking in tongues, baptism in the Holy Spirit and healing. This movement originated in the USA in the 1960s and spread to Latin America, where it has had an extraordinary impact on the Catholic laity. Endorsed by the Roman Catholic hierarchy and supported by Pope Paul VI (1897–1978), CCR became the most dynamic movement within the Catholic Church in Latin America, with a reputation for energetic evangelism.

For the most part, the growth of Latin American Pentecostalism has been brought about by indigenous initiatives and leadership, even if the original spark was lit by foreign agency or influences. The fact of the matter is that the Pentecostal–Charismatic experience has profound appeal precisely because it draws deeply on indigenous spirituality and tends to democratize religious power. The downside of this characteristic is that it fosters endless divisions and extensive fragmentation, since there is no shortage of charismatic individuals disposed to establish their own ministries or churches. By the 1960s even mainline Protestant groups had begun to transition from foreign control to indigenous leadership. The process was not without tensions; but gradually, mainline Protestant denominations were put on a national footing, headed by indigenous leaders. The Pentecostal movement did not suffer similar tensions, but it was marked by continuous division; though this divisiveness also contributed to its phenomenal growth.

❋ Revolution, persecution, liberation

From the late 1950s many Latin American nations experienced another period of intense political crisis and instability as the popular military dictatorships began to crumble. In Latin America's vastly uneven societies, economic development – assisted by various 'development packages' – benefited the already rich while plunging the masses even deeper into poverty. By the 1960s there was a growing consciousness among Latin American peoples that many of their countries were 'dependent' and 'oppressed' outposts of the United States and other developed countries. This opened the way for another cycle of revolutions, fomented by the appearance of leftist guerrilla movements, new military dictatorships (in Chile, Brazil, El Salvador and partly in Argentina), liberationist movements, and the emergence of socialist regimes during the 1960s and 1970s.

The rise of new military regimes added institutional violence and political repression to the huge economic hardships already being experienced by the lower classes. At the same time, Latin American intellectuals began to rediscover indigenous Latin American culture and question long-standing cultural dependence on Europe and North America. All these developments had direct repercussions on the Roman Catholic Church.

After the Second Vatican Council (1962–5) the leaders of the Catholic Church sought to find their voice and address the realities of the day. At the Second General Conference of Latin American Bishops of the Roman Catholic Church (CELAM), held in Medellín in Colombia in 1968, the bishops discussed the implications of the Second Vatican Council for the Catholic Church in Latin America. The meeting forcefully denounced the rampant injustices, foreign oppression and mass poverty which characterized Latin American societies and resolved that, unless the system could be changed, there would be no chance of any improvement. This signalled a bold new approach in which change and renewal was sought not through movements such as Catholic Action or politically through Christian Democracy, but through the active pursuit of liberation as integral to the message and ministry of the church.

Thus, at a time when the number of military governments in Latin America was on the increase, the Roman Catholic Church adopted a new radical position. Whereas in the past it spoke out to defend its own rights and privileges, it now began to speak out in favour of justice for the poor, and freedom for Christians and non-Christians alike. Leaving behind its old, defensive self-preservation, it now took upon itself a prophetic role, denouncing evil and tyranny where necessary, with all the political consequences of doing so.

In presenting itself as a defender of democracy, human rights and justice, the Roman Catholic Church became a thorn in the side of military dictatorships in many parts of Latin America. It paid a heavy price. In Brazil, for instance, hundreds of Brazilian Catholics were tortured, imprisoned and killed in the 1960s and 1970s. In El Salvador, the military government responded to calls for social reform and economic equality with brutal violence. In 1979 alone, four priests were assassinated, along with many hundreds of catechists. In all, at least 75,000 to 80,000 Salvadoreans were slaughtered – mainly *campesinos* (peasants or villagers) but also students, clergy and journalists. Few stories capture this era of state persecution more vividly than that of Archbishop Oscar Romero (1917–80), the Salvadorean Roman Catholic priest whose denunciation of human rights abuses and calls for social reform earned him martyrdom at the hands of Salvadorean death squads on 24 March 1980. Romero's ideas embodied the new consciousness within the Catholic Church that siding with the poor and oppressed and seeking their liberation was integral to the gospel. He wrote:

> Every time we look upon the poor . . . there is the face of Christ . . . The face of Christ is among the sacks and baskets of the farm worker; the face of Christ is among those who are tortured and mistreated in the prisons; the face of Christ is dying of hunger in the children who have nothing to eat; the face of Christ is in the poor who ask the church for their voice to be heard.
>
> (Archbishop Oscar Romero, Homily, 26 November 1978, in Marie Dennis, Renny Golden and Scott Wright, *Oscar Romero: Reflections on his life and writings* (Maryknoll, NY: Orbis, 2000), p. 35)

Central America

Romero was shot to death while celebrating Mass inside a church on the grounds of the Divine Providence Hospital, San Salvador.

The Liberation Theology movement

By 1960 there were over 600 bishops all over Latin America, living in isolation from one another. The Vatican II meetings brought them together for the first time, and this not only allowed a sense of collective identity to develop but also fostered active collaboration in addressing the continent's immense problems. Entrenched poverty and injustice immediately emerged as foremost concerns. At the same time, lay people in Latin America became more insistent on playing an active role in the life of the Catholic Church, which many still saw as a clergy-centred institution. The older lay movements such as Catholic Action had lost their attraction and many young people preferred to join secular trade unions or even enrol in militant leftist groups. It was in this context that 'base communities' emerged. These were small groupings of Christians at the parish

147

level who came together to help and support one another in living out the faith. In north-eastern Brazil, where the movement started, there were some 1,500 base communities by the mid 1970s, each consisting of about 150 Christians.

Christians in the universities also began to move away from the old ways of thinking. They now made efforts to relate their work more closely to the needs of society and to the liberation of an oppressed and dependent people. Among some theologians, there was a new recognition of the inadequacy of European theology to address the priorities and concerns of the Latin American context. More specifically, these theologians began to apply the insights of Scripture to the problems confronting Latin American societies, particularly the economic and political oppression to which large sections of the population were subjected.

Liberation Theology emerged out of these complex strands and impulses that marked the post-Vatican II era. One of its foremost thinkers, often regarded as 'the father of Liberation Theology', is Father Gustavo Gutiérrez (b. 1928), a Peruvian who studied theology and philosophy in Europe. Gutiérrez' book *A Theology of Liberation* (1971) explains that a commitment to the poor and oppressed – often expressed in the formula 'a preferential option for the poor' – is the core element of Liberation Theology. In this approach the whole of Scripture is constantly examined from the viewpoint of the oppressed. Gutiérrez argued that

> in the final analysis, an option for the poor is an option for the God of the kingdom whom Jesus proclaims to us . . . The entire Bible, beginning with the story of Cain and Abel, mirrors God's predilection for the weak and abused of human history.
>
> (Gustavo Gutiérrez, *A Theology of Liberation*, rev. edn (New York, NY: Orbis, 1988), p. xxvii)

Early Liberation Theologians tended to be Roman Catholic priests and laymen, although there were important exceptions, such as the nun Ivone Gebara (b. 1944), and Protestants were also represented. Though primarily addressed to pressing problems in the Latin American context, the rich and deeply provocative insights of Liberation Theology spread throughout the world as Christians and theologians (even in industrialized countries) applied its perspectives to the enormous challenges of poverty and oppression in their own contexts.

By the beginning of the twenty-first century Liberation Theology appeared to have lost its allure as a major strand of the theological discourse. Critics despaired that, while its focus on socio-economic problems is legitimate, it tends to minimize the spiritual dimensions of human sinfulness. That said, the impact and legacy of Liberation Theologies (the plural best captures the varieties of insight and application globally) are enduring. Few Christian communities today, in Latin America and elsewhere, would question the need to apply the claims of the gospel to contextual issues of poverty and oppression in every form. Indeed, it is correctly observed that as long as there are poor, marginalized or excluded persons, there will be Liberation Theology.

For the most part, the Protestant churches in Latin America looked at the situation differently. Though the growth of Protestantism contributed to the emphasis on reading the Bible that fed the thinking on liberation, most Protestant churches were reluctant to address the burning social, economic and political issues of the continent. Some even supported right-wing governments, no matter how repressive, out of a fear that the only alternative was communism, which they regarded as even worse. However, this outlook changed after the 1980s when Pentecostal movements entered the political arena in decisive fashion and became major political actors in countries such as Brazil. Indeed, Pentecostal–Charismatic movements also began to reflect the thinking and practices associated with Liberation Theology. This is not surprising, for Pentecostalism by its very nature involves social protest – since it stresses the need for social transformation and upholds the liberative power of the Holy Spirit in the lives of ordinary people. As explained below, its tremendous success has produced political action.

✳ Christianity and democracy since 1980

The 1980s witnessed the collapse of military regimes and the emergence of unstable democracies throughout the continent. Neoliberalism (an economic model which emphasizes free-market enterprise without state control), the privatization of state-owned enterprises and the cutting of public spending on social services was imposed throughout the region. Mixed with the forces of globalization, continuing political corruption, enduring socio-economic divisions and extensive rural-to-urban migration, this development contributed to increased poverty, massive underemployment and other major ills. With the new democracies the Roman Catholic Church turned even more conservative and defensive, championing issues such as anti-abortion laws, opposing same-sex marriage, and trying to keep control of education. Church leaders succeeded in frustrating the development of the dynamic base ecclesial communities and the Charismatic movement. They were more interested in holding meetings to do politics and to reinforce the ecclesiastical bureaucracy than in keeping in contact with real people and their needs.

Pentecostals and politics

As for Protestants in this period, they were hyperactive in evangelizing and planting churches. Their institutions increased notably and made major inroads into the Latin American scene. For the first time in history,

Protestantism came to constitute the majority of the population in some places, such as Guatemala and El Salvador. Latin American Pentecostalism has continued its phenomenal growth and produced a vast array of ministries and movements, from start-ups that adopt primal religious practices to megachurches defined by 'prosperity' teaching. To what extent this growth has been at the expense of Roman Catholicism is difficult to say. What is clear is that both Protestants and Catholics continue to draw on the deep religious and spiritual capacity of Latin American peoples.

Spectacular growth, ownership of public media (made possible by financial success), growing concerns about the breakdown of traditional values, as well as a more open and democratic political climate, all helped to facilitate Pentecostal involvement in politics – most notably in Brazil. Not surprisingly, the largest and most successful Pentecostal ministries and movements – for example Assemblies of God (AG), Universal Church of the Kingdom of God, and Four Square – have produced the most prominent political candidates and elected officials. In 1986 Benedita da Silva (b. 1943), a black female AG member of the Brazilian Socialist Party, became the first Brazilian woman to be elected to the National Congress. In 2005 Universal Church founded its own political party, the Partido Republicano Brasileiro (PRB), which had four of the 513 seats in the Federal Chamber of Deputies. This extensive political involvement has been tainted by scandals involving corruption; but the capacity for socio-political action fully demonstrates the extraordinary potential within Latin American Christianity (both Catholic and Protestant) for concrete social transformation.

✳ Conclusion

Challenges for Latin American Roman Catholicism

Roman Catholicism has good opportunities for church action today in Latin America. Many Latin American countries are experiencing a deep social and economic crisis, along with a lack of political leadership because of a lack of civic education and democratic exercise for many years, and are being plunged into serious moral decadence and corruption. In the midst of this, the Catholic Church represents a reconciliatory power that could mark the road to follow. The Church of Rome continues to be considered by all social sectors as a great moral reservoir. Its influence has markedly increased in the past few decades because in some way it has moulded itself to the various circumstances of the complex Latin American situation. It would be very difficult for the Catholic Church to lose its privileged position in most of the countries of the continent. With the experience it has gained during the centuries, the church always finds a way to mould itself to changing situations without losing its influence.

Some important positive elements are a more open attitude on the part of the Catholic Church towards Protestantism and other religions, the recommendation and spread of the Bible, the development of youth organizations, some cautious evangelization, the search for an authentic spirituality, the building up of the church from a popular base rather than relying on the hierarchy, identification with popular movements and the involvement of lay people.

However, there are some dangers that have to be addressed. Latin American Catholicism is not homogeneous. Its development is varied. The need for priests is critical. In recent decades, special efforts have been made to increase the number of priests, without success. The condition and status of the Roman Church differs from country to country and from administration to administration, but shortage of clergy has been and continues to be one of its major problems. Another important problem for today's Catholicism is the old issue of the relationship between church and state. To a great degreee, the continent presents a poor picture with regard to religious freedom. In general, the Catholic Church continues to act on the defensive and adopt a rather conservative attitude. And most of all, because there is no serious evangelization strategy, Roman Catholicism is losing most of its constituency to Protestantism, particularly to Pentecostalism. The acceptance of popular religiosity and popular Catholicism helped to somehow keep the masses under the umbrella of the church, but has corrupted its moral, spiritual and theological integrity, fostering syncretism and an increasingly nominal Catholicism.

Challenges for Latin American Protestantism

The present situation of Protestantism is not homogeneous. Mainline Protestant churches and those of immigrant origin are in decline. Eighty per cent of all *evangélicos* in Latin America today are involved in various Charismatic–Pentecostal groups. Rapid numerical growth, however, is creating new dangers. Among them are triumphalism, the corruption of the Christian gospel for a gospel of prosperity, the concentration of power in the hands of charismatic leaders, the lack of a deep process of discipleship for new believers, a kind of imbalance between mind and heart that can result in religious emotionalism and sentimentalism, and an increasing institutionalism that weakens the commitment to the kingdom of God. Besides, Evangelicals in this region tend to love the Bible but are often biblically illiterate. About 80 per cent of all pastors lack formal theological training, Bible teaching in local communities is scarce or of poor quality, and the traditional Evangelical zeal for Bible reading and attachment to God's word is disappearing. Unity continues to be a major challenge not only for Evangelicals but also for Roman Catholics. Efforts have been made which proved to be successful, but the road to Christian unity, to better fulfil the mission entrusted, continues to be elusive; it is a prayer waiting for response (John 17.21, 23).

The Caribbean

In geographical terms, 'the Caribbean' loosely refers to the subregion of island countries surrounding the Caribbean Sea with a total population of about 42 million. The name derives from 'Carib', the term used by Spanish colonizers in the sixteenth century to describe the local inhabitants. Territorial seizures by competing European nations – notably France, Britain and the Netherlands – continued the process. Today, the vast majority of the Caribbean population (perhaps as high as 90 per cent) are descended from the huge number of slaves imported from Africa. The rest comprise descendants of European settlers and the sizeable group of Asians (from India and East Asia) recruited as labourers during the colonial period. To these are added other immigrants from the Middle East and elsewhere.

Foreign occupation and waves of immigration over centuries make the Caribbean a place of remarkable ethnic and cultural diversity. Christianity is the dominant religion (Catholics and Protestants account for 59 per cent

Caribbean

and 24 per cent respectively), but indigenous Afro-Caribbean religions such as Rastafarianism (Jamaica), Santeria (Cuba) and Voodoo (Haiti) also flourish, alongside Asian faiths such as Hinduism and Sikhism, which in turn jostle with Islam and Judaism.

The islands of the Caribbean remained European colonial possessions much longer than other colonies. Only Haiti, the Dominican Republic and Cuba gained independence before 1900. One reason for this was the tremendous wealth generated by the sugar plantations and factories on these islands. By 1770 they accounted for almost 90 per cent of sugar exports globally. This also meant that the Caribbean islands used a significant proportion of enslaved Africans. In the eighteenth century the region absorbed some 60 per cent of the slaves taken to the Americas. With the exception of the islands of the Dominican Republic, which gained self-rule (from France) and abolished slavery in 1801, the abolition of slavery in the Caribbean was an extended process. Cuba, the last to do so, only ended slavery as a legal institution in 1886.

Caribbean Christianity (Catholics and Protestants)

Roman Catholicism came to the Caribbean with Spanish conquest and colonization. France, another major colonizer, was also Catholic, as were many Irish and Dutch immigrants. Throughout the colonial era, the Roman Catholic Church fully supported the domination and exploitation of non-European peoples. The church's complicity in the brutality of slavery presented a formidable barrier to mission. In any case, the Roman Church suffered from a severe and chronic shortage of priests, and evangelization of the African slave population was often neglected. That said, some African slaves were already Christian or familiar with Christianity before enslavement. Catholicism in Haiti, for instance, was largely imported by the large numbers of slaves from the Catholic Kingdom of Kongo in western Africa. Since much of Caribbean Catholicism developed without (or with little) clerical oversight and institutional control, what prevailed among the non-European population was a form of folk Catholicism blended with indigenous beliefs and African religion. In public life its most prominent features were the patronage festivals and the cult of the saints.

Like Roman Catholicism, the Protestant faith arrived in the Caribbean through colonization by Protestant nations – primarily Britain and the Netherlands. The Anglican Church was established in British territories and the Dutch Reformed Church in Dutch territories. But, in contrast to the territories of Spain, British and Dutch colonies in the Caribbean were marked by much religious diversity. For one thing, some of these colonies had previously been Spanish or French settlements (and therefore predominantly Catholic). When the Dutch captured Curaçao from the Spanish in the 1630s, they allowed the Catholic Church to continue its work. Lutheran congregations also emerged because some Dutch settlers were Lutheran.

The constant influx of European immigrants, including Quakers, Baptists, Methodists, Moravians, Scottish Presbyterians and even Jews (fleeing persecution in Europe), added other denominations and faiths to the mix. Importantly, the evangelization and religious instruction of the slave population came not from the national churches (which generally resisted such efforts) but from marginalized groups such as the Quakers, Baptists, Methodists and Moravians.

Despite widespread fears among colonial authorities and planters, the abolition of slavery and emancipation of former slaves in the early 1800s did not lead to violent uprisings and reprisals. Emancipation was accompanied by a massive influx of the newly liberated slaves into churches, which acted as new focal points for African communities. Before long, however, these African churches began to face tremendous challenges in the form of limited financial resources, a lack of trained clergy, and migrations. More than other Christian communities, they also tended to be characterized by emotional or expressive worship – religion overtly connected with music and dance – and an emphasis on demonstrations of spiritual power, all reflecting African religiosity.

As was the case in Latin America, the Catholic Church in the Caribbean experienced significant challenges in the wake of political independence because of its strong association with Spanish colonial rule. But, despite its weak institutional reach and influence, Catholicism emerged as a major element of Caribbean society. Adapted to the unique spirituality and religious ethos of Caribbean culture, the Roman Catholic faith became a pervasive feature of everyday life. Today, it is the dominant faith in the region, accounting for some 60 per cent of the Caribbean population. The highest concentrations of Roman Catholics are to be found in the Dominican Republic (95 per cent), Guadeloupe (95 per cent), St Martin (85 per cent) and Puerto Rico (85 per cent).

Protestant faiths have also taken firm root and continue to flourish in the Caribbean, though most Protestant denominations have lost ground to Pentecostalism (see below). At the same time, the postcolonial era has witnessed significant strides in ecumenical collaboration between the varieties of Protestant denominations, especially in addressing the huge need for theological and ministerial training. In 1966 for instance, the United Theological College of the West Indies (now the theological school in the University of the West Indies) was established in Jamaica when several denominations merged their training institutions. Founded in 1973, the Caribbean Conference of Churches, comprising 33 members in 33 countries by 2011, has sought to overcome the divisions (of race, creed, language, culture and distance) created by colonialism as well as provide a forum for united action against the region's colossal socio-economic challenges.

Due to the Caribbean's unique history and heritage, the impact of Liberation Theology on the region has been limited. What has emerged is a distinctive Caribbean theology which, though influenced by Liberation

Theology, is critical of its preoccupation with poverty. In response to the particular challenges of their context, Caribbean theologians seek to address not only issues of poverty but also those of culture, race and identity. The religious diversity of the Caribbean and the questions it raises for Christian theological reflection make up another significant strand. Much remains to be done, with the help of the region's growing body of theological training institutions. The linguistic diversity of the Caribbean hampers theological collaboration somewhat, and there is a continuing need for contextual relevance to be balanced with meaningful dialogue and interaction with other postcolonial theologies in the wider region and diaspora.

The 1900s witnessed the end of colonialism and the emergence of independent states throughout the Caribbean, followed by the rise of a few dictatorships (notably in Haiti and the Dominican Republic). The departure of European powers also allowed the United States to assert its hegemony and influence in the region from the late nineteenth century, leading to US occupation of several Caribbean territories. Expansive Protestant missionary activity from the United States and the explosive spread of Pentecostalism brought religious transformation to many areas.

The wide array of American missionary initiatives met with mixed responses. In the Dominican Republic, Protestantism was associated with US occupation and it made little headway. In Cuba, however, where Catholicism was linked to Spanish colonial oppression, Protestantism symbolized democratic values and enjoyed strong appeal. Importantly, also, the missionaries were Cuban-born exiles. Protestantism in Cuba flourished until the communist revolution of 1959, which led to the establishment of an atheistic state. Among former Catholic (Spanish-speaking) colonies, the highest rate of Protestant growth occurred in the US territory of Puerto Rico, where an estimated one quarter of the population are Protestant. Here, as in Haiti, the majority of Protestants are Pentecostal.

The growth of Pentecostalism

Introduced into the Caribbean from the USA, Pentecostalism took root in the Caribbean and spread rapidly through indigenous initiatives and organizations. Its explosive growth reshaped Caribbean Christianity. Heavily influenced by black spirituality, which emphasizes spiritual power, healing and ecstatic worship, American Pentecostalism resonated deeply with the predominantly African population of the Caribbean. But even if it was introduced by foreign sources, Pentecostal faith in the Caribbean assumed a variety of indigenous forms of expression. This contributed to its mass appeal. The Pentecostal surge in the region was greatly augmented by the spread of the dynamic and evangelistic Catholic Charismatic Renewal movement in the Catholic (former Spanish) states. By the mid 1950s, Pentecostals accounted for 25 per cent of Protestants in Puerto Rico. And, despite heavy restrictions on religion by the communist regime, in Cuba the Assemblies of God could claim 100,000 members and 756 congregations by the 1990s.

The growth of Pentecostalism has been even more dramatic in Jamaica. The long heritage of Protestant religion – established along with colonization by Britain – had something to do with this. But the emergence of Pentecostalism on the island was also linked to local initiatives, notably that of J. Wilson Bell (c.1860–1938), a Kingston preacher who invited missionaries from the Church of God, Tennessee, to come to his community in 1918. This connection led to the establishment of two of the largest Pentecostal denominations in Jamaica: the New Testament Church of God (NTCG) and the Church of God of Prophecy. Other Pentecostal groups affiliated with US Pentecostalism (including the mainly white Assemblies of God and the mainly black Church of God in Christ) also flourished. The influence of US culture in the wake of Jamaica's independence from Britain in 1962 gave further impetus to Pentecostal expansion. By the early 1980s, 30 per cent of the island's population identified as Pentecostal. The largest Pentecostal denomination is the New Testament Church of God which, in 2008, comprised 361 churches with over 92,000 active members (and some 200,000 worshippers on a typical Sunday).

Everywhere, the growth of Caribbean Pentecostalism has been at the expense of mainline Protestant churches. One reason for this is that Pentecostal churches and initiatives are mainly centred on urban areas and often have the most effective ministries aimed at the huge influx of migrants from rural locations. As elsewhere in the region, urbanization and Pentecostal growth have gone hand in hand.

Rastafarianism

The powerful intermingling of cultural influences and faith traditions in a context marked by violent oppression and suffering has produced a wide array of spiritual beliefs and religious phenomena in the Caribbean. Alongside the more orthodox forms of Christianity are Afro-Christian faiths which combine elements of African religious traditions and practices with elements from Christianity (or even Islam). The best known of these is Rastafarianism, which originated in Jamaica in the 1930s as part of the struggle against colonial oppression and white domination.

The Rastafarian movement traces its roots to the teachings of Marcus Garvey (1887–1940), a Jamaican-born political activist who championed black pride and black nationalism. Rastafarianism emerged shortly after Ras Tafari Makonnen (1892–1975) was crowned emperor of Ethiopia and took the title 'Haile Selassie, King of Kings and Lord of Lords, Conquering Lion of the Tribe of Judea'. Local Jamaican preachers, who identified the event as a fulfilment of Garvey's ideas, proclaimed that Haile Selassie was Christ returned as a black messiah to liberate Africans. Neither Haile Selassie's denial of divinity nor his subsequent death (in 1975) led devotees to abandon the claim. Additionally, the movement adopted Christian ideas and selective Old Testament writings. Notions of liberation, exile, ritual purity and food taboos (based on prohibitions in the book of Leviticus) are prominent; the biblical reference to 'Ethiopia' (in the King James Version) is recognized as indicating black Africa (the motherland) and fuels calls for mass repatriation; and the biblical imagery of 'Babylon' is explicitly applied to oppressive white society (or the West in general).

The lack of a single founder, central organization or distinctive text means that Rastafarianism is a rather fluid movement with a variety of practices and interpretations. Two particularly notable traits among committed followers are the practice of smoking ganja (the cannabis weed) and wearing 'dreadlocks'. Some explain ganja smoking, which is often done ritually in community, by referring to the tree in the New Jerusalem whose leaves are 'for the healing of the nations' (Revelation 22.2 NIV). Wearing dreadlocks emerged out of a commitment to both natural living and an African image (in contrast to the straight blond-haired European appearance), but is also explained as representing the image of the Lion of Judah or fulfilment of the vow taken by the Nazirites to refrain from cutting their hair (see Numbers 6.15).

Rastafarianism was initially denounced by the wider Jamaican society as a fringe movement comprising undesirable elements. But its message of social protest, affirmation of an African heritage and condemnation of all systems of oppression made it attractive to Jamaican youths. Its appeal increased even more after it began to influence Jamaica's musical culture in the 1960s and fashioned reggae music, which in turn became a powerful vehicle of Rastafarian thought and social critique from the 1970s. The catchy reggae beat and message increased the movement's popularity at a time when widespread economic poverty and entrenched social inequalities had created disillusionment with the promise of political independence and fuelled a culture of protest. The worldwide spread of reggae music – notably by legendary Jamaican musician Bob Marley (1945–81) – and the mass emigration of Jamaica's youth to Europe and North America contributed greatly to the global spread of Rastafarianism and the acceptance of some of its elements. Today, it is reckoned that followers around the world number about one million.

Beyond paradise

In response to the post-Second World War recruitment drive by devastated European nations, hundreds of thousands of people from the Caribbean migrated to the United Kingdom for work. Between 1955 and 1962 about a quarter of a million Afro-Caribbeans are estimated to have arrived and settled permanently in the UK. They encountered widespread racism and discrimination. But these immigrants and their descendants not only contributed to the country's economic success but also enriched UK society with their unique culture and helped to redefine what it means to be 'British'. Most importantly, Caribbean immigrants established their own churches and congregations, typically marked by dynamic worship and Pentecostal ministries – in contrast to the rather reserved home-grown churches. Along with African immigrants, the Afro-Caribbean community has helped, through the vibrant growth of its churches, to counter the decline of Christianity in the UK and transform the country's religious landscape.

Meanwhile, American influence in the Caribbean region and the passing of the historic 1965 Immigration Act by the US government saw the United States gradually replace the UK as the major destination of Caribbean migrants. By 1970 more than half a million Caribbean immigrants had settled in the USA; in 2009, they numbered 3.4 million (with the vast majority coming from Cuba, the Dominican Republic, Jamaica and Haiti). They form an important segment of the massive influx of non-white, post-1960s immigration that has changed the face of American Christianity. Like other immigrants, they have established new churches or revitalized existing congregations with vibrant and unique expressions of faith. The twenty-first century, in effect, sees Caribbean Christian expressions and initiatives playing a notable role in the globalization of Christianity.

DISCUSSION QUESTIONS

1 Explain the meaning and significance of the agreement known as *patronato* (or *padroado*).

2 What impact did the Latin American independence movements (and the overthrowing of Spanish rule) have on the Roman Catholic Church?

3 Explain how the following factors contributed to the growth of Protestantism in Latin America:

   (a) political independence;

   (b) immigration;

   (c) US Protestant missions.

4 What is liberalism and how did the embrace of this ideology affect the relationship between church and society?

5 It is asserted that 'in presenting itself as a defender of democracy, human rights and justice, the Roman Catholic Church became a thorn in the side of military dictatorships in many parts of Latin America'. Describe the restrictions and persecutions that the church experienced with the rise of military governments and the spread of Marxist ideas.

6 What are some of the factors that led to the spectacular growth of Pentecostalism in Latin America and the Caribbean? In what way does your answer apply to your own region?

7 What are the main roots of the Liberation Theology movement? How did this movement revolutionize Christianity in Latin America and affect Christian thinking around the world?

8 In what ways can it be said that the chief concerns and insights of Liberation Theology remain very much alive in Latin American Christianity?

9 In what ways has the response of the Protestant churches in Latin America differed from that of the Roman Catholic Church?

10 How would you describe religious life in the Caribbean and what explains the dominance of the Christian faith?

11 How true is it to say that the influence of Caribbean religious traditions extends well beyond the Caribbean into the wider world?

12 The intricate relationship between Christianity, indigenous culture(s) and the experience of colonialism shaped Caribbean Christianity in important ways. Highlight some of these and comment on whether the results have been the same in your context (if applicable).

Further reading

Edmonds, Ennis Barrington and Gonzalez, Michelle A. *Caribbean Religious History: An introduction*. New York, NY: New York University Press, 2010.

Escobar, Samuel. *Changing Tides: Latin America and world mission today*. New York, NY: Orbis, 2002.

Freston, Paul. *Evangelicals and Politics in Asia, Africa, and Latin America*. New York, NY: Cambridge University Press, 2001.

Goodpasture, H. McKennie. *Cross and Sword: An eyewitness history of Christianity in Latin America*. New York, NY: Orbis, 1989.

Gutiérrez, Gustavo. *A Theology of Liberation*, rev. edn. New York, NY: Orbis, 1988.

Higman, B. W. *A Concise History of the Caribbean*. New York, NY: Cambridge University Press, 2011.

This chapter seeks to present the history of the Christian churches in Eastern Europe, Russia and several countries of the Commonwealth of Independent States (CIS) over the past two centuries. Most Christians living in these parts of the world belong to the so-called 'Orthodox' churches, also known as Eastern, Greek or Greco-Roman. The term 'orthodox', translated from Greek as 'correctly glorifying' God, was adopted by this church to distinguish itself from non-orthodox Christian denominations. These churches base their faith primarily upon the dogmatic definitions of the seven ecumenical councils (AD 325–787). The Orthodox churches should be distinguished from the Oriental Orthodox churches, which rejected the Christological teaching of the Council of Chalcedon in AD 451. Chalcedonian Orthodox churches therefore include the Ecumenical Patriarchate of Constantinople, the Greek and Russian Orthodox churches, and the Orthodox churches of the former Soviet bloc countries and the CIS countries which were formed after the fall of the USSR. All these churches are geographically located in Eastern Europe and Russia.

Non-Chalcedonian Orthodox churches in Eastern Europe and the CIS are represented by the Armenian Apostolic Church. Aside from the Orthodox churches, Roman Catholic and various Protestant churches are also represented in Russia and the Eastern European countries. In covering the story of the Orthodox churches we shall also look at the history and development of these other Christian denominations.

Churches in the Eastern European countries

Bulgaria

In the nineteenth century Bulgaria was ruled by the Ottoman Turks. The Greek Ecumenical Patriarch in Constantinople assumed responsibility over Christians within the Ottoman Empire. In Bulgaria he upheld the tradition of appointing only Greek-speaking bishops and priests to purely

Bulgarian parishes. By the 1840s, however, the Bulgarian communities demanded that they be given bishops who could understand their language. Such priorities reflected the development of Bulgarian culture throughout the nineteenth century. Schools were founded which taught the Bulgarian language and propagated the idea of liberation. The consciousness of their cultural identity led many Bulgars to clash with both the Ottoman state and the Ecumenical Patriarchate. The leading figures in the struggle for independence were Neofit Bozveli (1785–1848) and Ilarion Makariopolski (1812–75).

In 1860 Bishop Ilarion Makariopolski declared the independence of the Bulgarian Orthodox Church. The Ecumenical Patriarch resisted, while the Ottomans were content to observe from the sidelines. In 1870 the sultan recognized the Bulgarian Church as a separate community headed by an exarch (or bishop, usually ranked between a patriarch and a metropolitan), Antim I (1816–88), who was elected to this post by the Holy Synod of the exarchate in 1872. The Patriarch excommunicated the new church two

Europe

years later for the heresy of phyletism – the creation of a separate bishopric by the Bulgarian community of Constantinople for parishes open only to ethnic Bulgars. The Bulgarian exarchate now became the focus of the continuing national revival and was a likely agent of the later Bulgarian claim to political freedom.

Bulgaria achieved independence in 1878 and the Bulgarian Church was granted state subsidies, with Orthodoxy declared the official religion. This declaration caused differences of interpretation on the ownership of power, leading to confrontations between church and state until the communist takeover. The Orthodox Church was prevented by the government from organizing itself into a patriarchate and even became part of the state machinery, which further alienated it from the Christian population.

After the Second World War the Ecumenical Patriarch recognized the autocephaly (the state of being self-governed or under its own national head) of the Bulgarian Church. The communist government brought church–state relationships to a logical conclusion and the Orthodox Church came mostly under state control. Nevertheless, the patriarchate was restored in 1953 with the election to this position of the Metropolitan of Plovdiv, Cyril (1901–71). The communist leaders paid tribute to the key role of the Orthodox Church in preserving Bulgarian identity over the centuries. After the collapse of communism, the Bulgarian Orthodox Church suffered a serious schism, due in part to the legacy of political involvement on the part of its hierarchs (heads of dioceses).

The Roman Catholic Church has been present in Bulgaria since the sixteenth century. In 1869 the Bulgarian Greek Catholic Church, which uses an Eastern type of service, was established. The Catholic Church was subjected to persecution by the communist authorities because nominally it was considered the religion of fascism. Bishops and priests were put to death, others spent many years in labour camps and prisons and church property was confiscated. After the fall of the communist regime in 1989 Roman Catholics in Bulgaria enjoyed greater religious freedom. In 1990 Bulgaria re-established relations with the Vatican. In present-day Bulgaria the Roman Catholic Church has two dioceses and one exarchy.

Protestant churches constitute only 0.5 per cent of the total population in Bulgaria. The Pentecostal message was brought to Bulgaria in 1920 by four Slavic emigrants to the USA and their families: the Russian Ivan Voronaev (1886–c.1936), the Ukrainian Dionisy Zaplishny (1888–1935), his Bulgarian wife Olga Zaplishny (1887–1982, née Popova) and the Belarusian Vasily Koltovich (1888–c.1936/7). On their way to Soviet Russia they visited Bulgaria, where the Congregationalist family of Olga Zaplishny extended hospitality to the group in the city of Burgas. As a result of the fervent preaching of these founders (Olga was an accomplished preacher in her own right), numerous Pentecostal groups sprang up around the country. These were characterized both by their multi-ethnic make-up (comprising Bulgarians, Armenians, Jews, Roma, Turks and Russians who had fled the Bolshevik Revolution) and by the fact that women were empowered alongside men. In Varna, where Ivan Voronaev and Vasily Koltovich went to minister, the Methodist Sijka Dryanova (1882–*c*.1954) became the leader of the Varna church.

In 1928 the movement went in three directions. The first group was registered through the work of the eminent Assemblies of God minister Nicholas Nikolov (1900–64), who was the nephew of Olga Zaplishny. The other two groups remained unregistered until 1990 – the group of Stoyan Tinchev (1880–1965) or Churches of God, and the family group Grozdanovi-Tomovi, which remained in the form of house churches consisting only of family members. During the communist regime numerous ministers were convicted of treason, among them Haralan Popov (1907–88) and Yoncho Dryanov (1907–86), the son of Sijka Dryanova. The Pentecostal movement not only became resilient to this oppressive regime but also multiplied. By 2000 the Bulgarian Pentecostal movement had the second-largest number of congregants after the Bulgarian Orthodox Church, with almost 100,000 adherents. Other strong Protestant groups in Bulgaria are the Methodists and the Congregationalists. The growth of Protestant churches took place after the collapse of communism in 1990 and was prompted by spiritual hunger, active evangelism and the enthusiastic support of missionaries from the USA.

The Czech Republic and Slovakia

During the nineteenth century Czechoslovakia was part of the Austro-Hungarian Empire, with Roman Catholicism as its official religion. With the dawning of the twentieth century, Czech political leaders and intellectuals expressed their commitment to national independence by embracing Orthodoxy. In 1918 Czechoslovakia became independent and was free to establish Orthodox parishes. Before that time, existing Orthodox parishes were under the Serbian diocese of Dalmatia. In 1921 the Serbian patriarch consecrated Bishop Gorazd (1879–1942) as head of the newly recognized Orthodox Church of Czechoslovakia. Almost all members of the church were converts from Roman Catholicism. The establishment of the church and the conversion of people from other faiths represented an attempt to return to Slavic roots and the teaching of Cyril (826–69) and Methodius (815–85), who had converted Moravia and Slovakia to Christianity in the ninth century.

In 1942 Bishop Gorazd was arrested and executed by the Germans. Around 300 priests and prominent believers were either executed or sent to German labour camps. During the communist regime, Czechoslovakia saw the most consistent and sustained application of a repressive policy. In order to ensure that Catholic clergy were sufficiently compliant, and to limit their numbers, the state required them to be licensed. Not until 1951 would the Czechoslovakian Orthodox Church gain independence and be declared autocephalous (or free from external ecclesiastical authority).

After the fall of the Soviet regime in 1991 and the establishment of independent Czech and Slovak states, the Christian churches began to act freely. The Orthodox Church established four dioceses, with the Bishop of Prague also being metropolitan. In 1998 the Ecumenical Patriarch recognized the autocephaly of the Czech and Slovak Orthodox churches. These churches are among the smallest Christian denominations in these countries.

The Roman Catholic Church is the largest Christian denomination in the Czech Republic, with one fourth of the population considering themselves Catholic. More than 60 per cent of Slovak citizens identify with Roman Catholicism. There is also the Evangelical Church of Czech Brethren, which was formed in 1918 through the unification of the Lutheran and Reformed Protestant churches. In addition, the Church of the Brethren, an Evangelical free church, has more than 250 local congregations with about 120,000 members.

Poland

Historically, Poland's population was Roman Catholic. After Napoleon's defeat in 1815 the victorious Russians assumed control over most of the Duchy of Warsaw. Under the Russian *tsars* (rulers), the new Kingdom of Poland became dependent on Russia, while the formerly eastern regions of Poland were now incorporated into the greater Russian Empire. The community of Byzantine Catholics (members of churches using an Orthodox liturgy but in communion with the Roman Catholic Church) living there were thus forced to 'convert' to Eastern Orthodoxy. After the First World War the revived Polish state had four to five million Orthodox citizens. By 1922 the Polish Orthodox Church had proclaimed its autocephaly, and in 1924 the Ecumenical Patriarchate recognized its new metropolitan, Dionizy Waledynski (1876–1960).

During communist rule, the Catholic Church in Poland retained greater authority and legitimacy than the communist government. A pattern of church–state relations evolved in Poland which was different from that in any other Eastern European country. The identification of the Catholic Church with the nation was bolstered under the communist regime, and the church was presented as a real alternative to the official ideological system.

In the mid 1970s there existed an established tradition of resistance to communist rule in Poland among intellectuals and the working classes, resulting in both groups identifying with the Roman Catholic Church by the 1980s. When Archbishop Karol Wojtyla (1920–2005) was elected in 1978 as the first Polish pope, communism as an ideology in Poland became thoroughly discredited. At the end of the twentieth century the Roman Catholic Church remained the leading church in Poland with nearly 10,000 parishes and with 95 per cent of the Polish population declared Catholic.

Former Yugoslav countries (Serbia, Croatia, Bosnia and Herzegovina, North Macedonia, Slovenia and Montenegro) and Albania

After two successive revolts against the Ottoman Empire in the early 1800s, Serbia gained international recognition as an independent state in 1830. The Serbian Church was transformed into a department of state and later gained its autocephaly with Serbia's complete independence from Turkey in 1882. As in other Balkan countries, there was friction between the church and the new political leadership; however, the Serbian constitution of 1903 recognized Orthodoxy as the state religion.

The establishment of the Kingdom of Serbs, Croats and Slovenes in 1918 was seen by the Serbian Church as an opportunity for the unification of Orthodox Christians and for potential growth. In 1920 the Serbian patriarchate had been re-established and soon absorbed the Church of Montenegro and the Serbian dioceses in Austria and Hungary. Church membership grew from 2.3 million in 1910 to seven million in 1925. However, the government retained firm control over the church, and in the 1920s non-Orthodox denominations complained that the Serbian Church was manipulating the state in its own confessional interests. In 1935 a resulting concordat between the Vatican and the Yugoslav government gave privileges to the Roman Catholic Church. After the Second World War the communist authorities in Yugoslavia tried to reduce the influence wielded by the Serbian Orthodox and Croatian Catholic churches in society. The authorities labelled religion as a superstition to be given no room in the public sphere dominated by atheistic materialism. Furthermore, links between these denominations and nationalist identities allowed for their potential to be used against the centralized communist state. The disintegration of Yugoslavia in the early 1990s revealed these fault lines had been shelved rather than wiped out.

In Bosnia and Herzegovina, national identity and religion again became more tightly bound together during this period. However, unlike in Serbia and Croatia, the Orthodox, Roman Catholic and Muslim communities are more balanced in size. The nineteenth century was more characterized by coexistence, but by the end of the twentieth century the fusing of nationalist and religious identities resulted in horrific conflict and persecution during the 1992–5 Bosnian War. By this point, to be Orthodox was to be Serbian, Roman Catholic to be Croat, and Muslim to be Bosniak. During the previous two centuries, each successive political regime had favoured one group over and against the others, producing successive fluctuations in their fortunes and numbers, apart from the communist regime which attempted to diminish the role of all religions in public life.

In contrast, Albania is a predominantly Muslim country, and throughout the nineteenth century its Christian minority was under the jurisdiction of the Ecumenical Patriarch of Constantinople. By 1924, however, the

Albanian Orthodox Church gained its autocephaly with the help of the politician and Albanian bishop Fan Noli (1882–1965). Under the communist regime, the Church in Albania suffered the most in comparison to other countries in Eastern Europe, with manifestations of religious faith outlawed in 1967 and all places of worship closed. However, the collapse of communism in 1991 led to a remarkable revival of religion, albeit in the midst of many economic problems. In 1992 Anastasios Yannoulatos (b. 1929) was elected as archbishop of Tirana and all Albania. Protestant missionaries from Western countries have tried to plant churches and operate relief ministries, with some success. But the future of the Orthodox Church in Albania is uncertain because of continuous clashes between the church and Albanian authorities who oppose the election and consecration of bishops by the Ecumenical Patriarch.

Romania and Hungary

In 1864 the Romanian Orthodox Church declared its independence from Constantinople, and Romania as a nation achieved independence from Turkey in 1877. In order to diminish Greek influence over the church, the Romanian authorities confiscated monastic property held by Phanariots, Greek Christians from Constantinople. The Romanian Church gained autocephaly in 1885 and the following year the Romanian constitution recognized the Orthodox Church as the dominant religion of the country. In 1890 a theological faculty was opened at the University of Bucharest. Church–state relations in Romania developed along similar lines to those in other Balkan states. The church and the Romanian political leadership worked together towards a reunited Romania, eventually achieved in 1918. After the First World War, Romanian territories increased with the addition of Bessarabia, Bukovina and Transylvania. The Orthodox Church grew in size to 15 million members, and the Romanian patriarchate was founded in 1925.

The first patriarch of the Romanian Church, Miron Cristea (1868–1939), was made prime minister of Romania in 1938, but he failed to assert his influence to combat the rise of the Iron Guard, a fundamentalist and populist movement within the church led by Corneliu Codreanu (1899–1938). This organization was founded in 1922 and went through several different name-changes before becoming 'the Iron Guard' in 1930. The supporters of this movement were young men and women, including university students, who were opposed to Western secularism. The major aims of Guardism were to strengthen and purify the life of the Romanian Church and to propagate anti-Western and anti-Semitic ideology.

In 1928 a new piece of Romanian legislation, the Law of Cults, was passed to regulate the national churches – that is, those which could be identified with a particular ethnic group within the state – and protect them from foreign 'sects' such as Baptists and Adventists. The first Baptist churches in Romania were founded independent of each other by immigrants: in

Bucharest by Germans in the late 1950s and in Cataloi by Ukrainians in 1862. An ethnic Romanian, Constantin Adorian (1882–1954) led the formation of the Baptist Union of Romania in 1920. Evangelical activity also helped to create 'born again' movements within the Orthodox Church. One such group was expelled from the church and became a neo-Protestant denomination called the Evangelical Christians. The Lord's Army movement, founded by the Transylvanian priest Iosif Trita (1888–1938) in 1923, was an Orthodox response to foreign Evangelical proselytism.

Following the communist takeover in Romania in 1944 the Orthodox Church was gradually removed from state life. In 1948 religious education was banned in schools, religious services in hospitals and the army were forbidden, and the church's theological schools were closed down. More than a thousand priests and lay people were imprisoned. Three archbishops, including the patriarch, Nicodim (1864–48), died in suspicious circumstances. Roman Catholics, as well as Baptists, also suffered discrimination. Under Nicolae Ceaușescu (1918–89), who came to power in 1965, the persecution of the Orthodox Church was brought to an end. The government began to pursue a liberal foreign policy and used the Orthodox Church as a national institution to secure the state's position against the pressure of the USSR. By the 1980s, 17 million of Romania's 21 million citizens were baptized Orthodox Christians.

The situation of the Church in post-Soviet Romania is complex and confusing. The Orthodox patriarch, Teoctist (1915–2007), resigned in 1989 following protests about his collaboration with the dictatorship of Ceaușescu. He was, however, reinstalled by the Holy Synod in 1990. The Greek Catholic Church was fully recognized in 1990, but fell into dispute with the Orthodox Church over the ownership of property. The Baptist Union of Romania had grown to more than 1,500 churches and 110,000 members by 2000 and remains the largest Baptist union in Eastern Europe. This growth resulted from religious freedom in the country and active evangelism led by the Baptist churches. The Pentecostal Church, present in Romania from 1922, has over 300,000 members and is the fourth-largest religious body in the country.

In the nineteenth century Hungary was ruled by the Austrian royal House of Habsburg and from 1867 became part of the Austro-Hungarian Empire. The Roman Catholic Church remained dominant in the Austro-Hungarian Empire during the 1800s. The emergence of the Hungarian Reformed Church was closely linked to Hungarian nationalism and the progress made towards Hungary's political independence following a major revolt against the Habsburgs in 1848.

By the end of the twentieth century, the Hungarian Reformed Church was the second-largest denomination in Hungary with about 1.5 million members. Other Protestant churches, such as Baptists and Pentecostals, have fewer than 30,000 members in total. The membership of the Hungarian Orthodox Church is mainly confined to certain national minorities in the country, mostly Romanians, Serbs and Ukrainians. After the Second World War, the ethnically Hungarian Orthodox communities were formed into an autonomous entity linked to the Moscow Patriarchate.

✳ The Orthodox Church and Christianity in Russia

From the end of the tenth century the Orthodox faith was the prevailing religion in Russia. In the nineteenth century the Orthodox Church in Russia was governed by a collegiate body, the Holy Synod, under a chief procurator appointed by the tsar. Originally, the procurator was supposed to communicate the tsar's wishes to the synod, but in practice he effectively ruled the church. After the Napoleonic Wars (1803–15), however, Russia experienced a national revival, with Tsar Alexander I (1801–25) attracted to German Pietism and non-Orthodox initiatives. Openness to Protestantism led to the founding of the Russian Bible Society in 1814. Yet during the reign of Nicholas I (1825–55) this policy was reversed. The Bible Society was closed and a decade of work destroyed.

Despite the overall reaction, which had followed the failure of the Decembrist revolt in 1825 (by Russian army officers protesting about the imperial succession), monks in the Orthodox Church maintained the Hesychast movement's tradition of mystical prayer of the heart. This tradition can be traced back to a group in fourteenth-century Byzantium, whose goal was full unity with God on a level beyond images and language, and who considered seclusion from the world as the only way to attain this goal (*hesychia* in Greek means 'silence' or 'speechlessness'). In the monastery of Optina Pustyn, near Tula, many leading intellectuals discovered genuine Christian teaching which followed the patristic traditions of Eastern Orthodoxy. Optina's influence was also spread through its publications, including Russian translations of Greek patristic texts. Prominent Russian writers and philosophers such as Gogol (1809–52), Dostoevsky (1821–81), Tolstoy (1828–1910), Soloviev (1853–1900) and Rozanov (1856–1919) visited this monastery. There they found holy men (*startsy*, or elders) who stood outside the church's hierarchy, in which the Russian intellectual elite was completely disappointed. The most famous monk among them was the ascetic St Serafim of Sarov (1759–1833), who devoted himself to the service of others as a healer and seer.

By the mid nineteenth century, the Russian Church had developed unprecedented missionary activity in remote regions of the Russian Empire. Restricted by state control from making any changes in church life and structure, and at the same time financially supported by the government, the Orthodox Church was able to channel its activities into establishing parishes in those regions, as well as creating written languages for the indigenous peoples and translating Christian and secular literature. By 1899 the Russian Church had 20 missions inside the empire and five foreign missions, in Alaska, Korea, China, Japan and Persia.

Among the few progressive leaders in the Orthodox Church was Filaret Drozdov (1782–1867), Metropolitan of Moscow from 1821 to 1867, who was politically liberal, tolerant and opposed to the idea that only the Orthodox Church had the right to exist in Russia. He lived long enough to see the liberal reforms, including the Emancipation Reform of 1861, that were implemented during the reign of Alexander II (1855–81). Filaret drafted the 1861 Emancipation Manifesto, which resulted in the passing of new legislation freeing Russian peasants from serfdom on the estates of landowners and granting them full rights as citizens. He also participated in the translation of the Bible into Russian, with the first complete translation published in 1876 and considered the standard in Russian churches to this day.

All of this brought a quickening of spiritual activities among the Russian aristocracy as well as the freed serfs. In the second half of the nineteenth century the Evangelical (Baptist) faith was introduced into Russia via St Petersburg, Ukraine and the Caucasus region. Lord Radstock (1833–1913) from Britain, invited by Countess Elizabeth Chertkova (1834–1923), preached among the Russian aristocracy in St Petersburg from 1874 to 1878. In 1884 Colonel Vasily Pashkov (1831–1902) convened the first congress of Evangelical communities in Russia. Several Russian aristocrats, among them Pashkov himself and Baron M. M. Korf (1842–1933), who actively participated in the distribution of Evangelical literature, were later deported to Europe by the Russian tsar. The Baptist movement in Ukraine originated from the so-called *stundists*, a group of dissenters founded in about 1860 in a village near Odessa. This group had apparently been influenced by German Mennonites who practised one-hour Bible-reading sessions (*Stunde* is the German word for 'hour' or 'lesson').

Secular authorities welcomed the help of the Orthodox Church in combating non-Orthodox denominations. By the end of the nineteenth century, the Russian Orthodox Church had failed to develop any programme for social or political engagement, while remaining strongly resistant to all innovations. This produced widespread anti-clericalism (opposition to the authority of the clergy) within Russian society.

Widespread changes took place in the religious life of Russia with the 1905 Russian Revolution and the edict on religious tolerance which granted religious freedom to non-Orthodox denominations. In order to be placed on an equal footing with other religions, the Orthodox Church needed to be freed from state control. Thus, the church began preparing for a 'local council' (*pomestny sobor*) – the supreme authority in the Russian Orthodox Church, periodically convoked, and consisting of bishops, clergy and laity. The Council convened on the eve of the October Revolution in 1917; but due to renewed resistance, the only decision it managed to implement was the election of the new patriarch, Tikhon Bellavin (1865–1925) – the first in nearly two centuries.

After the Soviet revolution, the Orthodox Church was divided into two camps. On one side, the so-called Living Church (Obnovlentsy) movement collaborated with the communist state; on the other, the traditionalists expressed opposition to communism. During the period from 1917 until 1928, other Christian denominations, such as the Baptists, Evangelicals and Pentecostals, grew and actively developed. While seeking to establish its power and fighting on all fronts, the communist state had no time to deal with religion. But the Decree on Separation of Church from State and School from Church (in 1918) opened the way for the confiscation of the Orthodox Church's schools and welfare establishments, the seizure of church property, and violence against clergy and laymen. By 1929 the state had issued the Law on Religious Associations banning all Christian denominations.

Patriarch Tikhon's eventual successor, Metropolitan Sergius of Moscow (1867–1944), issued a declaration of loyalty, which divided the Orthodox Church into alternative organizations: the Russian True Orthodox Church (Russian Catacomb Church) and the Russian Orthodox Church Outside of Russia led by Metropolitan Anthony Khrapovitsky (1863–1936). With religion remaining a powerful force among the people, massive persecutions were organized. Yet religion did not disappear as easily as the communists had planned. Although nearly every last sanctuary was closed in the USSR from 1928 to 1940 (under Stalin's rule), some 50 million Soviet citizens still classified themselves as Christians according to the 1937 census.

The situation would change with the outbreak of the Second World War, as the Soviet government and the people of the USSR would soon answer the call of Orthodox leaders to defend Holy Russia. With Iosif Stalin (General Secretary of the Communist Party of the USSR, 1922–53) seeking support against Germany, and with the UK and the USA (allies of the Soviet Union) expressing concerns about religious freedom in Russia, active persecution abated. By 1943 the communists had released Orthodox clergy from prisons and labour camps, and several churches were reopened. Stalin even allowed the Orthodox Church to elect a new patriarch. However, the Orthodox hierarchy in the Soviet Union was under extensive control by the KGB (Committee for State Security) and subject to excessive manipulation and oppression. The same was true for Evangelicals. In fact, the main Evangelical groups (the Baptists and the Pentecostals) were forced to form one Baptist union.

After the Second World War the Soviet government continued to tolerate the Orthodox Church due to its wartime effort and its usefulness to Soviet foreign policy. The Soviet authorities also encouraged the church to extend its authority over the Orthodox churches in the countries of Eastern Europe which had come under Soviet political control. In 1961, with the consent of the Soviet authorities, the Russian Orthodox Church became a member of the World Council of Churches.

A new anti-religious campaign was begun by Nikita Khrushchev (1894–1971), lasting from 1959 to 1964. During this time, Protestant and Catholic churches were persecuted with increasing degrees of intensity. The so-called Initsiativniki Baptists, an 'initiative group', broke away from the mainstream Baptist Church in the 1960s in protest against Soviet demands to stop missionary activity and religious instruction to children. They were concerned that the leadership of the Baptist Union was controlled by the KGB. Initsiativniki refused state registration and functioned as an underground church. As a result they were vigorously persecuted. Later, the Ukrainian Uniate (Greek Catholic) Church was forced to join the Russian Orthodox Church, while the Roman Catholic Church in Lithuania, Latvia and Estonia saw its bishops and priests arrested.

Persistent persecution only began to wane with the Millennium Celebration of Christianity in Russia in 1988. The last Soviet ruler, Mikhail Gorbachev (b. 1931; in power from 1985 to 1991), felt compelled to come to terms with the international and social role of ecclesiastical institutions as well as believers' faith commitments. The state began the return of confiscated churches and monasteries. In 1990 the Russian parliament passed a new law regulating the freedom of religion. Religious liberty became a part of the new civil order.

As the twentieth century came to a close, the Orthodox Church faced its biggest problem in providing spiritual care to the masses of people who had flooded through its doors at a time when its leaders were unprepared to deal with such numbers. The Orthodox hierarchy needed to regain lost or confiscated property and urgently build new churches across Russia, thereby giving people access to the services of the church. Preoccupied with preserving its jurisdiction – including establishing better relations with the state, dealing with internal problems of leadership and the education of clergy, engaging in social work, and reviving parish and monastic life – the Orthodox Church did not look sympathetically upon the growth and development of other Christian denominations. But the collapse of communism in Russia had also witnessed a massive religious boom, with many religious movements appearing seemingly out of nowhere.

In addition, the close of the twentieth century saw a restoration of the Russian Orthodox Church of Old Believers, a denomination distinct from the Russian Orthodox Church. The Church of Old Believers has existed in Russia since the 1650s, and before the revolution of 1917 a full 10 per cent of Russians belonged to this type of Orthodox church. Its members included the most wealthy and influential Russian capitalists. Nearly crushed by the communists, the Church of Old Believers had continued to exist in several forms, each community seeking to preserve and develop its own religious way of life.

After the fall of the Iron Curtain (in 1989), Russia was also flooded with missionaries from Western Europe and the USA, joining indigenous Protestant efforts at evangelization. Thousands of new Protestant churches of various denominations were planted in Russia, including Lutheran, Methodist, Baptist, Evangelical and Pentecostal congregations. The Pentecostal churches, present in Russia since the 1920s, belong to two major unions and several associations. Pentecostals have several thousand churches across the country and are the fastest-growing denomination. Protestant churches in Russia are actively engaged in social ministry to the poor, sick, orphaned and imprisoned. The biggest challenge they face comes from increasingly negative representations in the mass media, which derides them as sects. By the 1990s, however, people were beginning to see more clearly the differences between the Orthodox Church and all other Christian denominations.

Since the last decade of the twentieth century the Roman Catholic Church, which saw its entire institutional structure destroyed under communism, has also revived its activity in Russia. The Catholic Church acknowledges the primacy of the Orthodox Church in Russia, but it also directs its message and services to three specific groups of people: (1) those who kept their Catholic faith during communist times; (2) those who were baptized Catholic as infants but have since ceased to practise their faith; and (3) those who were raised without any religious affiliation. Partly due to such focused efforts, there were more than 200 Catholic churches in Russia by the year 2000. Little wonder then that the Catholic Church has been accused of expansionist proselytism by the Orthodox Church in Russia in recent years.

For all this, the passing of a new law on religion in 1997 formally reinstated state control over religious life. This effectively restored the status of the Orthodox faith as the traditional religion of Russia.

✳ Christianity in the CIS countries

The Baltic states: Estonia, Latvia and Lithuania

In the nineteenth century Estonia was governed by Russia, and the Russian tsars granted vast privileges to the resident Baltic-German nobility of the country, including freedom of religion. Religion in Estonia was represented by Orthodox, Lutheran and Roman Catholic churches. The Russian Orthodox Church established the Diocese of Riga (Latvia) in 1850, which governed the Estonian parishes. The Russian Orthodox hierarchy promoted Russification (the adoption of Russian culture and language) and the active building of churches. Some 65,000 Estonian Lutherans were converted to Orthodoxy following a rumour about free distribution of land in Russia. When this rumour turned out to be a hoax, people returned to the Lutheran Church. The Roman Catholic Church began its revival through the consecration of Catholic cathedrals in 1845 in Tallin and in 1899 in Tartu.

After the collapse of the Russian Empire in 1917 Estonia became an independent state and the Estonian Orthodox Church became autonomous. In 1919, during the Estonian War of Independence, the church's first hierarch, Plato Kulbusch (1869–1919), and many others were martyred by the communists. The Russian patriarch Tikhon recognized the Estonian Orthodox Church as being independent in 1920. However, the church's elected head, Archbishop Alexander Paulus (d. 1953), turned to the Ecumenical Patriarchate to receive canonical recognition. This provoked a split among the Orthodox Christians in Estonia. During the Second World War, the Soviet invasion restored the Estonian Church to the jurisdiction of the Moscow Patriarchate. Most of the Estonian clergy were deported to Siberia soon thereafter. Later, Metropolitan Alexander Paulus established the Estonian Orthodox Church Abroad and a new synod was formed, having been reorganized from Sweden. By the 1990s the Estonian Church had re-emerged in Estonia, resulting in the existence of two Orthodox churches: the Estonian Apostolic Orthodox Church subordinate to the Ecumenical Patriarch of Constantinople, and the Estonian Orthodox Church of the Moscow Patriarchate.

The Latvian Orthodox Church, including ethnic Latvians as well as Russians, dates back to the 1840s, when native Latvians petitioned the Russian tsar to be allowed to conduct services in their native language. After the revolution in Russia in 1917 the Latvian Orthodox Church became autonomous. Bishop John Pommers (1876–1934), released from Soviet captivity in 1920, became its leader. He reorganized the church structures and came to an understanding with the Latvian authorities, who had persecuted the Orthodox for their perceived links with Russia. Pommers held together the Latvian and Russian Orthodox churches. It is believed that Soviet agents were responsible for his murder in 1934. In 1936 the Latvian Orthodox Church, led by Augustins Petersons (1873–1955), came under the auspices of the Ecumenical Patriarchate.

The Soviet invasion in 1940 brought the Latvian Church into forced subjection to the Moscow Patriarchate. Sergii Voskresenskii (1898–1944) was installed as metropolitan of all Lithuania, Latvia and Estonia. When Germany occupied the region in 1941 Sergii was recognized as exarch of 'Ostland', but he was murdered in 1944, possibly by the Germans. Augustins Petersons led many of his flock into exile and organized the Latvian Orthodox Church Abroad in 1944. The Latvian Orthodox Church only re-emerged in the 1990s with Latvian independence. In modern Latvia there are 350,000 Orthodox Christians.

The Evangelical Lutheran Church has existed in Latvia since the sixteenth century. In the following centuries it was influenced by the Herrnhuter Brotherhood, a German Pietist movement. In 1919 there were 194 Lutheran congregations in Lativa. Lutheran pastors received their training in the theological faculty at the University of Tartu. As the Russian army approached Latvia in 1944 Archbishop Teodors Grinbergs (1870–1962) and two thirds of the clergy went into exile and the Lutheran Church came under Soviet control, a situation that lasted until 1990. There are more than 400,000 Lutherans in present-day Latvia.

Lithuanians accepted Eastern Orthodoxy during the Byzantine evangelization of the East Slavs in the tenth and eleventh centuries. However, the Lithuanians became predominantly Roman Catholic after the systematic campaign of baptism of the Lithuanian nation in the fourteenth century. Several Orthodox monasteries founded in the 1500s were preserved among the country's ethnic minorities. In the nineteenth century the major part of Lithuania was incorporated into the Russian Empire. The Roman Catholic Church struggled against Russification and the attempts made to force conversions to Orthodoxy. During the First World War, Eleuthery Bogoiavlenskii (1868–1940), the Russian Orthodox Bishop of Vilnius, led the autonomous Lithuanian Orthodox Church. Bogoiavlenskii moved to Kaunas when the country was annexed to Poland in 1923, but he assumed leadership of the Latvian and Estonian Orthodox churches during the Second World War.

After the Second World War, all Christian denominations in the Baltic republics suffered persecution under the USSR. After the Baltic states gained their independence in the 1990s, Protestant and Roman Catholic churches, spurred on by support from Christians in the West, began to function freely and quickly developed their churches' life and ministry. Lithuania is the most Catholic of all the Baltic states. There are almost three million Catholics, around 80 per cent of the total population. More than 15 per cent of the people of Latvia consider themselves Catholic. Now, however, Pentecostal and Charismatic churches are growing in both Latvia and Lithuania.

Belarus

By the late eighteenth century, Belarus had been incorporated into the Russian Empire. With this development, the influence of the Russian Orthodox Church grew considerably, even as the influence of Polish Catholicism weakened. By the early twentieth century, four Orthodox dioceses existed in Belarus. In 1921 Belarus was divided between Poland and Soviet Russia. In Polish areas more than half of the Orthodox churches were closed down. The Metropolitan of Belarus remained in the Soviet half. In 1942 the Council of Minsk declared the Belarusian Orthodox Church autocephalous, but at the end of the Second World War it was reincorporated into the Soviet Union and subjected to the Moscow Patriarchate. In 1990 the Orthodox Church of independent Belarus was again recognized as autonomous. Other Christian denominations in Belarus, such as the Roman Catholics, Baptists and Pentecostals, were supported by missionaries from the USA and other Western nations and experienced growth and development during the 1990s.

Ukraine

Throughout the nineteenth and early twentieth centuries, the Orthodox Church in Ukraine existed as part of the Russian Orthodox Church.

However, with the fall of the Russian Empire in 1917, the establishment of an autocephalous church in Ukraine coincided with the move towards independence. In 1921 the Ukrainian Autocephalous Orthodox Church (UAOC) came into existence with the establishment of new clergy. Although utterly destroyed by the communists, the UAOC was officially registered after the collapse of the Soviet Union and, after proclaiming itself a patriarchate, elected its first patriarch. The UAOC grew mostly at the expense of the Russian Orthodox Church and by the end of the twentieth century had more than a thousand parishes.

In 1992 the Russian Orthodox Church deposed the Metropolitan of Kiev, Filaret Denysenko (b. 1929), and replaced him with another metropolitan, Volodymyr Sabodan (1935–2014), who became the head of the Ukrainian Orthodox Church of the Moscow Patriarchate (UOC-MP). By 1998 this patriarchate had more than 6,000 churches in Ukraine. Denysenko, who was close to the president of Ukraine, Leonid Kravchuck (b. 1934), rejected the decision to depose him and established the Ukrainian Orthodox Church of the Kiev Patriarchate (UOC-KP). In 1995 he was elected as patriarch of this church, which by then had around 2,000 parishes. Thus, by the end of the twentieth century, Ukraine had three separate Orthodox churches with two patriarchs.

There also exists in Ukraine the Ukrainian Greek Catholic Church. In the 1500s, the Catholics in Western Ukraine left the Orthodox communion for various political and theological reasons and entered into communion with the Church of Rome. When Western Ukraine was incorporated into the Soviet Union, the Greek Catholic Church there was suppressed and, in 1946, was aggregated to the Russian Orthodox Church. The clergy who refused to accept this incorporation died in prison camps. Yet in 1989 a meeting of the hierarchs of Ukraine pursued the re-establishment of the Ukrainian Catholic Church, and by 1993 more than 1,000 Catholic churches had been registered.

At the present time the majority of Ukraine's population is divided among the Ukrainian Autocephalous Church, the Ukrainian Orthodox Church and the Ukrainian Catholics. None of these churches has a leading position in Ukraine. Aside from the Orthodox and Catholics, Evangelical, Pentecostal and Charismatic churches are also strongly represented in the country and are growing rapidly. Ukraine has the highest number of Pentecostals of any European nation.

Georgia

Georgia became Christian in AD 330, and the Georgian Orthodox Church gained autocephaly in 1057. Although Russia actively annexed Georgian kingdoms from the late 1700s, the Georgian Church retained its autocephaly, and its head gained a seat on the Holy Synod of the Russian Orthodox Church. As a result of revolts in Georgia in the early nineteenth century, the church lost its autocephaly in 1811. A Russian archbishop was appointed exarch of the Georgian Church and plans were put in place to replace Georgian with Slavonic rites. In the late 1800s growing Russian control clashed with the developing Georgian national consciousness, and in 1886 a student at Tiflis seminary fatally stabbed the Russian rector.

The Georgian Church's autocephaly was restored in 1917 when, as a result of the October Revolution in Russia, Georgia regained its independence for a short period. This change was accepted neither by the Russian Orthodox Church nor by the Soviets, who invaded Georgia in 1921 and subjected the Georgian Orthodox Church to intense harassment. Hundreds of churches were closed by the government and hundreds of monks were killed during Stalin's persecution.

During the Second World War the Russian Orthodox Church finally recognized the autocephaly of the Orthodox Church in Georgia. However, the Georgian Church became increasingly dependent upon Soviet power, and in the 1970s its leadership fell into moral decay and corruption. However, the 1980s saw the church becoming more popular and influential due to growing nationalist sentiment in Georgia. In 1990 the Patriarch of Constantinople recognized and approved the autocephaly of the Georgian Church and the patriarchal honour of its primate (or 'catholicos'). Georgia's independence in 1991 gave more opportunities for the development of the Orthodox Church. The special role of the Georgian Church and its close relationship with the state is enshrined in the Georgian constitution. By the end of the twentieth century, the Georgian Church consisted of 15 bishoprics headed by the catholicos-patriarch, Ilia II (b. 1933), whose residence is in the Zion Cathedral in Tbilisi. There is also a minority Armenian Apostolic Church (accounting for around 6 per cent of the population) and tiny Roman Catholic and Baptist communities (both less than 1 per cent).

 Conclusion

During the final decade of the twentieth century, after the collapse of communism in Eastern Europe and Russia, significant changes took place in the life and development of various Christian churches present in those countries, which had suffered intense oppression and anti-religious ideology. The churches could now legally function in freedom and security, but they all faced the primary task of re-establishing themselves as properly functioning organizations within society. Church leaders needed to learn once again how to properly develop their own responses to social and political problems, as well as how to establish proper state–church relations.

Another major difficulty for the Christian Church is to overcome the overall ignorance of ordinary people in matters of faith and religion, and to find a language with which to communicate with its flock. The best possible way to resolve this issue is to provide structured education for the clergy. In summary, at the dawn of the twenty-first century, the Christian churches in Eastern Europe and Russia looked forward to the new opportunities and challenges which freedom of religion and growing economic development could bring to the lives of their people.

? DISCUSSION QUESTIONS

1 What were some of the peculiar features of the Eastern Orthodox churches in the nineteenth century?

2 Describe the reform movements within the Church in nineteenth-century Russia, including their origins; how did these movements relate to wider political reforms in the country?

3 What were the relationships between church and state in Russia and the Eastern European countries during the twentieth century?

4 What part did Catholic and Protestant churches in Eastern Europe and Russia play in the development of Christianity in that region during the twentieth century?

5 How did Christianity develop in the CIS countries during the twentieth century?

6 What changes took place in the life of the Eastern Orthodox churches after the fall of communism in Eastern Europe and Russia?

7 In a number of countries during this period, there is a close connection between ethnic and denominational identity; for example, to be Russian is to be Orthodox. How did this hinder or help the mission of the Church and are there parallels in your own situation?

Further reading

Angold, Michael. *Cambridge History of Christianity*, Vol. 5, *Eastern Christianity*. Cambridge: Cambridge University Press, 2005.

Binns, John. *An Introduction to the Christian Orthodox Churches*. Cambridge: Cambridge University Press, 2002.

Clendenin, Daniel B. *Eastern Orthodox Christianity: A Western perspective*, 2nd edn. Grand Rapids, MI: Baker, 2003.

McGuckin, John A. *The Orthodox Church: An introduction to its history, doctrine, and spiritual culture*. Malden, MA: Blackwell, 2008.

Nielsen, Niels C., Jr (ed.). *Christianity after Communism: Social, political and cultural struggle in Russia*. Oxford: Westview Press, 1994.

Parry, Ken and Melling, David J. (eds). *The Blackwell Companion to Eastern Christianity*. Oxford: Blackwell, 2007.

Pospielovsky, Dmitry. *The Russian Church under the Soviet Regime 1917–1982*, 2 vols. Crestwood, NY: St Vladimir's Seminary Press, 1984.

Ware, Timothy. *The Orthodox Church*. New York, NY: Penguin Putnam, 1991.

9

The Middle East (or South-West Asia and Egypt)

Issa Diab

The Middle East experienced major transformations from the year 1800 onwards, including both colonial rule and political independence. Many changes also occurred in Middle Eastern Christianity. The Christian faith in this part of the world was in a state of weakness in the late eighteenth century, and although the Catholic and Protestant missions pumped life into it, this only happened through schismatic crisis, the creation of union or reunion movements, and the establishment of new churches.

Despite the historic decline of Christianity in the region (since the Middle Ages), Middle Eastern churches are proud of their ancient history and origins. Two writers note that:

> For them, history is ever present: they celebrate their origins at the first Pentecost. They view the Western fascination with counting current members as superficial. Amid the icons of the saints, they feel constantly surrounded by 'the cloud of witnesses.' They also believe that Western Christians too often ignore the promise that the Lord of the church is present 'where two or three' gather in Christ's name.
>
> (Betty Jane Bailey and J. Martin Bailey, *Who Are the Christians in the Middle East?* (Grand Rapids, MI: Eerdmans, 2003), p. 43)

❈ Background and major historical developments

The term 'Middle East' was popularized around 1900 in Britain as a loose definition for the area traditionally encompassing countries or regions in Western Asia and parts of North Africa. As a political reference, the Middle East has no clear boundaries. This chapter mainly covers the following countries: Egypt (and Sudan), Iraq, Syria, Jordan, Lebanon, Israel and the Palestinian territories; the Arabian Peninsula: Saudi Arabia, Kuwait, Bahrain, Qatar, the United Arab Emirates, Oman, Yemen; Central Asia: Turkey and Iran.

The region is the birthplace of the world's great monotheistic religions: Judaism, Christianity and Islam. Located at the intersection of three continents, the Middle East has always been a major centre of world affairs. In modern times, it has attained great geopolitical, economic and religious significance, in part because many countries located around the Persian Gulf have large quantities of crude oil. The Middle East witnessed the emergence of the most ancient Christian denominations: the Greek Orthodox Church, the Coptic Church, the Armenian Orthodox Church, the Syriac Orthodox Church, the Assyrian Church and the Ethiopian Orthodox Church – not to mention the Eastern Catholic churches.

Christological conflicts

While the period 1800 to 2000 is our main concern, events dating back to the fourth century are crucial to the story and must be mentioned briefly. In particular, the Christological conflicts (conflicts on the nature of Christ) that

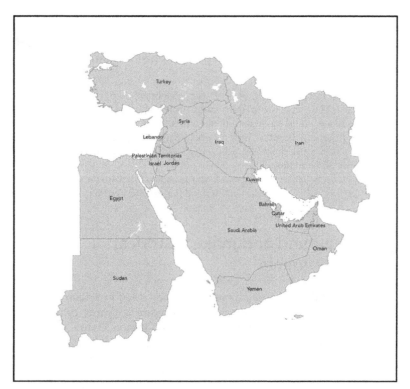

South-West Asia and Egypt

took place in the fourth and fifth centuries divided Christianity into a number of antagonistic bloc communities: the Nestorians, excommunicated at the Council of Ephesus (AD 431), fled from persecution and gathered in northern Mesopotamia and Persia, where they founded what is called today the Assyrian Church of the East. The Syriacs and Copts, who were also excommunicated, in their case at the Council of Chalcedon (AD 451), fled from persecution and gathered in two regions: the Syriacs in Syria, where they founded the Syriac Orthodox Church; and the Copts in Egypt, where they founded the Coptic Orthodox Church.

The emergence of Islam

From the seventh century, a new power arose in the Middle East, that of Islam, while the Byzantine Roman and Sassanid Persian empires were both weakened by centuries of stalemate warfare. In a series of rapid Muslim conquests, the Arab armies swept through most of the Middle East, reducing the Byzantine lands by more than half and completely engulfing the Persian lands.

In Anatolia, the Muslim expansion was blocked by the still capable Byzantines with the help of the Bulgarians. The Byzantine provinces of Roman Syria (Syria, Lebanon and Palestine), Egypt and North Africa, however, could not mount such a resistance. The non-Chalcedonian churches (Syriacs and Copts) welcomed the advent of new rule as a means to gain freedom from Byzantine animosity. The Greek Orthodox patriarch, Sophronius of Jerusalem (560–638), negotiated with Caliph Umar (579–644) in 637 for the peaceful transfer of the city into Arab control, and the Muslim conquerors swept through those regions. Thus, two of the five patriarchates (Jerusalem and Alexandria) came under Muslim rule. Two others (Constantinople and Antioch) would be taken later by the Muslim Ottomans. Only Rome would remain free.

The cracks and fissures in Christian unity led to 'the Great Schism'. Although 1054 is the date usually given for the factual beginning of the Great Schism, needless to say this schism, in fact, took place progressively. What really happened was a complex chain of events whose climax culminated in the excommunication of the Byzantine Church by Rome, brought about by the excommunication of the Roman Church by the Byzantine Church.

The Ottoman Empire

In 1453 the Byzantine Empire came under the control of the Ottoman Turks. In 1516 Antioch also fell into the hands of the Ottomans, and by the end of the sixteenth century the Ottomans had founded a huge empire and the whole Middle East, with the exception of Persia, was under their rule. As a result of the Ottoman conquest of the Byzantine Empire, all the Orthodox churches in the Middle East were suddenly isolated from the West. With only rare interferences by the Western 'Christian' nations, they would be confined within the Islamic world. It is, in part, due to this geographical confinement that the voice of Eastern Orthodoxy was not heard during the Reformation in sixteenth-century Europe.

In 1638, with the threat of war (in the form of Muslim jihads against the Christians within the Ottoman Empire), France offered to protect the Christian minority and signed the 'protocol of Christian Minorities Protection' with the Ottomans. France then established special ties with the Maronites (members of an Eastern Catholic church). This protocol encouraged Catholic missionaries to establish missionary work in Syria, Lebanon, Palestine and Egypt, and start working to reunite the Eastern churches with Rome by means of schools and seminaries, in addition to the Eastern Catholic schools opened in Rome after the Council of Trent in 1545. In the same way, British intervention in the affairs of the Middle East encouraged Protestant missionaries to establish missionary work and found Protestant churches in Turkey, Syria, Lebanon, Palestine and Egypt.

By the nineteenth century the Ottoman Empire was increasingly under the financial control of the European powers who wanted to get involved in the matters of the Middle East. The French annexed Algeria in 1830 and Tunisia in 1878. The British occupied Egypt in 1882, though it remained under nominal Ottoman sovereignty. The British also established effective control of the Persian Gulf, and the French extended their influence into Lebanon and Syria. In 1912 the Italians seized Libya.

In November 1914 the Ottoman Empire entered the First World War on the side of the Central Powers. Ottoman authorities had begun a propaganda drive to present Armenians living in the Ottoman Empire as a threat to the empire's security. On the night of 24 April 1915, the Ottoman government rounded up and imprisoned an estimated 250 Armenian intellectuals and community leaders. This date became the traditional memorial day of the Armenian Genocide. On 29 May 1915, the Ottoman authorities passed the Temporary Law of Deportation, authorizing the Ottoman government and military to deport anyone it 'sensed' as a threat to national security – implicitly targeting the Armenians and other Christian minorities such as Assyrians and Syriacs. This was followed by another law, the Temporary Law of Expropriation and Confiscation, which stated that all property, including land, livestock and homes, belonging to Armenians was to be confiscated by the authorities.

Thereafter, the Armenians were marched out to the Syrian town of Deir ez-Zor. Ottoman troops escorting them not only allowed others to rob, kill and rape the Armenians but also often participated in these activities themselves. Deprived of their belongings and forced into the desert, hundreds of thousands of Armenians perished. A lesser number of people from other Christian minorities – Greeks, Syriacs and Assyrians – met the same destiny. Massacres of Armenians and other Christians were committed in various other places in Turkey.

The fall of the Ottomans in the First World War allowed Kemal Atatürk (1881–1938) to seize power in Turkey and embark on a programme of modernization and secularization. He abolished the caliphate (Muslim rule), emancipated women, enforced Western dress, advocated the use of a new Turkish alphabet (based on the Latin alphabet in place of the Arabic alphabet) and abolished the jurisdiction of the Islamic courts. In effect, Turkey, having given up its rule over the Arab world, now determined to secede from the Middle East and become culturally part of Europe.

The 400 years of Ottoman rule in the Middle East had a complex impact on Christianity. Following the fall of Constantinople in 1453, Muhammad II (1432–81) did not distance himself from the Greek Orthodox Patriarch of Constantinople (called the Ecumenical Patriarch) but instead brought the church under close control by installing Gennadius II Scholarius (c.1400–73) as patriarch, after demanding a heavy fee. He established him as the ruler and representative of the Millet of Rum (a group of Christians), thus gathering the Orthodox Christian subjects of the empire, regardless of their ethnicity, under one ecclesiastical jurisdiction.

Under the 'millet system', conquered people were considered subjects of the empire but not subject to the Muslim faith or Muslim law. The word *millet* is a Turkish and Arabic word that means 'community'. The millet system was instituted by the Ottoman authorities, according to which each millet (community) had limited autonomy to manage the affairs of its members relating to marriage and divorce, adoption and heritage, and other matters. The people living under this system were known as *dhimmi*, that is, non-Muslims living under the protection of Muslims, but they were not always treated as such. According to Islamic law, *dhimmi* were required to pay a special tax, called *jizya*, and were subject to a number of restrictive regulations. As the largest group of non-Muslim subjects, the Greek Orthodox millet was granted a number of special privileges in the fields of politics and commerce, in addition to having to pay higher taxes than Muslim subjects.

Although the Ottoman state did not pursue a policy of forced individual conversion, it did decree that, for reasons of outward distinction, the people of the different millets should dress in certain ways, for instance wearing specific colours of turbans and shoes – a policy that was not, however, always followed by Ottoman citizens. Moreover, from the time of Murad I (1326–89) to the seventeenth century, the Ottoman state also put into effect the *devshirme* – a policy of filling the ranks of the Ottoman army and administrative system by forcefully removing young Christian boys from their families and taking them to the capital for education and training. Being raised in a Muslim milieu, these children, as they grew up, would in practice become Muslims.

The world wars

During the First World War (1914–18), the Young Turks (a reform group that introduced constitutional rule to the Ottoman Empire) joined Germany and Austria–Hungary against Britain and France. The Arabs had lived more or less happily under Ottoman rule for 400 years, until the Young Turks tried to assimilate them into Turkish culture and change their traditional system of government. The British fomented revolution in the Ottoman domains by exploiting the awakening force of Arab nationalism. They found an ally in Sharif Hussein (1854–1931), the hereditary ruler of Mecca, and promised to support his revolt against the Ottomans and the formation of an independent Arab state. But when the Ottoman Empire was defeated in 1918, the British and French governments concluded a secret treaty (the Sykes–Picot Agreement) to partition the Middle East between themselves. Additionally, via the Balfour Declaration, the British promised the international Zionist movement their support in creating a Jewish homeland in Palestine. The Arab population saw these developments as an act of betrayal by the British.

Britain and France soon established control over the Middle East (by mandate from the League of Nations) and rearranged the region to suit their interests. Syria became a French protectorate, and the Christian coastal areas of Syria, as well as a big part of the Beqaa (a very strategic plain), were split off to become the Greater Lebanon. In this domain, Maronites became a majority, not only among Christians but also among the other religious communities. Iraq and Palestine became British-mandated territories. Iraq was named the 'Kingdom of Iraq'. Palestine became the 'British Mandate of Palestine' and was split in half. The eastern half of Palestine became the 'Emirate of Transjordan', and the western half was placed under direct British administration. The already substantial Jewish population was allowed to increase. Most of the Arabian Peninsula fell to another British ally, Ibn Saud (1876–1953). Saud created the Kingdom of Saudi Arabia in 1932, founded on the principles of Wahhabite Islam.

Catholic missionaries in the Middle East, the Maronite Church in particular, enjoyed the support and encouragement of the French mandatory authorities, while the British Mandate was supportive of Protestant missionary organizations.

After the First World War, the Greco-Turkish War (May 1919 to October 1922) – also called the 'War in Asia Minor' or the 'Greek campaign of the Turkish War of Independence' or the 'Asia Minor Catastrophe' – led to the establishment of the Republic of Turkey. In 1924 the independent Kingdom of Egypt was created. Although Egypt was technically 'neutral' during the Second World War, Cairo soon became a major military base for British forces and the country was occupied. In 1941 a coup d'état in Iraq led the British to invade. The British invasion of Iraq was followed by the Allied invasion of Syria–Lebanon and the Anglo-Soviet invasion of Iran.

In Palestine, the conflicting forces of Arab nationalism and Zionism created a situation which the British were unable to resolve. Meanwhile, the

Holocaust gave rise to a new urgency in the Zionist quest to immigrate to Palestine and create a Jewish state there. The establishment of the State of Israel in 1948 resulted in the displacement of hundreds of thousands of Palestinians, who were housed in refugee camps in Lebanon, Syria and Jordan. Throughout the rest of the twentieth century, most of the Middle Eastern countries restored their independence.

Other major developments

The discovery of oil in the Middle East was a major turning point in its history. Oil was found first in Persia (1908) and later in Saudi Arabia (1938) and the other Persian Gulf states, and also in Libya and Algeria. The Middle East possessed the world's largest easily accessible reserves of crude oil. Given the influence that oil has in international commerce and industry, the oil-producing countries in the Middle East became the economic and political target of the great international powers. The oil wealth of these countries allowed their governments to plan and execute huge infrastructure and construction programmes that attracted Western experts and companies as well as migrant labour from around the world, creating an international community. Among these foreigners were Christians, who established churches in most of the Muslim countries.

The Israeli–Palestinian conflict

The struggle between the Arabs and Jews in Palestine culminated in the 1947 United Nations plan to partition Palestine. The objective was to create an Arab state and a Jewish state in the narrow space between the River Jordan and the Mediterranean Sea. While the Jewish leaders accepted the plan, the Arab leaders rejected it. On 14 May 1948, when the British Mandate expired, the Zionist leadership declared the State of Israel. In the 1948 Arab–Israeli War which immediately followed, the armies of Egypt, Syria, Transjordan, Lebanon, Iraq and Saudi Arabia intervened and were defeated by Israel. About 800,000 Palestinians fled from areas annexed by Israel and became refugees in neighbouring countries, thus creating the 'Palestinian problem' which has bedevilled the region ever since.

The Israeli–Palestinian conflict remains unsettled; the list of Arab–Israeli wars includes major wars such as the 1948 Arab–Israeli War, the 1956 Suez War, the 1967 Six Day War, the 1970 War of Attrition, the 1973 Yom Kippur War, the 1982 Lebanon War and a number of lesser conflicts. In 1979, Anwar Sadat (1918–81), the third president of Egypt and successor of Gamal Nasser (1918–70), concluded a peace treaty with Israel, ending the prospects of a united Arab military pact. The Israeli–Palestinian conflict continued in many ways, mainly on the Palestinian and Lebanese front.

The departure of the European powers from the region, the establishment of Israel and the increasing importance of the oil industry marked the creation of the modern Middle East. In an effort to protect its interests in the region, including access to oil, the USA established a strong alliance with the conservative monarchies of Saudi Arabia, Jordan, Iran and the Persian Gulf emirates, despite the failings of these regimes. In Iran this arrangement ended with a revolution led by the Shia clergy that overthrew the monarchy in 1979 and established a theocratic regime which was even more anti-Western than the secular regimes in Iraq or Syria.

The fall of the Soviet Union and the collapse of communism in the early 1990s had several consequences for the Middle East. It allowed large numbers of Soviet Jews to emigrate from Russia and Ukraine to Israel, further strengthening the Jewish state. It cut off the easiest source of credit, armaments and diplomatic support to the anti-Western Arab regimes, weakening their position. It opened up the prospect of cheap oil from Russia, driving down the price of oil and reducing the West's dependence on oil from the Arab states. And it discredited the model of development through authoritarian state socialism which Egypt (under Nasser), Algeria, Syria and Iraq had been following since the 1960s, leaving these regimes politically and economically stranded. Rulers such as Saddam Hussein in Iraq increasingly turned to Arab nationalism as a substitute for socialism.

These developments led Iraq into its prolonged war with Iran in the 1980s and then into its fateful invasion of Kuwait in 1990. Kuwait had been part of the Ottoman province of Basra before 1918 and thus in a sense part of Iraq, but Iraq had recognized its independence in the 1960s. The USA responded to the invasion by forming a coalition of allies which included Saudi Arabia, Egypt and Syria. Having gained approval from the United Nations, it evicted Iraq from Kuwait by force in the Persian Gulf War (January–February 1991). The war and its aftermath brought about a permanent US military presence in the Persian Gulf region, particularly in Saudi Arabia, something which caused great offence to many Muslims.

The rise of Islamic fundamentalism
The nineteenth and twentieth centuries also witnessed the emergence of 'Islamic fundamentalism', an attempt to reform the Islamic community along traditional lines that largely rejected modern values. The most important reasons for the emergence of Islamic fundamentalism were the social problems of Islamic society, the impact of Western colonialism, the abolition of the Islamic caliphate in 1924 and the adoption of secularism by Turkey (then the largest Muslim country). Islamic fundamentalism is based on Salafism, the principle of going back to ancient Islam. The aim is to reform Islam by eliminating impurities and restoring the faith as it was practised in the beginning. Muslim fundamentalists, called also Islamists, work for the implementation of Islamic law and the establishment of an

Islamic state in all Arab and Islamic countries, notwithstanding the presence of Christians and non-Muslims in these countries.

The history of Middle Eastern Christianity from 1800

In addition to the weakness of the Middle Eastern churches at the beginning of the nineteenth century (and long before), four major developments triggered dramatic demographical changes in Middle Eastern Christianity. First, the creation of the Greater Lebanon by the Sykes–Picot Agreement in 1916 – by which Britain and France divided the Ottoman Empire – allowed the (Catholic) Maronites to become a majority among other religious groups living in Lebanon. Second, the 'Christian [Armenian] Genocide' by the Ottomans (see above) caused the extermination of thousands of Christians residing in different areas of Asia Minor. The rest of these Christian communities emigrated mainly to neighbouring countries: Syria, Lebanon, Iraq, Egypt and Palestine. Third, the exchange of population between Turkey and Greece meant that thousands of Turks residing in Greece were allowed to go and reside in Turkey, and thousands of Greeks residing in Asia Minor were allowed to go and reside in Greece. Due to the Ottoman massacres against Armenian, Syriac and Assyrian Christians, and the exchange of the Greeks of Asia Minor for Turks from Greece, Anatolia had become empty of Christians by 1922.

Fourth, as a result of the Israeli–Palestinian conflict, accompanied by the threat of Islamic fundamentalism and other economic problems, thousands of Middle Eastern Christians have emigrated to the West. Consequently, the number of Christians in the Middle East is continually decreasing. Even the Palestinian territories, located in the region where Jesus was born and Christianity was founded, are in danger of becoming empty of Christians. With the end of the Christian presence in Asia Minor, the Christians of the Middle East became concentrated in the Arab Middle East and the valley of the Nile. In addition, the Assyrian, Armenian and Syriac churches were uprooted from Asia Minor and had to face, henceforth, the difficult experience of existing in various diasporas. The rupture between the Hellenic Greek and the Arab Greek Orthodox was absolute, except in Palestine.

In addition to the demographic changes, two major developments dramatically transformed the structure of the Church. In the first instance, the Eastern Catholic movement, which dated back to the seventeenth century, produced schismatic groupings: the Eastern Orthodox churches and a 'Uniate movement' (the latter connected to Rome). This gave rise to new Middle Eastern Catholic churches in addition to those already in existence. Second, the establishment of Protestant churches in the Middle East linked to Protestant missions challenged the Orthodox churches and generated many internal reform movements.

The Catholic missions, the Uniate movement, and the emergence and growth of Eastern Catholic churches

The Vatican had long tried to bring the Middle Eastern churches under its influence. As a result of the Crusades, a brief and rather superficial reunion between parts of Eastern churches and Rome took place at the Council of Florence (1439). However, when the Middle East came under the control of the Mamluk Turks in the thirteenth century and then the Ottoman Empire in the sixteenth century, all connections between the Christians of the Middle East and western Europe were cut. After the fall of Constantinople in 1453 new efforts at reunion came from three sources: the Eastern schools in Rome, the Catholic missions and supportive Catholic nations such as France.

In the wake of the Council of Trent (1545), Rome understood that reunion with the Eastern churches would only be established with careful preparation. This took two forms: (1) opening Eastern schools in Rome and inviting Eastern Christian students, and (2) encouraging Catholic missionary work in the Middle East. Pope Gregory XIII (r. 1572–85) opened St Athanasius School for the Greeks in 1576 and two other schools in 1584 – one for Maronites and another for Armenians. A number of Eastern clergymen studied in these schools during the sixteenth, seventeenth and eighteenth centuries, and thus prepared people in their countries to accept reunion with Rome.

Regarding the second factor, between the 1570s and 1590s, Pope Gregory XIII sent several delegations of Jesuits to Syria purposely to work on the reunion of the Middle Eastern churches with Rome. While these attempts were unsuccessful, they had planted the idea of reunion in the minds of many Christian leaders. Furthermore, in 1840, France signed an agreement with the Ottoman sultanate, according to which France was allowed to protect the Christians of the region against any kind of discrimination or persecution, and Western Christian missionaries were allowed to work in the Middle East. Consuls from Europe's Roman Catholic nations built good social relationships with many Christian leaders, and facilitated the activities of Catholic missionaries.

The Franciscan order was already active in the Holy Land from the time of the Crusades. As a result of the 1840 'French Agreement', a number of Catholic orders were encouraged to send missionaries to the Middle East. The Carmelite, Capuchin and Jesuit orders sent missionaries to Syria, where the city of Aleppo became a centre of their activities. Catholic missionaries opened schools, preached, translated Christian books into Arabic, established para-church organizations and cultivated friendships with many lay-leaders, priests and bishops. These interactions with Middle Eastern Christians, made possible by the charity and educational activities of Catholic missionary groups, encouraged positive attitudes towards Rome. They also created an acceptance of the idea of reunion with Rome.

In time, the Maronite Church, and a number of bishops from almost all the Middle Eastern churches, declared their reunion with Rome. This step created much commotion within Middle Eastern Christianity; but Rome, from its side, welcomed the reunited bishops and recognized the ordinations of their 'Catholic' patriarchs. The list of these 'Uniate churches' (the official name that was given to the Middle Eastern churches that reunited with Rome) is as follows:

- the Chaldean Catholic Church (the Patriarchate of Babel);
- the Greek Catholic Church – the Melkite (the Patriarchate of Antioch and the Holy Land);
- the Syriac Catholic Church (the Patriarchate of Antioch);
- the Coptic Catholic Church (the Patriarchate of Alexandria);
- the Armenian Catholic Church (the Catholicosate of Cilicia).

The Catholic Middle Eastern churches comprised the churches in the above list as well as the Maronite Church and the Latin Church in the East.

The emergence of Catholic churches in the Middle East was tumultuous because it involved 'separation movements' within the different Orthodox churches. Neither the original Orthodox churches nor the Ottoman authorities recognized these 'new churches'. Consequently, the 'new Catholics' were persecuted until France and Austria intervened and asked the Ottoman rulers to stop all forms of persecution and to recognize the Middle Eastern Catholic churches as independent Christian communities. Then, in 1830, the Ottoman rulers recognized the Middle Eastern Catholics as one community and appointed an Armenian priest, who took the title of Patriarch, as their representative. When Ibrahim Pasha (of Egypt, 1789–1848) entered Syria in 1832 persecution against Catholics stopped and Middle Eastern Catholic churches were allowed full recognition and freedom. Catholic missionary work was revived and Eastern Catholic churches entered their 'golden age'. At that time, Protestant missions also began work in the Middle East.

To help the Uniate churches, Rome issued the necessary decrees in the Roman Apostolic See that allowed these churches to keep their autonomy under the authority of their local patriarchs. They were also allowed to practise their oriental liturgies after submitting them to a few changes to become harmonious with the doctrines of the Roman Catholic Church. Since 1917 the Eastern Catholic churches have been represented in the Holy See and the Roman Curia through the Congregation for the Oriental Churches, in which members by right are the patriarchs and the major archbishops of these churches. The 'Congregation' organizes the relationships between the Holy See and the Eastern Catholic churches.

Towards the end of the Ottoman era the Middle Eastern Catholic churches experienced a cultural and theological renaissance by virtue of the oriental schools opened in Rome and the connections with Rome that had been built by the Uniate movement. Religious books were edited and schools were opened throughout the empire. This Arab cultural renaissance brought about religious reform through the training and education of the clergy. Thus, Middle Eastern Catholic churches opened theological seminaries, new religious orders were founded, and printing facilities were widely utilized. Under the French Mandate in Syria and Lebanon (1918–46), the Eastern Catholic churches prospered in many senses – materially, culturally, theologically and spiritually.

The Holy See has an episcopal ecclesiastical jurisdiction with the following Eastern Catholic churches, including countries (date of union or foundation in parentheses):

- Alexandrian liturgical tradition:
  - Coptic Catholic Church (patriarchate): Egypt (1741);
  - Ethiopian Catholic Church (metropolia): Ethiopia, Eritrea (1846).
- Antiochian (Antiochene or West Syrian) liturgical tradition:
  - Maronite Church (patriarchate): Lebanon, Cyprus, Jordan, Israel, the Palestinian territories, Egypt, Syria, Argentina, Brazil, USA, Australia, Canada, Mexico (union reaffirmed 1182);
  - Syriac Catholic Church (patriarchate): Lebanon, Iraq, Jordan, Kuwait, the Palestinian territories, Egypt, Sudan, Syria, Turkey, USA and Canada, Venezuela (1781);
  - Syro-Malankara Catholic Church (major archiepiscopate): India, USA (1930).
- Armenian liturgical tradition:
  - Armenian Catholic Church (patriarchate): Lebanon, Iran, Iraq, Egypt, Syria, Turkey, Jordan, the Palestinian territories, Ukraine, France, Greece, Latin America, Argentina, Romania, USA, Canada, Eastern Europe (1742).
- Chaldean or East Syrian liturgical tradition:
  - Chaldean Catholic Church (patriarchate): Iraq, Iran, Lebanon, Egypt, Syria, Turkey, USA (1692);
  - Syro-Malabar Church (major archiepiscopate): India, USA (at latest, 1599).
- Byzantine (Constantinopolitan) liturgical tradition:
  - Albanian Byzantine Catholic Church (apostolic administration): Albania (1628);
  - Belarusian Greek Catholic Church (no established hierarchy at present): Belarus (1596);
  - Bulgarian Greek Catholic Church (apostolic exarchate): Bulgaria (1861);
  - Byzantine Church of the Eparchy of Križevci (an eparchy and an apostolic exarchate): Croatia, Serbia and Montenegro (1611);
  - Greek Byzantine Catholic Church (two apostolic exarchates): Greece, Turkey (1829);

- Hungarian Greek Catholic Church (an eparchy and an apostolic exarchate): Hungary (1646);
- Italo-Albanian Catholic Church (two eparchies and a territorial abbacy): Italy (never separated);
- Macedonian Greek Catholic Church (an apostolic exarchate): Republic of Macedonia (1918);
- Melkite Greek Catholic Church (patriarchate): Syria, Lebanon, Jordan, Israel, Jerusalem, Brazil, USA, Canada, Mexico, Iraq, Egypt and Sudan, Kuwait, Australia, Venezuela, Argentina (1726);
- Romanian Church United with Rome, Greek-Catholic (major archiepiscopate): Romania, USA (1697);
- Russian Byzantine Catholic Church: (two apostolic exarchates, at present with no published hierarchs): Russia, China (1905); currently about 20 parishes and communities scattered around the world, including five in Russia itself, answering to bishops of other jurisdictions;
- Ruthenian Catholic Church (a sui juris metropolia, an eparchy and an apostolic exarchate): USA, Ukraine, Czech Republic (1646);
- Slovak Greek Catholic Church (metropolia): Slovak Republic, Canada (1646);
- Ukrainian Greek Catholic Church (major archiepiscopate): Ukraine, Poland, USA, Canada, UK, Australia, Germany and Scandinavia, France, Brazil, Argentina (1595).

With a revived Latin Church of the Middle East, Bishop Joseph Valerga (1813–72) was appointed Latin Patriarch of Jerusalem. Though officially superseding the Franciscans, Valerga was also the Grand Master of the Order. On Valerga's death in 1872 Vincent Braco (1835–89) was appointed, and following his death in 1889 the Ottoman sultan authorized the re-establishment of a Latin hierarchy. The Grand Masters of the Order continued to be named as Latin patriarchs until 1905.

Western Protestant missions: the emergence and growth of Eastern Protestant churches

Congregational and Presbyterian missionary work

At the beginning of the nineteenth century, Protestant missionaries from churches of the Reformed tradition in the USA and Scotland, as well as from the Anglican Church in Britain and the Lutheran Church in Germany, came to minister in the Middle East. They arrived with the goal of proclaiming the message of the gospel, first to the Jews, then to the Muslims and Eastern Christians. Prior to their coming, these Protestant missionaries had very little knowledge about the Middle Eastern churches. The churches founded in the Middle East by these Protestant denominations are usually known as 'Evangelical churches'.

In Syria and Lebanon

Since they were forbidden by Ottoman laws to acquire property in Jerusalem, Congregational and Presbyterian missionaries (from the American Board of Missions) chose Beirut as the mission's headquarters in 1823. At that time, Beirut was a minor port on the Syrian coast. From there, the missionaries directed their work towards Mount Lebanon and regions in Syria, Palestine, Asia Minor and Mesopotamia. Through their connections with Armenian clergymen in Sidon (Lebanon), the missionaries came to know about the existence of a large Armenian community in Istanbul (ancient Constantinople). Thus, in 1831, they started a mission work in the Ottoman capital.

These Protestant missionaries did not come with the intention of establishing a Protestant church in the Middle East. But the difficulties they faced with the millet system, and negative reactions from the different Middle Eastern churches, forced them to establish local Protestant churches in many areas of Turkey, Lebanon and Syria from the 1840s onwards. Thereafter, they also opened schools, and later universities. Many of these schools and universities are still functioning today.

The translation of the Bible into vernacular languages was a major focus of Protestant missions. In 1834 the American Mission moved the Armenian and Turkish section of what was the American Press from Malta to Istanbul, and moved the Arabic section to Beirut. An Armenian translation of the Bible was completed in 1853 and an Arabic version in 1864. The Arabic translation is still used today in the Evangelical and Orthodox churches.

In Egypt and Sudan

In 1854 a group of missionaries from the Reformed Church (Presbyterian) in the USA arrived in Egypt to begin an Evangelical ministry. The Evangelical Church of Egypt was formed in 1860 in Cairo. In the following years the ministry extended to many places in the Nile Delta and in Upper and Middle Egypt: Asyūt in 1865; Mansūrah, 1866; al-Fayyūm, 1866; Alexandria, 1875; al-Qalyūbiah, 1894; Suez, 1900; Zaqaziq, 1905; and other places. Thus, the Evangelical ministry grew and spread throughout all of Egypt. By 2000 there were over 300 Evangelical churches grouped into eight presbyteries, with many schools and other humanitarian and educational institutions. A theological seminary, now situated in Cairo, also started offering courses in 1863.

In 1899 these Presbyterian missionaries in Egypt travelled to Sudan to explore the possibility of starting an Evangelical ministry there also. Egyptian Evangelical churches joined the effort, sending ministers to Sudan at their own expense. Consequently, Evangelical work started in Sudan in 1901; and from that time on, many Presbyterian churches were formed in different places. The work in Sudan was carried out through collaboration between the Egyptian Presbyterian Church and American Presbyterian missionaries working in Egypt.

In Iraq and the Gulf

Protestant missionary work in Iraq began in the 1820s. Mission agencies focused on the north of Iraq and what is now south-eastern Turkey. The American Board of Commissioners for Foreign Mission (ABCFM), a coalition of US Reformed denominations, and the Arabian Mission of the Reformed Church in America (RCA) undertook the foundation of the Presbyterian work in Iraq. A coalition of three US denominations founded the United Mission in Mesopotamia in 1924 (later renamed the 'United Mission in Iraq'). The result of the 'Reformed ministry' was that two officially recognized Protestant churches emerged: the National Protestant–Evangelical Church and the Assyrian Evangelical–Protestant Church, in addition to the Seventh-day Adventist Church, which was also officially recognized.

Protestant mission work began in the Gulf in 1891 when the Arabian Mission of the Reformed Church in America (RCA) established its base in Basra (Iraq). The result was the establishment of at least partly indigenous worshipping communities in Bahrain, Oman and Kuwait. These churches were able to serve expatriate Christians belonging to Protestant, Orthodox and Catholic communities in the different countries of the Arab Gulf. Up until today, this missionary work is associated with greatly appreciated medical and educational services. The National Evangelical Church in Bahrain was recognized as a national church by the Bahrain government in 1968.

In Oman, following the handover of the Arabian Mission's medical work to the Omani government in 1973, the fragile indigenous Omani Christian community melted away. The surviving church, now known as the Protestant Church in Oman, was allowed to exist under an agreement between the ministry and the Episcopal Diocese of Cyprus and the Gulf and the Reformed Church in America, signed in 1977. In addition to the two recognized National Evangelical churches in Oman and Bahrain, we should mention the National Evangelical Church in Kuwait, which was also recognized. In recent times, the countries of the Arab Gulf have shown an openness and readiness to recognize national Christian churches.

The Anglican and Lutheran missionary work

From 1823 Anglican missionaries were sent to Jerusalem from the London Society for Promoting Christianity Amongst the Jews – also known as the London Jews Society, and today referred to as the Church's Ministry among the Jews (CMJ). After the 1840 treaty between Britain, Prussia, Austria and Russia and the Ottoman Empire, Wilhelm IV, King of Prussia (1795–1861), convinced Queen Victoria (1819–1901), the Archbishop of Canterbury and the Bishop of London to grant the national Protestant Church of Prussia an equal standing with the United Church of England and Ireland in the Holy Land. An agreement was set up between the two sides according to which their two churches were to work jointly and in a united way in a bishop-ric for all Protestant churches that might wish to join it, and the two sides would rotate in nominating the Bishop of Jerusalem. The first nomination was made by England. In 1841 the Archbishop of Canterbury consecrated Revd Michael Solomon Alexander (1799–1845) as the first Anglican bishop of Jerusalem. The Jerusalem diocese included Syria, Chaldea, Egypt and Ethiopia. Later, Prussian bishop Samuel Gobat (1799–1879) formed the native Evangelical communities and dedicated the first church in 1847. In 1851, Gobat also solicited the help of the Church Missionary Society (CMS), which sent missionaries to work in Jerusalem until 1918, when indigenous leaders took over the work.

In the Palestinian territories and Jordan

The Protestant community was officially recognized by the Ottoman gov-ernment's decree of 1850. It consisted of the Evangelical and Episcopal groups who were under the Church of England in Palestine and Jordan and the Reformed Presbyterian and Congregational communities in Syria and Lebanon. In 1905 a new body, the Council for the Evangelical Episcopal Community, was set up; though the Palestinian Evangelical Episcopal com-munity was not recognized until 1970. In the Hashemite Kingdom of Transjordan, however, it was officially recognized in 1938. After 1948, when the Palestinians were displaced, the community was split into two parts: one council was in Jordan and the other in Israel. But the two councils re-united in 1976 when an independent province was created for the Episcopal Church in the Middle East. The province included the two dioceses of Iran and Egypt, a new diocese of Cyprus and the Gulf, and the Diocese of Jerusalem, which now included Jordan, Lebanon, Syria, the West Bank, Gaza and Israel. The church council's long demand for an Arab bishop was eventually granted in 1957.

In 1869 the ministry in Bethlehem, Beit Jāla and Beit Sahūr, where there were small Protestant or Evangelical groups, was handed over by Bishop Gobat and the CMS to the Berlin Missionary Society. Ludwig Schneller (1858–1953), the son of the founder of the Syrian Orphanage in Jerusalem, Johann Ludwig Schneller (1820–96), was pastor to the community in Bethlehem. There he built the Lutheran Church of the Nativity, which was inaugurated in 1893. Native Evangelical Lutheran communities were formed, and churches and schools were built in many places in Palestine and in Jordan. The ministry of Johann Schneller extended to Amman in Jordan and to Khirbet Qanafar in Lebanon.

In Egypt

In 1819 the Church Missionary Society (CMS) in Britain sent its first mis-sionary to Egypt. He was followed later by others. In 1833 the CMS mis-sionaries opened a school for boys and another for girls in Cairo. In time, a school of theology was opened, and one of its earliest graduates was a bishop who was consecrated in Ethiopia. It is worth noting that the CMS did not set out to establish an Anglican church; rather it aimed to revive the Coptic Church.

In Iraq and the Gulf

The CMS founded an Anglican ministry in Iraq in the 1820s. When 'the Christian Genocide' in Ottoman Turkey forced Arabic-speaking Armenians and Syriacs to migrate from the Diyārbekir–Mardin–Midyat triangle to Iraq, the CMS missionaries took care of them and formed Anglican-like communities. The outbreak of the First World War forced the CMS to cease its work in Iraq; but personnel of the Arabian Mission, a missionary agency belonging to the Reformed Church in America, filled the gap in Baghdad from 1920 to 1924. Afterwards, these Anglican-like ministries became part of the National Protestant–Evangelical Church in Baghdad. Since the First World War, the Anglican presence in Iraq has been exclusively linked to expatriates. It currently comes under the authority of the Diocese of Cyprus and the Gulf of the Episcopal Church in Jerusalem and the Middle East.

Evangelical missionary work

In the twentieth century new Evangelical missions also arrived in Lebanon, including the Society of Friends (Quakers), which had already started outreach in Palestine and moved to Lebanon in 1873. In 1895 the first Evangelical Baptist church was founded in Beirut as a result of missionary work by the Southern Baptist Convention of the USA. In 1912 US missionaries from the Church of God (Anderson, Indiana) were established near Beirut, and their first national congregation was formed in 1920. There are also other Evangelical churches in Syria, Lebanon and Jordan, including the Alliance Evangelical Church, the Church of the Nazarene, the Church of the Brethren (Plymouth) and the Seventh-day Adventists. Pentecostal–Charismatic churches such as the Assemblies of God also started ministries from the 1950s onwards.

At the same time, the same Evangelical missions that worked in Lebanon extended their work to include other parts of the Middle East such as Jordan, Egypt and Sudan. In the 1950s Evangelical missionary work also began in North Africa. It is not easy to provide a precise account of the ministry of Evangelical missions in the different countries of the Middle East because of many sudden changes and a lack of continuity.

Organization of the Evangelical communities in the Middle East

After decades of Evangelical ministry in the Middle East, it became obvious that the plurality of Evangelical churches did not fit in with either the 'patriarchal churches', which had strict hierarchical structures, or the millet system that remained after Ottoman rule. In response, the Evangelical communities in almost every country formed a representative body or council that officially represented them in ecclesiastical courts and promoted their interests in various official, governmental and religious bodies. The Supreme Council of the Evangelical Community in Syria and Lebanon was formed in 1937; and a similar council was established in Egypt, now known as the 'General Evangelical Council'.

The following Evangelical churches or denominations established representative councils: the Presbyterian Church, the Congregational Church (in Lebanon only), the Reformed Church (in Egypt only), the Armenian Evangelical Church, the Anglican–Episcopal Church, the Lutheran Church (in the Palestinian territories and Jordan only), churches from the Wesleyan tradition (Church of Grace, Church of God (Anderson, Indiana), the Nazarene Church, the Methodist Church, the Gospel Preaching Church and the Church of Faith), the Brethren Church (Plymouth Brethren), the Open Brethren, the Baptist Church (mainly Southern Baptist), Pentecostal churches, the Seventh-day Adventist Church, the Christian Alliance Church and the Free Evangelical Church.

Assyrian Church of the East

At the start of the twentieth century and during the outbreak of the First World War, Assyrians entered an era of new hostilities with the Ottoman Turks during which villages were burned and churches plundered. Hundreds of precious old Christological books were looted and destroyed, with only a few reaching the world's famous museums. The Christian Assyrians were scattered and are still being scattered. Wherever they went, in Iraq, Iran, Syria, Lebanon, Kuwait, Greece, Italy, Sweden, Russia, the USA, Canada and Australia, they clustered together and found communities in which they could adhere to their ancestral faith.

The non-Chalcedonian churches

In general, all the Eastern Orthodox churches were affected by the ministry of the Catholic and Protestant missions in the Middle East. Protestant missions, and the Uniate movement, caused these churches to lose members. The need to stem the loss of members, as well as the impact of the cultural renaissance of the nineteenth century, saw the Eastern Orthodox churches introduce many reforms. But the cultural renaissance also infused churches and society with the spirit of nationalism, which the Ottoman rulers met with repressive measures. Two of the three non-Chalcedonian churches suffered severe persecution, which reached its height in 1915 when the Ottoman commander Jamal Pasha (1872–1922) killed thousands of Syriac and Armenian Christians residing in Turkey. From there, these Christians fled and took refuge in the neighbouring countries, mainly in Lebanon and Syria.

The Coptic Orthodox Church of Alexandria

During the nineteenth century, Egypt witnessed important historical events that formed the basis for a revival in various fields. This was possible because the Ottoman governor, Muhammad Ali Pasha (1769–1849), and his son, Ibrahim Pasha (1789–1848), encouraged Western missionary work in Egypt. In particular, the Coptic Orthodox Church of Egypt experienced spiritual renewal. The main elements in this revival included founding new schools, launching the ministry of the Sunday school in the church, setting up a printing house, establishing a theological seminary, refreshing the monastic life and opening or reopening vocational monasteries, launching new religious and secular publications and periodicals, and translating the Coptic liturgy into English. Church buildings were repaired and renovated, and new structures put up, after centuries of neglect due to the fact that the Islamic Ottoman rulers forbade the repair or erection of church buildings.

General episcopacies for social services, education, religious institutes and research were founded. And, for the first time, the Holy Synod of the Coptic Church instituted the consecration of females in the church for practical and social work. The revival also produced missionary initiatives to other parts of Africa and beyond. Not only were missionaries commissioned to offer pastoral care for Copts living outside Egypt, but Coptic churches were also established in Sudan, and for the first time in Kuwait, North America, Canada and Australia. These efforts were greatly aided by the translation of church liturgy into the English language. A committee of the liturgy was instituted and commissioned to review the rituals of the Coptic Church.

From its earliest beginnings, the Orthodox Church of Ethiopia was under the leadership of the Coptic Orthodox Church in Egypt. In 1959 Patriarch Cyril VI of Egypt (1902–71) ordained the first Ethiopian catholicos (ruling bishop), which also opened the way for the Ethiopian Church to ordain its own bishops and exercise greater autonomy (see Chapter 3 above). Finally, in 1970, the Ethiopian Orthodox Church (and the Eritrean Orthodox Church) became totally autonomous – free from Egyptian ecclesiastical oversight and control.

Under Cyril VI's successor, Pope Shenouda III (1923–2012), the Coptic Church experienced its greatest expansion. Shenouda III not only established good relations with Egypt's Muslim rulers but also made strenuous efforts to end the long-standing isolation of the Coptic Church. In 1973 he visited the Catholic pope Paul VI (1897–1978), becoming the first Coptic pontiff to visit the Vatican in over 1,500 years. The two pontiffs signed a declaration about the unity of the Church to mark the resumption of relations. The Alexandrian pope also exchanged visits with the Ecumenical Patriarch in Constantinople, the Orthodox patriarchs of Moscow, Romania, Bulgaria and Antioch, and the Catholic patriarchs in the Middle Eastern countries. The Coptic Church also expanded globally under Shenouda's leadership and became a member of the Middle East Council of Churches. The death, in March 2012, of this popular and charismatic leader who had headed the Coptic Church for more than four decades was greeted with a public outpouring of grief by Egypt's Christian population.

The Syriac Orthodox Church of Antioch and All the East

Under the Ottoman rulers, the Syriac Orthodox Church endured severe persecution and was greatly affected by the massacres of 1915, which reportedly took the lives of a quarter of a million Syriac Orthodox Christians. Religious persecution also triggered huge migrations of the church's members to other parts of the world, including Europe and North America. The patriarchate moved first to Homs, in Syria, and subsequently to Damascus (in 1957). This church preserves the Semitic elements of early Christianity in its liturgy (in the Syriac language) and is considered one of the most ancient churches. Today, its adherents are to be found mainly in the Middle East and the Indian state of Kerala, with many dispersed throughout the world. The Syriac Orthodox Church is one of the founding members of the Middle East Council of Churches. It became a member of the World Council of Churches in 1960.

The Armenian Orthodox Church

In reaction to the Uniate movement and the establishment of the Armenian Protestant Church in 1850 the Armenian Orthodox Church undertook major reforms. In 1860 it produced the 'Regulation of the Armenian Nation', a sort of constitution which established a national assembly formed in majority by laymen. This assembly was given power to elect the Patriarch of Istanbul and play a leading role in the affairs of the community. However, the move towards an autonomous organization and the strengthening of nationalism provoked persecution by the Ottoman powers. The Christian population in south-eastern Anatolia and Cilicia experienced massacres during 1894–5. The horror of the Armenian Genocide came to a climax in 1915, during the First World War. Accused of a treacherous sympathy for the Russians, the Armenians of Eastern Anatolia were systematically exterminated. The genocide caused the death of approximately 700,000 Christians, mainly Armenians.

These events forced the Armenians to abandon their homeland in huge numbers. Most settled in Syria and Lebanon. In 1930 a new catholicosate was established in Antelias, Lebanon. This was followed by the organization of dioceses and the founding of a new theological seminary. A chapel commemorating the death of one and a half million Armenian Christians was also erected. This catholicosate remains the centre for the Armenian Orthodox Church and its worldwide diaspora.

✳ Ecumenism in the Middle East

Undoubtedly, the ecumenical spirit in the Middle East derives mainly from initiatives taken by the World Council of Churches (WCC), beginning in 1948. Ecumenism in the Middle East had four indirect sources: the announcement by Pope John XXIII (1881–1963) on 25 January 1959 of a council of the Catholic Church, in which ecumenism would be a major theme; the first pan-Orthodox conference in the summer of the same year, convoked by Athenagoras I, Patriarch of Constantinople (1886–1972), with a view to harmonizing the Orthodox position in the face of the developments of the ecumenical movement; the creation, in 1960, of the Secretariat for the Promotion of the Unity of Christians by Pope John XXIII; and the third general assembly of the WCC in December 1961 in New Delhi, which was attended by Orthodox churches from Eastern Europe and emphasized dialogue between Eastern and Western churches. The Orthodox Ecumenical Council (OEC), comprising all the churches of the Middle Eastern members of the WCC, also came into existence.

The first step towards ecumenism had been taken in 1932 when the Protestant and Evangelical communities regrouped in the 'Near East Christian Council'. After New Delhi, however, this council enlisted for the first time a new non-Protestant member, the Syriac Orthodox Church of Antioch, and thus became the 'Near East Council of Churches'. It was this new council that would see the beginning of negotiations between the Greek Orthodox churches and the non-Chalcedonian Orthodox churches of the region, resulting in the creation of the 'Middle East Council of Churches' (MECC) in 1974. The MECC groups the Middle Eastern churches into 'ecclesiastical families'. To the initial group of three families – the Orthodox family (Chalcedonian), the Oriental Orthodox family (non-Chalcedonian) and the Evangelical family (Anglican, Lutheran, Presbyterian and Congregational) – was added the Catholic family in 1990. The joining of the Assyrian Church of the East to the MECC was due to be considered in 1994, a few days after the signing of the Common Christological Declaration by Pope John Paul II (1920–2005) and Patriarch Denkha IV (1935–2015), but other issues delayed the church's membership.

The MECC is intended to be a transitory structure with a view to a collective advance towards a unity in plurality. The priority objectives of the MECC are: (1) the continuity of the Christian presence in the Middle East, particularly in counteracting the causes of Christian emigration; (2) the renewal of the spiritual quality of churches through and beyond their socio-cultural identity; (3) Christian unity; and (4) the common testimony of churches in multireligious societies. By the beginning of the twenty-first century, and after more than 30 years of existence, the MECC initiative was a vital mechanism for enabling all the Middle Eastern churches to work together to counteract the challenges put in their way by the complexity of the Middle East – challenges relating to their existence, witness and indeed survival.

 Conclusion

Middle Eastern Christianity is an enduring and suffering Christianity. Its history is highly controversial and complicated; its present is very problematic; and its future is quite uncertain. The Ottoman Empire was but another Islamic regime that devastated and weakened Middle Eastern Christianity. With the defeat of the Ottomans and the dissolving of their empire, Christians hoped to enter an era of freedom, revival and prosperity. But the rise of Islamic fundamentalism and the counter-emergence of a kind of 'Christian fundamentalism', in the same region where Judaic fundamentalism also exists, makes the existence and mission of Middle Eastern churches very precarious. The huge decrease in the number of Christians due to mass emigration and a low birth-rate also presents its own challenges. Even so, it is difficult to imagine a Middle East without Christians.

 DISCUSSION QUESTIONS

1 What is meant by 'Chalcedonian' and 'non-Chalcedonian' churches?

2 Describe how the Eastern Latin or Eastern Catholic Church came into existence.

3 What was the impact of Islam on Middle Eastern Christianity during the second half of the first millennium AD?

4 Explain the following expressions:

    (a) *jizya*;

    (b) *dhimmi*;

    (c) patriarch;

    (d) catholicos.

5 What were the results of the Christian or Armenian Genocide?

6 Try to assess the impact of the Catholic and Protestant missionary work in the Middle East.

7 What are the main causes of the decrease in the number of Christians in the Middle East, and how can we stop this decrease?

Further reading

Badr, Habib (ed.). *Christianity: A history in the Middle East*. Beirut: Middle East Council of Churches, 2005.

Bailey, Betty Jane and Bailey, J. Martin. *Who Are the Christians in the Middle East?* Grand Rapids, MI: Eerdmans, 2003.

Lewis, Bernard. *The Middle East: A brief history of the last 2,000 years*. New York, NY: Scribner, 1995.

Mansel, Philip. *Constantinople: City of the world's desire, 1453–1924*. London: John Murray, 1995.

Scudder, Lewis R. *The Arabian Mission's Story: In search of Abraham's other son*. Grand Rapids, MI: Eerdmans, 1998.

10

The South Pacific

Hugh Morrison

 Introduction

Māori are the indigenous people of New Zealand, whose presence dates from the late thirteenth century CE. They are descended from Polynesians who migrated from South-East Asia across the Pacific. They had to adapt

South Pacific

to living on a larger land mass in a more temperate climate. Legends were one way by which they made sense of this new environment. Māori legends include the story of the demigod Maui. With his magical fish hook he pulled up a great fish (Te Ika a Maui) that is today's North Island of New Zealand. The work of geologists indicates that New Zealand, and the many islands of the Pacific, did rise up out of the sea. In effect the Pacific is a vast 'continent' of ocean dotted by land masses shaped by volcanoes and mountain-building. To the north and west lie the true continental 'islands' of Papua New Guinea and Australia. Modern humans came into this region between 60,000 and 30,000 years ago. They came first to the Australian and New Guinea land masses (joined during the Ice Ages and known as the continent of Sahul). Later people-groups moved in an eastwards direction as sea voyagers, through what we now know as Melanesia and Polynesia. They reached as far east as Easter Island by about 500 CE, and as far south as New Zealand no later than 1300 CE.

When the first Europeans entered the Pacific, from the early sixteenth century onwards, they encountered a wide range of Polynesian and Melanesian cultures and social structures. These societies incorporated indigenous religious systems of varying sophistication. Early missionaries and other Europeans did not always understand the religions they first encountered. To some, such as Wesleyan missionary James Stack, Māori religion, for example, seemed like a 'long round of absurdities'. Prolonged exposure and observation, however, led most to admit more correctly (such as John Davies in Tahiti) that 'these islanders are Religious people, and their religion (or if you please Superstition) influences all their affairs . . . everything they do'.

✳ Christian origins

European influences and Christianity moved into the Pacific from east to west, beginning with the sixteenth-century voyages of Magellan (1480–1521), Mendaña (1542–15) and Quirós (1565–1614). The earliest sustained influence was in the Spanish-dominated Philippines. To the south the Solomon Islands were the first island group to receive Roman Catholic explorers, with the first baptisms occurring by about 1606. Yet some of the more remote islands of this group were still being evangelized by Protestants and Catholics in the early 1900s.

In the modern era the earliest introduction of Christianity dated from about 1774, with a short-lived Franciscan mission to French Polynesia. The main thrust dated from the 1820s (see Table 1 for details). This 'arrival' is often popularly associated with European missionaries. British interest in the South Pacific was partly precipitated by the initial voyaging of Captain James Cook (1728–79) in 1768–71. Christian interest was further tied to the impact of eighteenth-century Pietism, evangelical awakening,

Table 1 The formal arrival of Christianity in named Pacific countries

Country/Territory	Formal Roman Catholic presence	Formal Protestant presence
Solomon Islands	1568	1849
Vanuatu	1606	1839
Mariana and Caroline Islands	1668	1852
French Polynesia	1774	1797
Australia	1820	1788
New Zealand	1838	1814
Hawaii	1827	1818
Cook Islands	1894	1821
Tonga	1842	1797 and 1822
Samoa	1845	1830
Fiji	1844	1830
Niue	?1842	1830
Wallis and Futuna Islands	1837	1835
New Caledonia and Loyalty Islands	1851	1840
New Guinea	1840s and 1882	1855
Tokelau	1861	1858
Kiribati and Nauru	Early 1880s	1857
Marshall Islands	1899	1857
Tuvalu	?	1861

Sources: Ian Breward, *A History of the Churches in Australasia* (Oxford: Oxford University Press, 2001); John Garrett, *To Live among the Stars: Christian origins in Oceania* (Geneva: WCC, 1982)

Enlightenment thinking and missionary enthusiasm in Europe. Protestant missionary societies such as the London Missionary Society (LMS) and Church Missionary Society (CMS), two of the earliest in the Pacific, were a direct product of such fervour and thinking.

In the Australian colonies, Protestant British chaplains, accompanying the convict settlers, first mediated Christianity from 1788. Their focus was on convicts and then on settlers, not on the Aborigines. Likewise Revd Samuel Marsden (1764–1838), colonial chaplain in Sydney, was Christianity's first official European ambassador to New Zealand in December 1814. In this case, however, Marsden's actions were prompted by direct contact with Māori in Sydney and in Britain, and marked the beginning of missionary work in New Zealand. Among others, the Marist Brothers, Picpus Fathers, the LMS, the CMS, American Congregationalists (ABCFM) and British Wesleyans were all instrumental in the introduction of Christianity to wider Polynesia, Melanesia and Micronesia.

European missionaries were not always the first to herald the Christian message or to mediate a Christian presence. While this was a marked feature of Protestant Christianity, the same was also true of Roman Catholic evangelization. Many Tahitian *katekita* (from the French *catéchiste*) such as Athanase Tuamea (b. 1837), in the Tuamoto group, were instrumental in taking Christianity to the scattered atolls of French Polynesia. The progress of the LMS provides representative evidence for the early transmission of Christianity by Pacific evangelists more than by European missionaries. Twenty-nine LMS British missionaries and their wives landed in Tahiti in March 1797. Prevailing ideas of missionary strategy, Tahitian suspicions, political manipulations and traditions of religion and culture all combined to hinder immediate 'progress'. The nucleus of a Tahitian 'church' had slowly emerged by 1815, nearly 20 years later. From that point the church was better organized by a second wave of LMS missionaries. Some of its Tahitian members took on the role of Christian missionaries to their own peoples and further abroad. The key person for this strategy was LMS missionary John Williams (1796–1839, killed on the island of Erromanga, Vanuatu).

Tahitians briefly introduced Christianity to Hawaii in 1818–19. More significantly such notables as Papeiha (d. 1867) and Vahapata (no date), from the island of Ra'iatea, went west to the Cook Islands in 1821. They predated the first European LMS missionaries to the Cooks by at least six years. Over the next decade Tahitian Christians were instrumental in the initial evangelization of Tonga, Samoa and Fiji. In turn, Cook Island and Samoan Protestant Christians were significant missionary vanguards to Samoa, Wallis and Futuna, Niue, Kiribati, Nauru, New Caledonia, the Loyalty Islands, the Solomon Islands and New Guinea over the course of the nineteenth century. This is not to say that European missionaries were absent, or that the Europeans were all ready to hand over church control to Polynesian or Melanesian Christians. Yet indigenous evangelization was one of the most important ways by which Christianity was ultimately accepted within Pacific communities. To the south a similar story unfolded in New Zealand. Māori also became pioneering evangelists among the many New Zealand tribes (*iwi*) in the 1830s, especially in the North Island. Various Roman Catholic and Protestant missionary societies then consolidated this process over the next two decades.

The LMS story indicates two things that occurred many times across the South Pacific. First, initial Christian evangelization of many parts of the Pacific often predated British, European and American colonization. At the same time, Christianity, colonization, commerce and Western culture were as inextricably related in the Pacific as in other parts of the non-Western world in the eighteenth and nineteenth centuries. Second, the early experience of the LMS in Tahiti also reflected a story commonly told in the early nineteenth century. Missions and missionaries, in their pioneering stages, were often dependent on local patronage and political circumstances for their initial survival and continuing presence.

 Oceanic Christianity

European migrations, capitalism and imperial rivalries transformed the Pacific region throughout the nineteenth and early twentieth centuries. Christianity arrived in a range of ways and progressed at varying rates. By the early 1900s Christianity had reached every land mass of the Pacific region, but not every part of those land masses. A 1930 survey indicated that just over 30 per cent of the region's population could be considered 'Christian', and that 60 per cent of these were Protestant. Apart from Australia and New Zealand, the island groups considered to be 'wholly evangelized' included French Polynesia, the Cooks, Samoa and Tonga. Yet New Guinea, Vanuatu (New Hebrides) and the Solomon Islands were still considered to be only 'partly evangelized'. In the case of Papua and New Guinea, with its complex mountain-and-valley landscape and tribal structures, evangelization has been a major feature of the era following the Second World War. By the late twentieth century, however, commentators regularly referred to Christianity as a Pacific religion, indicating the ways in which it has been seamlessly incorporated into a wide range of socio-cultural practices and structures across the region.

Pacific indigenous peoples encountered forms of Christianity that were introduced and mediated by Polynesian, Melanesian and European missionaries of both genders. The study of this process, in a range of settings, reveals that Christianity was accepted, rejected, adopted and adapted by local peoples in ways that were important for the region's emerging identity. Christianity often came in 'European clothing', depending on the country of origin. How it developed partly reflected these influences. Spanish or French Roman Catholic and Protestant influences were felt in territories such as French Polynesia, New Caledonia, the Mariana Islands and Nauru. Distinctive American or British Congregational and British Wesleyan Methodist structures emerged in Hawaii, the Cook Islands, Samoa, Tonga, Fiji, Niue, Kiribati, the Loyalty Islands and parts of the Caroline and Marshall Islands.

The situation was more complex among the Melanesian territories. Vanuatu and the Solomon Islands were sites of negotiated Wesleyan Methodist, Presbyterian and Anglican missions, from a mixture of Britain, Canada, Australia and New Zealand. From colonial New Zealand Bishop George Selwyn (1809–78) forged enduring Anglican links between the Solomon Islands, Australia and New Zealand with the formation of the Melanesian Mission (1847) and the Diocese of Melanesia (1861). Solomon Islands Protestant Christianity was also significantly influenced by the creation of the Queensland Kanaka Mission in 1886 (for Melanesian 'labourers' in Queensland, Australia) and of the South Seas Evangelical Mission in 1904 (which in 1975 became the independent South Seas Evangelical Church). Papua and New Guinea territories attracted all-comers, with a notable Dutch and German Protestant influence in the decades up to the First World War. Over the bulk of the twentieth century, Australian and New Zealand missions and churches were most prominent in their Papua and New Guinea involvement both before and after the birth of the independent nation of Papua New Guinea in 1975.

Christianity was partly a European 'import', along with disease, muskets, commerce, capitalism and cultural customs and conventions. But as an 'import' it was reshaped by its Pacific recipients in many different ways. It was not simply a belief system thrust upon unwilling and passive populations. John Garrett refers to 'each church distinct', wherein Pacific churches became marked by 'exceptional variety in local and denominational forms' (John Garrett, *To Live among the Stars: Christian origins in Oceania* (Geneva: WCC, 1982), p. 253). Two themes emerge that are useful to note for the historical development of these churches and groups through the nineteenth and twentieth centuries.

Indigenous ministry and leadership

The early Tahitian evangelists were the forerunners of many Polynesian teachers, preachers, pastors and catechists. For both Protestants and Catholics such an emphasis was a matter of both necessity and cultural expediency. There were simply not enough Europeans to cover the territory with the requisite linguistic and cultural skills. Protestant missionaries focused on the training of these evangelists. The LMS institute, established at Takamoa in the Cook Islands (1839), became something of a prototype of the initial Protestant strategy. LMS literature depicted this as a place that would educate 'a race of pastors and teachers for the native churches and of faithful Missionaries for the regions beyond them'. Residential training revolved around four years of biblical and doctrinal education, with an emphasis on preaching and school teaching. Similar Pacific institutions, such as Malua in Samoa (and the sister school at Papauta for women), later paved the way for training that aimed at producing and supporting indigenous church workers as well as evangelists.

The other Protestant strategy was to remove students to a neutral place of education. Between 1849 and 1867, under the Melanesian Mission, many Loyalty Islander, Melanesian and Māori male students went to St John's College in Auckland, New Zealand. Loneliness, illness and deaths contributed to the relative failure of this venture. In 1867 Anglican training was relocated to Norfolk Island. Its climate was warmer, but Melanesian students were still far-removed from their homes.

For Protestants the legacy of both training approaches remains. The former approach is represented by the strategic formation of leaders and thinkers offered at the Pacific Theological College in Suva, Fiji. The latter approach is represented by the continuing partnership that Auckland's St John's Anglican College has with churches across the south-west Pacific.

Indigenous catechists were also important in Roman Catholic spheres of activity. The Picpus Fathers established schools in Hawaii and French Polynesia during the 1830s and 1840s, with the hope that candidates for the priesthood might emerge. By the end of the 1800s only Tiripone Mama Taira Putairi (1846–81), from French Polynesia, had been ordained (1873). Marists under Bishop Pierre Bataillon (1810–77) responded to the call by Pope Gregory XVI (1765–1846), in his encyclical *Neminem profecto* (1845), to work towards an indigenous clergy. They established a seminary at Lano in the Wallis Islands in 1847. A second seminary was located at Kolopelu on Futuna Island. Lano was eventually developed into a boys' school. Various other attempts to train prospective priests included sending students to a seminary near Sydney, Australia, and taking them to Rome. All of these efforts were unsuccessful. A revival of Lano as a seminary from the 1870s led to the eventual ordination of four Wallis and Futuna priests in 1886, followed by ten more over the next decade. Earlier, in 1884, the first indigenous women religious were received into orders.

Over the course of the nineteenth and early twentieth centuries indigenous ministry did become more the norm and was integrated into the structures of Polynesian and Melanesian societies. However, an emphasis on training and on priestly formation did not immediately translate into indigenous ordination, ministry and leadership. Certainly it seems that this developed more easily for Protestants than for Roman Catholics, especially among the more egalitarian-minded LMS and Wesleyan Methodist churches. For example, in the Cook Islands, over 20 local men, known locally as *orometua* (teachers), served as unsupervised pastors by the 1850s. A number of these had sons who later also became pastors. Cook Island society respected oratory, and so preaching became the most important task of these leaders. By the early 1900s it had become the norm that Cook Island churches and their leaders would be financially self-supporting.

Late nineteenth-century racism and imperialism contributed to the slow relinquishment of power and oversight by European missionaries. In some Melanesian contexts autonomous indigenous leadership was often hindered by the attitudes of missionaries or by the view that ordained ministry could only be attained by formal, university-level education. Evangelists and teachers were valued but still not always respected on an equal footing. Presbyterian missionaries in Vanuatu, for instance, were still indecisive about indigenous leadership well into the 1900s. By 1900 there were significantly fewer ordained Roman Catholic indigenous priests than Protestant clergy. In some cases, as in Kiribati and Nauru, the first ordinations were not until the 1960s. In Melanesia the first indigenous Anglican bishops were appointed in 1963 (Solomon Islands) and 1979 (Vanuatu). Tonga's first Anglican bishop, Fine Halapua (1910–94), was not consecrated until 1967. At the same time, Pacific churches took a long time to allow women into church government. Significant changes for women did not happen until the 1960s, although such influential movements as the Anglican Mothers' Union had existed in some countries, for example Tonga, since the late 1950s.

Varied expressions of Pacific Christianity

The case of nineteenth-century French Polynesia typifies John Garret's broader notion of 'each church distinct' throughout the Pacific. Within a decade of the LMS churches launching out into Pacific-wide evangelization, the first cargo cult emerged in the form of the Mamaia Cult (Tahiti, 1826). Cargo cults were Melanesian movements that arose in response to European colonialism. They often revolved around a charismatic or prophetic figure, looked forward to a dramatic, other-worldly deliverance, and could be violent in nature while lacking political influence. The Mamaia Cult, for example, combined pre-Christian ecstatic religious behaviour with an expectation of Christ's imminent return, in reaction to the introduction of Christianity by the LMS. It spread and survived until 1841. Such movements emerged periodically among Pacific indigenous populations that simultaneously adopted Christianity and struggled with European colonialism or later Westernization.

From the 1830s Catholic priests and missionaries introduced a new form of Christianity. While this became the officially sanctioned form of Christianity in these islands, Roman Catholic Christianity did not always translate so easily into Tahitian cultural forms. French and British Evangelical Protestants were more successful. By the end of the nineteenth century, indigenous Protestants were singing hymns using traditional tunes and musical structures, and debating biblical texts in communal forums both inside and outside church buildings. Tahitian church business and liturgy were regularly expressed in the vernacular. As a result culture, language and chiefly virtues were preserved. On some islands, most notably in the Leeward, Tuamotu and Austral groups, this also resulted in a pronounced sense of Christian and cultural identity.

Throughout the nineteenth century Pacific adaptations of older Christian forms were commonplace. Under the influence of missionary James Chalmers (1841–1901), for instance, coconut milk became a substitute for 'wine' in communion services and local pastors were encouraged into ordained ministry. Sundays became a major cultural event and still are, both in the Cooks and for Cook Islanders now living in New Zealand and elsewhere. In Samoa, by 1900, the now prevailing pattern of local self-sustaining village churches was well established. In Tonga the Wesleyan Church was connected early on with royal approval and state identity. The breakaway Free Church of Tonga, formed amid political turmoil in 1885, was perhaps one of the first national indigenous churches in the Pacific region.

In Fiji, after 1879, both Roman Catholics and Protestants were perhaps the first Pacific Christian community to contend with religious pluralism, in the form of Hindu and Muslim indentured sugar-cane plantation labourers from India. In the many islands and dialects of Vanuatu, Presbyterian

Christianity provided a sense of identity, where Bislama (a variant of Pidgin) became the common language used by churches. By the end of the nineteenth century Roman Catholic and older Protestant churches were joined by a range of newcomers, namely the Latter Day Saints, the Churches of Christ and the Seventh-day Adventists. The full spectrum of Western Christianity, reshaped in a host of local environments, was evident across the Pacific.

During the twentieth century this process of growth and enculturation continued. Pacific Christians were now counted in terms of generations as well as numbers. Numerical growth was most evident in the valleys and mountains of Papua New Guinea and in many of the more remote Melanesian islands. By the 1970s such churches were self-sustaining, while training remained a partnership between local people and educators from Australia and New Zealand.

By then, Pentecostal churches and influences were also commonplace in the Pacific context. A well-documented revival among Evangelical Protestant churches in the Solomon Islands had a widespread impact on both local and Australian churches for the decade to follow. The long march to church self-determination finally reached its end in the 1960s and 1970s. At the same time, the influences on Christianity now came as much from North America (especially because of the war years) as from elsewhere – a trend that was also true for New Zealand and Australia. The latter two countries moved into a much closer relationship with the entire South Pacific after the First World War, when many territories were entrusted to them under a League of Nations mandate. Therefore the continuing relationship, working from dependency to self-determination, has been a close (and not always harmonious) one.

The creation of the World Council of Churches in 1948 was a strong motivator towards a sense of regional Christian identity and led to stronger connections between island churches and the wider world. This was expressed notably in the numbers of theological graduates completing further study in other countries before returning to local ministry. Similarly, Vatican II had a major impact on the indigenization of worship and liturgy, and helped to move Protestants and Catholics closer together. In 1966 the Episcopal Conference of the Pacific was fully accepted into membership of the Pacific Conference of Churches.

✳ New Zealand and Australian Christianity

Two Anglican English clergymen were the first people to officially introduce Christianity in the Australian and New Zealand colonies: Revd Richard Johnson in Sydney (1788) and Revd Samuel Marsden in the Bay of Islands (1814). In both sets of colonies parallel Christian 'streams' emerged – a missionary church and a British or European settler church. In Australia, ministry to convicts and then free settlers predated, by several decades, ministry

to Aborigines. In New Zealand, missions to Māori predated settler ministry and the two streams then coexisted until at least the turn of the nineteenth
and twentieth centuries, if not longer. There were many similarities between
the Australian and New Zealand stories. Traditionally, in this regard, historians have focused on two features.

The first is the supposedly 'secular' nature of settler societies. Low observed rates of church attendance, especially among the working classes
and males from the late 1800s onwards, have led many scholars to assume that Australians and New Zealanders were less religious than other
peoples. Steadily declining statistics of religious affiliation since the 1960s
have helped to cement this view. This assumption is now being seriously
questioned, as historians explore the nature of religious life at the local
and community levels. The second focus has been on the relationship between churches and the state. From early on, both sets of colonies rejected
the notion of an established state church such as the Church of England.
Governments sought to be fair to all denominations and to avoid the sectar-
ianism that divided British society. Arguments over the colonial government
providing some of Bishop Selwyn's salary, in the 1850s, perhaps forced a
wider split between church and state in New Zealand than in Australia. At
the same time, there was a general acceptance that both countries should be
'Christian societies'. Denominations and individual churches have played
an active role in negotiating with and challenging governments over a range
of social, economic and moral issues. Christians of all denominations have
been active and prominent as politicians and civic leaders, and in general
the churches were wholly in support of involvement in both the First and
Second World War. The following discussion of selective themes illustrates
some of the differences and similarities between the Australian and New
Zealand Christian stories.

Denominational patterns

Settler Christianity reflected its largely British origins in broad form, but
this differed with respect to such factors as geography, denomination and
the ethnicity of settlers. Australia was, until political federation in 1901, a
collection of self-governing colonies (later states). This, and its huge size,
continues to have an impact on politics, society and religion. New Zealand's
stretched-out geography initially encouraged a form of provincial government, but it was governed centrally from 1876. British Anglicanism was historically dominant in both countries (around 40 per cent of the population).

Roman Catholics were more important in Australia than in New Zealand,
and are now proportionally the largest Australian denomination. In both
countries the divide between Protestants and Catholics was most notice-
able between the late 1800s and the 1930s, and reflected political struggles
in Ireland. The trial of New Zealand Catholic bishop James Liston (1881–
1976), for alleged sedition in 1922, perhaps marked the height of this

tension. Presbyterians and Methodists were more numerically dominant in New Zealand than Australia. Due to post-1945 immigration, Orthodox churches grew substantially in Australia, with the Greek Orthodox being the largest community. An important Australian innovation was the creation of the Uniting Church of Australia (1977). This brought together churches from Congregational, Methodist and Presbyterian traditions, and made up about 10 per cent of the population by 1996.

Both countries also displayed distinctive geographical patterns. English Presbyterians were prominent in Victoria, and Scottish Presbyterians in southern New Zealand. German and Scandinavian Lutherans were to be found in Queensland, South Australia and Victoria. English Baptists were active and influential in such urban settings as Adelaide, Melbourne, Dunedin and Auckland. Baptist women from Adelaide, Dunedin and Christchurch were pioneering missionaries to eastern India from the early 1880s. Irish Roman Catholics were prominent in rural southern Queensland, Sydney and Melbourne, and on the west coast of New Zealand's South Island.

In the modern era the strength of 'denominationalism' has, to some extent, been diluted. This has been influenced by ecumenism, the Charismatic movement, the emergence of both Pentecostal and large metropolitan churches, and by social and political change. However, denominationalism was an important rallying point for nineteenth-century settlers, and became an important and enduring mark of identity. At times this was a fraught process. For example, New Zealand Presbyterians were split into two churches between 1866 and 1901 over theological and cultural disagreements. For smaller groups, such as Baptists and Open Brethren, denominational identity was one way of standing out in the new society. European ethnic distinctions became increasingly less important than overall denominational identity. At the same time, ethnically defined churches are now more prominent due to large-scale immigration, especially from East and South Asia. Today, there is a rediscovery of denominational identity by many older traditions as they face declining numbers and social influence.

Indigenous Christianity

Vigorous Māori Protestant and Roman Catholic churches already existed in New Zealand by the mid nineteenth century. The movement towards Christianity was marked by high levels of literacy and the same interest in the *mana* (power or prestige) of the written word displayed in other parts of the Pacific such as Hawaii and French Polynesia. In 1840 the Crown and Māori entered into a formal partnership by signing the Treaty of Waitangi. By this stage there was a definable Māori church with a New Testament and liturgies in the Māori language, indigenous preachers and catechists, and church buildings with elements of Māori architecture and design. By the 1850s a handful of Methodist and Anglican Māori had gone as missionaries to Tonga and the Loyalty Islands.

The tragic land wars of the 1860s reversed all of this. Conflict smouldered on through a number of one-off engagements between Māori and the Crown up to at least the First World War. Their net effect, among other things, was to diminish the goodwill of Māori towards Christianity and to set back progress by decades. Māori did not all abandon Christianity, even though large numbers left the Anglican, Methodist and Catholic churches. Most denominations, however, continued to treat Māori paternalistically as a focus for mission. The Latter Day Saints were particularly active as missionaries among Māori from 1881.

At the same time, these conflicts provided the opportunity for a number of distinctive Māori religious movements and communities to emerge. Most prominent among these were the Ringatu Church (1868), the peaceful communities of Parihaka (led by Te Whiti c.1830–1907) and Maungapohatu (led by Rua Kenana 1869–1937), and the Ratana Church (1918). These movements revolved around charismatic leaders and incorporated Christian elements, or redefined Christian theology in the light of injustices, illness and land deprivation. In the case of the Ratana Church there was an increasingly significant alliance forged with the Labour Party. Today, the support of the Ratana Church, as a major Māori Christian grouping, is sought by all main political parties. Commentators see some parallels between the Ratana story and the current popularity of the independent Destiny Church among many Māori, especially in its attempt to engage with modern social and political issues.

The rest of the twentieth century witnessed painfully slow progress towards Māori autonomy and power-sharing within church structures, including the ordination of clergy. Most progress was made after the mid 1970s, when the newly established Waitangi Tribunal began to seriously address Māori grievances through the political and judicial systems. The Anglican Church's separation into three self-governing bodies (Māori, Pacific Islander and Pākeha (European)) was indicative of wider forces at work for change in the last two decades of the twentieth century.

Australia did not witness the same potential for an early nineteenth-century indigenous Christian movement. Missions to Aborigines only began in the early 1830s, by which time the population had been seriously and deliberately decimated. This reflected a tragic mix of racism, land speculation and multiple cross-cultural misunderstandings. Various attempts by the 1840s to work sympathetically with Aborigines, by Wesleyan Methodists and Benedictines, signalled a more 'enlightened' approach. By the later nineteenth century this had broadened to missions and mission work in the south and east of Australia, conducted by the Moravians and Presbyterians, among others. Faith missions such as the United Aborigines Mission and the Aborigines Inland Mission modelled a more 'incarnational' approach, but their particular style and theology did little to advance the Christian cause among Aborigines. At the same time, churches and missions were both involved and implicated in the longer-term separation of

Aboriginal children from their families and localities, now referred to as the 'stolen generations'.

From the early twentieth century a succession of Catholic, Anglican and Methodist missions targeted the Aborigine communities that were more isolated from white populations. Their impact may have been greater due to this factor, and therefore more successful in fostering indigenous forms of Christianity. Aborigine ministry to Aborigine people was also slow to develop. Moses Uraiakuraia (1869–1954), an evangelist among the Aranda people of Central Australia in the early 1900s, was an isolated early example. By the 1930s and 1940s there were sporadic signs that white Australian mission workers understood the importance of finding Aborigine forms of Christian faith and expression. It took until at least the 1970s for this to be more fully accepted. Between 1964 and 1975 most of the main denominations began to accept Aborigines into ordained ministry.

The Charismatic movement and Pentecostal growth of the 1960s and 1970s coincided with significant revival or renewal movements among Aborigines. In hindsight this may have been more successful in propelling many Aborigine communities towards accepting Christianity because it encouraged expressions of worship and theology which had deep cultural resonances. The Mabo land-title case in 1992, and the declaration of a national apology to Aborigine peoples by the new Labour Government of Australia in 2008 (both of which had Christian influences), are signs of a new future for Aborigines within their homeland.

The role of women

Women and men were equally prominent in colonial Christianity from the beginning, but were not always equal in terms of leadership and public ministry. Women such as Marianne Williams (1793–1879, CMS, New Zealand) and Janet Matthews (1849–1939, Wesleyan Methodist, Australia) accompanied their missionary husbands and were expected to fulfil domestic roles. But they were more than simply 'missionary companions'. They were effective, busy and often independent missionaries in their own right, working with women and children and more particularly as teachers. In the later-nineteenth-century Australian context, such women were possibly responsible for mitigating some of the impact of European colonialism on Aborigine communities. In both sets of colonies the wives of clergy exercised important ministries, and were often strategically significant in public and private. From the late 1800s onwards hundreds of Protestant women, single and married, were active as missionaries (at home and abroad) and as deaconesses. Many more were involved in unheralded civic and church charitable work, in social welfare activism and reform, and in political campaigns for alcohol prohibition, votes for women, social morality and women's health.

Catholic women religious also had an early presence. A number of British and European nuns, for example, accompanied Bishop Pompallier (1802–71) back to New Zealand in 1848. Such women wielded an important influence within indigenous and settler communities alike, through locally founded orders, including the Sisters of St Joseph, of Mercy, and of Compassion. The educational work of Sister Mary MacKillop (1842–1901) in Australia among deprived children, and the efforts of Sister Suzanne Aubert (1835–1926) among Māori and New Zealand's urban poor, are well-known and representative examples of the broad impact of these groups. Mary MacKillop was canonized in 2010 and is now formally referred to as St Mary of the Cross MacKillop.

On both sides of the Tasman Sea women were often the mainstay of institutional, organized religion. Yet it took a long time for this to translate into equality for women within the churches. A paradox existed for a number of decades from the 1880s onwards. Australasian women missionaries overseas exercised roles and leadership that were often equivalent to those of ordained clergy. Meanwhile, their counterparts at home were barred from participating in synods, assemblies or presbyteries, and from ordained preaching and ministry roles. From the 1880s women were preaching and leading within the Salvation Army. By the 1950s in New Zealand, there were a handful of ordained women in Congregational, Assemblies of God and Methodist churches. However, they were the exception and not the rule. In both countries women were not admitted to bodies of church government until at least the 1920s. To be a Protestant deaconess or a Catholic religious was the closest that women could come to being ordained until the 1960s.

The fundamental social and cultural upheavals of the 1960s and 1970s, and second-wave feminism in particular, contributed to significant change. The ordination of women in Presbyterian and Anglican churches occurred first in New Zealand from the 1960s and 1970s and later, in the 1980s and 1990s, in Australia. Revd Dr Penny Jamieson (b. 1942) became the first Anglican woman bishop worldwide, appointed to the Diocese of Dunedin, New Zealand, in 1989. At the same time, women, ordained or not, have also been prominent in church leadership in both ecumenical groups and in church aid or development agencies.

While ordained ministry still remains out of touch for Catholic and Orthodox women, their roles and place within church and community remain important. The Vatican II reforms of the 1960s have been both burden and blessing in this regard. Women religious are declining in numbers, and the lack of formal vestments means that they are not so publicly obvious as in earlier decades. Yet they continue to play important social and community roles, to be influential through all levels of education, and to provide valuable guidance to Christians of all denominations and genders through retreat centres and as spiritual directors. The involvement of lay women in Catholic public worship is now commonplace.

A changing environment

Up until about the 1970s churches and Christian organizations were fundamentally important social and cultural institutions in the Australian and New Zealand contexts. Church buildings and facilities were valuable community resources in scattered rural areas, and a focus for community activities everywhere. Holiday seasons such as Christmas, New Year and Easter have been shaped and reshaped, in the colonial context, by the various denominational and ethnic traditions. In the 1950s and 1960s the 'baby boom' period witnessed the growth of city suburbs. To meet this demand there was a large programme of suburban church-building. The visit of American evangelist Billy Graham to both countries in 1959 marked the height of this optimism and growth. Generations of Australian and New Zealand children went to Sunday school and Bible class, attended their first Mass, took part enthusiastically in summer camps, attended church schools or interacted with clergy through weekly 'Bible in Schools' lessons (in state schools).

This has not always translated into adult participation in church services, especially for Australian or New Zealand men. Yet there is evidence that contact with churches in childhood did much to foster a set of ethical guidelines for public and private adult life. Ecumenical and Evangelical groupings, such as the Student Christian Movement, the Young Women's and Young Men's Christian Associations, Scripture Union, the Catholic Youth Movement and university-based Evangelical Unions were incubators for young and emerging church, political and community leaders. International movements, for example Youth for Christ and Youth with a Mission, were adapted to local circumstances to meet the changing social and cultural environment from the 1960s onwards. Each has catered for Australasian young people across the socio-economic spectrum, particularly among those not attending church.

Within churches the Charismatic movement and emerging Pentecostal-style groups also sought to respond to the changing environment. They may not ultimately add greatly to the Christian population of both countries. Yet they have helped to forge a loose form of ecumenism, and have introduced a greater informality to liturgy, worship and Eucharist. In particular, Protestants and Catholics have been brought closer together at the local level for worship and community involvement.

✳ South Pacific Christianity at the turn of the millennium

The Pacific region's share of both world and Christian population has never been huge. Modern statistics, however, suggest that it is a region that represents broader trends in the worlds of both the North and the South.

Steady but unspectacular growth in the numbers of Christians since the late twentieth century has mirrored that of North America. Numbers, however, are only part of the story. Pacific Christianity is vastly complex, and defies simple description or quantification. As elsewhere, it is both a 'transplanted' and a 'translated' religion, one that reflects the social and cultural complexities within which it is embedded. It is a mature religion, in that it is inhabited by several generations of indigenous members and leaders, and marked by a considerable depth of contextualized theological reflection.

Nevertheless, Christians and churches of the Pacific region face a host of environmental, economic, political and social issues that are no less complex than in other places. The Pacific is a truly globalized region, touched by the ravages of war (both international and local) and faced with acute issues of sustainability and growth. Its resources are much sought after by larger competing countries and multinational companies. What happens in the rest of the world happens in the Pacific, to greater or lesser extents. Because churches and culture are so intertwined in this region, these challenges are as much for the Church as they are for wider society. At the same time, one of the consequences of modernization has been to downplay the role and significance of religion, especially in the more Westernized south-west Pacific. The region as a whole needs to face the future together. Communities of faith still have a strategic role to play in moving towards that future.

? DISCUSSION QUESTIONS

1 To what extent was the evangelization of the South Pacific due more to indigenous evangelists than to European missionaries?

2 Compare and contrast the impact of Roman Catholic and Protestant Christianity across the various Pacific Island groups.

3 From your wider reading, why do you think European Christians throughout the Pacific (including Australia and New Zealand) took so long to develop indigenous leadership and churches?

4 To what extent did Christianity develop in the same way or differently in New Zealand and Australia?

5 How and why have the roles and place of women within churches and society changed in different parts of the Pacific region?

6 How have churches responded to widespread social and economic change since the Second World War and to what extent have they been a positive social influence?

7 To what extent do you think that Christianity has become a truly Pacific religion?

8 Compare and contrast the nineteenth- and twentieth-century development of Christianity in the Pacific with one other region you have studied in this volume.

Further reading

Breward, Ian. *A History of the Churches in Australasia*. Oxford: Oxford University Press, 2001.

Davidson, Allan. *Christianity in Aotearoa: A history of church and society in New Zealand*. Wellington: Education for Ministry, 2004.

Davidson, Allan (ed.). *Tongan Anglicans 1902–2002: From the Church of England mission in Tonga to the Tongan Anglican Church*. Auckland: College of the Diocese of Tonga, 2002.

Davidson, Allan K. and Lineham, Peter J. *Transplanted Christianity: Documents illustrating aspects of New Zealand church history*, 2nd edn. Palmerston North: Dunmore Press, 1989.

Emilsen, Susan and Emilsen, William W. (eds). *Mapping the Landscape: Essays in Australian and New Zealand Christianity*. New York, NY: Peter Lang, 2000.

Ernst, Manfred (ed.). *Globalization and the Re-shaping of Christianity in the Pacific Islands*. Suva: Pacific Theological College, 2006.

Garrett, John. *To Live among the Stars: Christian origins in Oceania*. Geneva: WCC, 1982.

Hutchinson, M. and Treloar, G. (eds). *This Gospel Shall Be Preached: Essays on the Australian contribution to world missions*. Sydney: Centre for the Study of Australian Christianity, 1998.

Lake, Meredith. *The Bible in Australia: A cultural history*. Sydney: NewSouth Publishing, 2018.

Lange, Raeburn. *Island Ministers: Indigenous leadership in nineteenth century Pacific Islands Christianity*. Canberra: Pandanus Books, 2005.

Lineham, Peter J. *Sunday Best: How the Church shaped New Zealand and New Zealand shaped the Church*. Auckland: Massey University Press, 2017.

Morrison, H., Paterson, L., Knowles, B. and Rae, M. (eds). *Mana Maori and Christianity*. Wellington: Huia Publishers, 2012.

Piggin, Stuart. *Spirit of a Nation: The story of Australia's Christian heritage*. Sydney: Strand Publishing, 2004.

Ross, Kenneth R., Tahaafe-Williams, Katalina and Johnson, Todd M. (eds). *Christianity in Oceania*. Edinburgh: Edinburgh University Press, 2021.

11

Pentecostal and Charismatic movements

Allan H. Anderson

 Historical overview

The significant changes in global Christianity during the twentieth century are in no small part due to the emergence of Pentecostalism. From being a predominantly European and American religion in the early twentieth century, not only has Christianity shifted southwards but it has also fundamentally changed in character. When Pentecostalism began in the first decade of the twentieth century there were several revival movements occurring in several parts of the world, the most notable being in Wales, Estonia, India, the USA and Korea. The Welsh Revival (1904–5) created worldwide expectations, especially among missionaries, that a Holy Spirit revival would sweep over the world before the imminent return of Christ. These revivals were accompanied by ecstatic phenomena, and those most significant for Pentecostalism were prophecy, healing and speaking in tongues.

The Welsh Revival emphasized the Pentecostal presence and power of the Spirit, as meetings were long, spontaneous, seemingly chaotic and emotional, focusing on the immediacy of God in the services and in personal experience. This revival was declared to be the end-time Pentecost of Acts 2, the 'latter rain' promised by biblical prophets that would result in a worldwide turning to God. These ideas were continued in other revival movements. Pentecostal-like movements had been known in South India since 1860, when speaking in tongues and other manifestations of the Spirit's presence were reported. In 1905 revivals broke out in North-East India where Welsh Presbyterian missionaries were working and at Pandita Ramabai's Mukti Mission in Pune near Mumbai, where speaking in tongues and other ecstatic phenomena occurred. This revival, which lasted two years, spread to various parts of India, and Mukti Mission became an international centre for the spread of Pentecostalism. The 'Korean Pentecost' of 1907–8 commenced at a Presbyterian convention in Pyongyang and soon spread throughout Korea, and was likened by eyewitnesses to the Day of Pentecost (see Acts 2).

All these revivals were characterized by emotional repentance with loud weeping and simultaneous praying and had the effect of creating an air of expectancy and longing for revival in many parts of the evangelical world. The signs that this revival had come would be based on the earlier reports: an intense desire to pray, emotional confession of sins, manifestations of the coming of the Spirit, successful and accelerated evangelism, and spiritual gifts to confirm that the Spirit had come. This coming of the Spirit was linked to a belief that the last days had arrived and that the gospel would be preached to all nations on earth before the imminent return of Christ. The stage was set for the coming of a new Pentecost to spread across the world in the new (twentieth) century.

The Azusa Street Revival in Los Angeles (1906–9) was the most significant dynamo for scores of early Pentecostal missionaries fanning out all over the world with the new message of Pentecost. Its African American leader William Joseph Seymour (1870–1922) had been invited to Los Angeles in 1906 to a small Holiness church, but it was locked against him after he preached that the phenomenon of 'tongues' was the sign of Spirit baptism. People continued meeting Seymour for prayer in a private house, where several individuals, including Seymour, received Spirit baptism. Within a week this rapidly growing group moved into a former African Methodist Episcopal church building on Azusa Street, where daily meetings, spontaneous and emotional, without planned programmes or speakers, commenced in the morning and usually lasted until late at night. Singing in tongues and people falling to the ground 'under the power' or 'slain in the Spirit' were common phenomena.

The racial integration in these meetings was unique at that time and Seymour led a fully integrated leadership team. Seymour became the spiritual leader of thousands of early Pentecostals as he directed the most prominent centre of Pentecostalism for the next three years, further promoted by his periodical, *The Apostolic Faith*. Visitors came to be baptized in the Spirit, and many of these began Pentecostal centres in other cities. Under Seymour the Apostolic Faith movement took on international dimensions, and from 1906 onwards Pentecostal missionaries began to migrate to various parts of the globe, reaching some 25 nations within two years. By 1926, only two decades after the revivals that had given birth to the movement, hundreds of Pentecostal missionaries were found in at least 42 countries outside North America and Europe.

In the second decade of the twentieth century, these movements expanded in various parts of Asia, Latin America and sub-Saharan Africa. The result of the opposition to these new emphases by established denominations and churches was the emergence of various forms of independent churches in the 1910s and 1920s, most of which were motivated by eschatological expectations about the imminent second coming of Christ and were characterized by emphases on healing and exorcisms, speaking in tongues and prophecy.

These independent churches were small at this stage and were marginalized by the established churches. They were mostly of a Pentecostal type, and those that emerged in the North were eventually known as 'classical Pentecostal' churches. In Africa the 'Spirit churches' emerged at the same time, often intersecting with 'classical Pentecostal' churches and missionaries; and in China and India as well as in other parts of Asia the same intersection formed independent churches that were mainly Pentecostal and biblical literalist in character. Pentecostalism soon suffered from many schisms and formed several new denominations and associations during the early years of the century. By 1930 there were several different kinds, including Holiness Pentecostals, 'Finished Work' Pentecostals, 'Oneness' (non-Trinitarian) Pentecostals, and a myriad of independent churches in several parts of the world that did not have Western origins, the most notable being in Africa and China.

The Charismatic movement

At various stages in the twentieth century these independent Pentecostal churches also interacted with older churches, leading to the development of Charismatic movements (Pentecostal expressions and practices in the older non-Pentecostal churches or denominations). This happened, for example, in France and South Africa in the 1930s and 1940s, and in North America in the 1950s. It was the birth of the 'Charismatic movement' in the Episcopalian Church in Southern California in 1960, however, that had the greatest impact on the older churches, and Charismatic renewal broke out in Catholic circles among American students in 1967. But these events were the culmination rather than the commencement of a movement that had already existed for decades. The commencement of Pentecostalism in Europe, the revivals in India, the 'Korean Pentecost' in the Presbyterian and Methodist churches, and the Pentecostal revival among Methodists in Chile at the beginning of the twentieth century were in fact 'Charismatic' and ecumenical movements in the established churches.

Several significant influences prior to 1960 helped change the attitude of older churches to the Pentecostal experience. Most notable were the independent healing evangelists who operated independently of classical Pentecostal denominations and through whom Christians outside these denominations were exposed to Pentecostal experience. The Full Gospel Business Men's Fellowship International, organized by Demos Shakarian (1913–93) in 1951, with the backing of mass healing evangelist Oral Roberts, brought the Pentecostal experience to laymen and introduced the healing evangelists to them. Meanwhile, South African David du Plessis (1905–87) travelled around the world from 1951 as a spokesperson for Pentecostalism in ecumenical circles and brought many 'mainline' church people into the Pentecostal experience.

Several ministers received Spirit baptism in these churches in the 1940s and 1950s and promoted spiritual renewal thereafter. One of the best known is Dennis Bennett (1917–91), Episcopalian rector of St Mark's Episcopal Church in Van Nuys (suburban Los Angeles), who, along with some of his members, received Spirit baptism in November 1959. Bennett testified to his experience in a Sunday sermon in April 1960 and was asked to resign. Many regard this event as the beginning of the Charismatic movement. The movement spread to most older denominations.

An important feature of the Charismatic movement in the early 1970s was the theological reflection made in publications by Catholic scholars, placing the movement firmly within Catholic tradition. The Catholic Charismatic movement spread in Europe to include significant communities in France, Belgium, Italy, Spain, Portugal, Hungary, Czechoslovakia and Poland, and is especially strong in India (perhaps five million) and in the Philippines (perhaps 11 million). In Kerala, India, Father Mathew Naickomparambil (1947–2021) led weekly healing and evangelism meetings that drew crowds of 15,000 and hosted conferences of 200,000. The Catholic Charismatic movement of El Shaddai in the Philippines led by layman Mike Velarde (b. 1939) is the largest of all these national Charismatic movements with some seven million members. By 2000 there were an estimated 120 million Catholic Charismatics, representing about 11 per cent of all Catholics worldwide and almost twice the number of classical Pentecostals combined. This remarkable achievement probably stemmed the tide of the exodus from the Catholic Church into classical Pentecostalism.

During the 1970s and 1980s, tensions between 'Charismatic' and 'traditional' groups within these older churches eventually led to the formation of more new independent churches. As the Charismatic movement began to decline in the late 1970s, new 'non-denominational' movements with much weaker links to older churches began to emerge. The 'restoration' movement emphasized house groups and 'radical' discipleship, while the 'Word of Faith' movement, with a major stress on prosperity and healing by faith, arose in North America. The latter, also known as 'positive confession', the 'faith message', the 'prosperity gospel' or the 'health and wealth' movement, is thought to have originated in early Pentecostalism and been influenced by Baptist pastor E. W. Kenyon (1867–1948). Kenyon taught the 'positive confession of the Word of God' and a 'law of faith' that works by predetermined divine principles.

The development of the prosperity gospel movement was also stimulated by the teachings of Pentecostal healing evangelists and the Charismatic movement. Its essence is that health, wealth and success are promised to the one who has faith. By 2000 this was a prominent teaching in many churches globally. Its leading North American exponents have been Kenneth Hagin (1917–2003) of Tulsa, Oklahoma (widely regarded as the 'father of the Faith Movement'), and Kenneth Copeland (b. 1936) of Fort Worth, Texas, among many others. Preachers in other parts of the world have propounded a modified form of this teaching to suit their own contexts, and such figures as David Paul Yonggi Cho (1936–2021) in South Korea, David Oyedepo (b. 1954) in Nigeria, Sunday Adelaja (b. 1967) in Ukraine and Edir Macedo (b. 1945) in Brazil have presided over megachurches with an emphasis on faith and prosperity.

Associations of different kinds of independent churches were formed, soon the fastest-growing Charismatic movements in the English-speaking world, becoming hundreds of independent global networks. Some of these became megachurches which today tend to occupy centre stage in discussions about global Pentecostalism.

✳ Understanding the concepts and numbers

Today, the proliferation and variety of global Pentecostalism is bewildering, and some attempt will be made here to make some sense of this by defining the terms we use. Broadly speaking, we may speak of 'Pentecostalism' as an umbrella term referring to movements and churches with a 'family resemblance' that emphasize the work of the Holy Spirit in the life of the believer. 'Pentecostal churches', 'the Charismatic movement' and 'independent churches', however, will have a more limited definition. After discussing the meaning of the terms, the chapter will look specifically at theological definitions and conclude with a recommended classification for understanding global Pentecostalism.

Defining Pentecostalism

Knowing more precisely what we mean by the term 'Pentecostalism' is very important, even if such precision is elusive. Indeed, is a label such as 'Pentecostalism', which emerged at the beginning of the twentieth century, an altogether appropriate term to use today for this global movement? It is probably more correct to speak of 'Pentecostalisms' in the contemporary context, even though the singular form will continue to be used to describe these movements as a whole. The task of defining any religious phenomenon is often necessary and useful; at the same time, fixed definitions can be inadequate and misleading. This is because definitions depend on which range of criteria is applied. Furthermore, such criteria are always subjective or arbitrary, and differences may not be perceived as significant by the movements themselves on which these criteria are imposed. There is also the possibility of overlooking differences that may be quite important to church members. 'Insider' and 'outsider' views always create such differences of viewpoint. The phenomenon of Pentecostalism is, however, much more complex than any neat categorizing will allow.

Pentecostalism began as a restoration or revitalization movement at the beginning of the twentieth century among radical Evangelicals and their missionaries, who were expecting a worldwide Holy Spirit revival before the imminent coming of Christ. The fundamental conviction of these early

Pentecostals was that, before the expected end-time disastrous events, the 'old-time power' of the Acts of the Apostles would be restored to the Church and 'signs and wonders' would enable the Christian gospel to be preached rapidly all over the world. The message travelled quickly as its messengers used the new steamship and rail networks and spread out into a world dominated by Western colonial powers.

As the world of the twentieth century lurched through two devastating world wars that created disillusionment with Western 'civilization' and the colonial empires crumbled, Pentecostalism changed with it. Like other forms of Christianity, Pentecostalism saw itself not as a form of Christianity imported from the West, but one of many national and international initiatives. By the end of the century it had developed thousands of local varieties ranging from urban megachurches comprising thousands of worshippers, high-tech equipment and sophisticated organizations to remote village house churches meeting in secret with only a handful of believers.

Pentecostal churches meet in living rooms, classrooms and rudimentarily constructed shelters as well as in enormous buildings. Pentecostal churches are found among all classes and ethnic categories, Western or Northern churches, Eastern and Southern churches, and urban and rural churches. All these churches show a variety of theological positions, many are fundamentalist (they emphasize fundamental or traditional principles and oppose modernism), but a few are liberal; and there are churches that combine several of these types and positions. Pentecostalism today is fundamentally and dominantly a global phenomenon. Its significant growth in North America and Europe occurs today among Hispanics, Africans, Asians and other minorities. More than three quarters of its members in the world today are not 'white', and this proportion continues to increase. In recent years, Pentecostalism has expanded most remarkably in sub-Saharan Africa, the Asian Pacific rim and especially Latin America, where the growth has been so significant that some countries, for example Guatemala, are now on the verge of having a Protestant majority.

Many opulent buildings holding thousands of worshippers reflect an emerging Pentecostal middle class in the cities of Africa, Asia and Latin America. Nevertheless, most Pentecostals belong to a grassroots movement appealing initially to the disadvantaged and underprivileged, whose desire for upward social mobility is nurtured and sometimes realized by what Pentecostalism offers. Many, if not most, of the rapidly growing Christian churches in the Majority World are Pentecostal in nature and operate independently of Western Pentecostalism.

The globalization of various kinds of Pentecostalism is a fact of our time. Large independent Pentecostal communities with no connections to older forms of Pentecostalism sprang up in many parts of the world, especially after the 1970s. They often formed international networks and loose associations, which have occasionally been organized into new denominations.

In the Majority World these are often the fastest-growing sections of Christianity and appeal especially to the younger, better-educated urban population. Some of these churches propagate a 'prosperity gospel' which seems to reproduce the worst forms of consumer capitalism in Christian guise. Some scholars have suggested that this is a form of 'Americanization', but there is also the danger of generalizing and failing to appreciate reconstructions and innovations made by Pentecostals in adapting to a very different social context.

Pentecostal and Charismatic Christianity in all its diversity (both inside and outside the older churches) was probably the fastest-expanding religious movement worldwide in the twentieth century. According to somewhat debatable statistics, it had well over half a billion adherents by the end of the century, a quarter of the world's Christian population, but much depends on what is included in such figures. The statistics are considerably inflated by including such large movements as African and Chinese independent churches and Catholic Charismatics. But even if these figures are inaccurate and overinflated, no observer of Christianity can deny the significance of Pentecostalism in today's global religious landscape. Considering that this movement had a minuscule number of adherents at the beginning of the twentieth century, it has been an astounding achievement.

The many varieties of Pentecostalism have contributed to the transformation of the nature of global religion itself and this has enormous implications. Its adherents are usually on the cutting edge of the encounter with people of other faiths, often confrontationally so. The future of Christianity is affected by this seismic change in the character of the global Christian faith – a change that some have referred to as its 'Pentecostalization'.

Although the term 'Pentecostalism' is now widely used by scholars of religion and most of them assume they know what it means, the term has been used to embrace churches as widely diverse as the celibacy-practising Ceylon Pentecostal Mission, the seventh-day Sabbath-keeping True Jesus Church in China with a 'Oneness' theology (explained below), the enormous, uniform-wearing, ritualistic Zion Christian Church in southern Africa, and Brazil's equally enormous and ritualistic, prosperity-oriented Universal Church of the Kingdom of God. These are put together with the Assemblies of God, various Churches of God, the Catholic Charismatic movement, 'neo-Charismatic' independent churches with prosperity and 'Word of Faith' theologies, the 'Third Wave' Evangelical movement with its use of spiritual gifts framed within a theology that does not posit a subsequent experience of Spirit baptism, and many other forms of Charismatic Christianity as diverse as Christianity itself. Clearly, such a widely inclusive definition is problematic and leads to wild speculations about the extent of the movement. Some Pentecostal scholars tend to use certain generalized statistics as proof of the numerical strength of their particular form of Pentecostalism.

Theological aspects

If we are to understand this global movement, we must include its more re-cent and often most public expressions in the independent, Charismatic and neo-Charismatic movements. Despite the seeming diversity within global Pentecostalism, the movement has 'family resemblances', certain universal features and beliefs throughout its many manifestations, most of which emerged in the early twentieth century. These churches embrace a form of Christianity where spiritual gifts such as speaking in tongues, prophecy and healing are widely practised and where services are usually both emotional and entertaining. Many of these churches allow participation in the services by any member of the congregation, and actively responding to the preacher with cries of 'Amen' and 'Hallelujah', dancing and singing enthusiastically and sharing in simultaneous prayer are encouraged. Although this is not at all a homogeneous movement, and acknowledging their very significant dif-ferences, the thousands of different denominations and movements show-ing the above features could all be described as 'Pentecostal' in character, theology and ethos.

There are dangers, however, in making theological definitions that tend to consider all forms of Pentecostalism as essentially the same, and even though, in most forms of Pentecostalism, experience and practice are usu-ally more important than dogmatic formulations, these experiences and practices also often differ and one cannot find a description that will fit all types. For example, Pentecostals often define themselves theologically in terms of the doctrine of the 'initial evidence' of speaking in tongues – the belief that speaking in tongues is the 'initial evidence' of Spirit baptism – which in the North sometimes separates 'classical Pentecostals' from 'Charismatics'. Yet Pentecostalism is more correctly seen in a much broader context where it is regarded as a movement or movements concerned pri-marily with the experience of the working of the Holy Spirit and the prac-tice of spiritual gifts. Although this definition is quite broad, it is a useful starting point.

On one hand, the word 'Pentecostal' is derived from the Day of Pentecost experience at the birth of the early Church. Acts 2.4 is probably the most important distinguishing 'proof text' in classical Pentecostalism, as the verse describes how the disciples in Jerusalem were 'filled with the Holy Spirit and began to speak in other tongues as the Spirit enabled them' (NIV). This experience of being 'filled' or 'baptized' with the Holy Spirit is what dis-tinguishes these Pentecostals, in their own opinion, from most others. But there is a difference between Pentecostalism in its first generation and that in the second – and it is usually in the third generation that a revitalization movement arises promoting 'revival', which often has a different emphasis from that of the first or second generation. In later forms of Pentecostalism this so-called 'distinguishing' doctrine is given less prominence; in fact, the insistence on 'tongues' is often absent and certainly of relatively minor significance. In any case, many contemporary Pentecostal churches seldom use speaking in tongues in public worship.

On the other hand, one can discern certain theological criteria for defining what Pentecostalism is. One of the earliest attempts to do this was made by the Swiss theologian Walter Hollenweger (*Pentecostalism: Origins and developments worldwide* (Peabody, MA: Hendrickson, 1997), pp. 18–19). He considered that the growth of Pentecostalism had taken place not because of adherence to a particular doctrine but because of its roots in the spirituality of nineteenth-century African American slave religion. In his well-known analysis, he outlines the main features of this spirituality to include an oral liturgy and a narrative theology and witness, maximum participation of the whole community in worship and service, visions and dreams in public worship, and an understanding of the relationship between the body and the mind manifested by healing through prayer.

The thousands of Spirit churches throughout Africa and the various house churches in China are 'Pentecostal' movements in this sense, where the features outlined by Hollenweger have persisted, although their form of Christianity is often quite different from Western forms of Pentecostalism. Hollenweger argues that the essence of Pentecostalism is found in its oral nature and that one should look for a founding figure who best represents that characteristic. He concludes that the founder is William Seymour (with his background in African American spirituality) and his Azusa Street Revival. His characteristics of this spirituality, mentioned above, constitute his theological criteria. We could also argue that the identity of Pentecostalism could be found in its 'glocalization' – that combination of a global meta-culture with a certain local particularity. The Pentecostal family resemblance transcends locality and denominational loyalty and displays striking similarities in different parts of the world. The vast majority of Pentecostals are situated in places where local cultural characteristics are resilient in the face of globalization, and where local perceptions are often very different from those found in Western contexts.

Some classical Pentecostal theologians see a distinction between themselves and 'Charismatics' and make charges of 'syncretism' against those closest to them in theology and history, such as the African independent Spirit churches. 'Syncretism' is not always a pejorative word, and Pentecostalism is permeated by syncretism of all kinds: from a mixture of American capitalism and the 'success' ethos of the Western world, to the shamanistic cultures of the East and the South. There are indeed substantial differences between classical Pentecostals and other Pentecostals and Charismatics; basic to my presentation is an emphasis on variety and difference. I would argue that even within classical Pentecostalism itself (sometimes within the same Pentecostal denomination) there are also fundamental differences, such as those between classical Pentecostals and Charismatics. For example, the eschatological emphasis of early Pentecostals that is still found in Latin America is no longer such a prominent feature of Western classical Pentecostalism.

The modern 'prosperity theology' that suggests that God's favour leads believers to experience success, prosperity and health is not really a stranger or newcomer to classical Pentecostalism's history. It may have mutated, but its themes go back to early healing evangelists and are implicit in much of its 'holistic' approach to Christian life. In many developing countries of the world this message is often attractive because it gives people hope in what are otherwise desperate economic and social conditions. But there are also far more commonalities between these different groups than there are differences; there are essential emphases common to all that distinguish them from the rest of Christianity; and these commonalities justify such an inclusive definition.

Pentecostals claim, as do many other confessing Christians, that their experiences are the result of encounters with God. There will always be religious or 'mystical' reasons given for people joining or continuing to adhere to religious movements, and Pentecostalism is no exception. An 'outsider' approach to studying Pentecostalism might exclude the possibility of a non-physical realm of reality, or what Pentecostals believe is the presence of the Holy Spirit in their experience. Acknowledging this non-physical reality in Pentecostal experience will better ensure that a theological approach to global Pentecostalism will have integrity and transparency. So, however we use the term 'Pentecostal', it has to be inclusive enough. This inclusive theological approach will avert both hasty generalizations and overlook obvious differences. In referring to many different kinds of churches as 'Pentecostal', we neither overlook their distinct character in liturgy, in healing practices and particularly in their different approaches to religion and culture nor ignore their unique contribution to Christianity in a broader global context.

✳ Different forms of Pentecostalism

Hollenweger's threefold classification of global Pentecostalism into classical Pentecostals, the Charismatic renewal movement, and Pentecostal or 'Pentecostal-like' independent churches is a useful starting point. To these three groups I will add another. Although no working definition answers all the objections or altogether avoids generalizations, parameters acceptable to most can at least be set. Using a narrower theological definition such as 'initial evidence', 'speaking in tongues' or even 'baptism in the Spirit' is fraught with difficulties when there are exceptions all over the world, even in the case of those who can indirectly trace their origins to the USA, such as in most forms of European classical Pentecostalism. Similarly, a historical definition that depends on established links alone is difficult to maintain in the plethora of different mutations of Pentecostalism worldwide.

Although we must resist any simple definition in such a diverse movement, a multidisciplinary definition of Pentecostalism will not rely exclusively on theological dogma, cultural characteristics or historical precedent. Situating Pentecostalism within the broad framework of those movements and churches whose main emphasis is the experience of the working of the Holy Spirit and the practice of spiritual gifts may be a satisfactory way of dealing with the problem of overly narrow theological definitions.

Within this inclusive definition in terms of an emphasis on the Spirit and spiritual gifts, a broad taxonomy of global Pentecostalism can be further divided into at least four overlapping types, each with its own family resemblance. These include the following, each with its own subtypes:

1 Classical Pentecostals

Belonging to this group are those whose roots can be traced back to the early twentieth-century revival and missionary movements. Theologically, these have been divided into (a) Holiness Pentecostals, with roots in the nineteenth-century Holiness movement and a belief in a second work of grace called 'sanctification'; (b) Baptistic or 'Finished Work' Pentecostals, who differ in their approach to sanctification, seeing it as an outgrowth from conversion; and from the latter stem, (c) Oneness Pentecostals, who reject the doctrine of the Trinity and posit a Unitarianism that includes the deity of Christ; and (d) Apostolic Pentecostals, both Oneness and Trinitarian, who emphasize the authority of present-day 'apostles' and 'prophets'. These categories apply mostly to Western-originating Pentecostals, and the last one includes the significant number of West African Apostolic Pentecostals influenced by the British Apostolic Church. All of these groups have a theology of a subsequent experience of Spirit baptism usually accompanied by speaking in tongues.

2 Older church Charismatics

These include Roman Catholic Charismatics, Anglican Charismatics and Protestant Charismatics. In other words, they belong to movements that remain in established older churches, are widespread and worldwide and often approach the subject of Spirit baptism and spiritual gifts from a sacramental perspective. In some countries, for example France, Nigeria, Brazil and the Philippines, they constitute a significant percentage of the Christian population.

3 Older independent and Spirit churches

These are commonly found in China, India and sub-Saharan Africa and may or may not have historical ties with classical Pentecostalism. These churches do not always have a clearly defined theology or necessarily see themselves as 'Pentecostal', but their practices of healing, prayer and spiritual gifts are decidedly so. They are referred to in the literature by many different terms.

Here I rely on the continent I know best, Africa, where these churches can be grouped together as (a) African churches of the Spirit, although they are known by a plethora of names. In southern Africa there are Zionists and Apostolics, 'Zion-type' and 'Spirit-type' churches; in West Africa 'spiritual', 'prophet-healing' and Aladura (prayer) churches; and in East Africa they include 'Pentecostal' and 'spiritual' churches. Most prefer to be known as 'churches of the Spirit'. Some observers feel that these churches should be separated from Pentecostal ones because of the relative enormity of this African phenomenon. Others in 'classical Pentecostalism' in the West try to distance themselves from churches they pejoratively view as 'syncretistic'. When looked at from a global perspective, however, this tends to blur the Pentecostal identity of these churches and obscure common characteristics and historical links. The various terms used to describe these churches also suggest that at least they are *inclined* to be Pentecostal. These churches are indeed, says Harvey Cox, 'the African expression of the worldwide Pentecostal movement' (*Fire from Heaven: The rise of Pentecostal spirituality and the reshaping of religion in the twenty-first century* (Reading, MA: Perseus, 1995), p. 246), and scholars increasingly recognize their Pentecostal character, as do the churches themselves.

In China, independent churches that arose in the early twentieth century are known as (b) 'Old Three-Self' churches; and (c) many other independent Pentecostal churches emerged in Asia and Latin America from the 1920s to the 1960s.

4 Neo-Pentecostal and neo-Charismatic churches

These have arisen since the 1970s and are often regarded as 'Charismatic' independent churches. They include megachurches and consist of various kinds: (a) 'Word of Faith' churches and similar churches where the emphasis is on physical health and material prosperity through faith; (b) 'Third Wave' churches, who usually conflate Spirit baptism with conversion and see spiritual gifts as available to every believer; (c) new Apostolic churches, who have reintroduced an apostolic leadership to their governance not unlike that of the earlier Apostolic Pentecostals; and (d) probably the largest and most widespread group, consisting of many other different independent churches that vary considerably in their theology between 'Third Wave', 'Word of Faith' and 'classical Pentecostal', and are therefore difficult to categorize.

Some of the churches in the 'neo-' or 'new church' category are among the largest Pentecostal churches in the world, including the Brazilian Universal Church of the Kingdom of God and the Nigerian Redeemed Christian Church of God, whose widespread use of the media and public relations is becoming a defining characteristic. It should also be noted that 'neo-Pentecostal' is a fluid term that has been used in various ways over the past 50 years, at one stage referring to older church Charismatics (see 2, above), later to independent Charismatic churches, then to 'Third Wave' churches, and more recently to a wide range of newer independent Pentecostal churches that embrace contemporary cultures, use fashionable methods of communication, media and marketing, form international networks or 'ministries', and often have a 'prosperity' emphasis.

Pentecostalism has quickly become a non-Western, Majority World church movement. With its offer of the power of the Spirit to all, regardless of education, language, race, class or gender, it emerged as a mission movement that subverted the conventions of the time. Its methods were not so dependent on Western specialists and trained clergy and the transmission of Western forms of Christian liturgy and leadership. Within less than a century, Pentecostal and Charismatic Christianity in all its diversity has expanded into almost every country on earth. By the twenty-first century, Pentecostalism in its many forms has become extremely significant both inside and outside the older 'historic' churches and probably ranks as the fastest-growing religious movement of the twentieth century.

? DISCUSSION QUESTIONS

1 Discuss the relationship between revivalism and Pentecostalism.

2 The Azusa Street Revival is often considered the beginning of the Pentecostal movement. Is this a fair historical assessment?

3 What is the difference between 'classical Pentecostalism' and the 'Charismatic movement'? How has this distinction changed in recent years?

4 What forms of Pentecostalism are you familiar with in your area?

5 Describe how some Pentecostal groups view others as syncretistic. Explain why you support or challenge this evaluation.

6 What criteria can be used in defining Pentecostalism?

Further reading

Anderson, A. H. *An Introduction to Pentecostalism: Global Charismatic Christianity*, 2nd edn. New York, NY: Cambridge University Press, 2014.

Anderson, A. H. *To the Ends of the Earth: Pentecostalism and the transformation of world Christianity*. New York, NY: Oxford University Press, 2013.

Cox, H. *Fire from Heaven: The rise of Pentecostal spirituality and the reshaping of religion in the twenty-first century*. Reading, MA: Perseus, 1995.

Hollenweger, W. *Pentecostalism: Origins and developments worldwide*. Peabody, MA: Hendrickson, 1997.

Martin, D. *Pentecostalism: The world their parish*. Oxford: Blackwell, 2002.

Miller, D. and Yamamori, T. *Global Pentecostalism: The new face of Christian social engagement*. Berkeley, CA: University of California Press, 2007.

Robeck, C. *Azusa Street Mission and Revival*. Nashville, TN: Thomas Nelson, 2006.

Wilkinson, M., Au, C. and Haustein, J. (eds). *Brill's Encyclopedia of Global Pentecostalism*. Leiden: Brill, 2021.

Afterword: Towards world Christian history

Angus Crichton

The previous chapters have described Christian history across six continents and through two centuries. A large number of individuals and Christian groups have been encountered. Some have pointed towards God's reign of justice and righteousness, while others have obscured this reign; some have done both. At first glance, this appears to be a series of separate regional narratives, isolated from one another by boundaries of sea, sand or geographic convention, mirrored in the separate chapters here. And yet attentive readers will note connections between the regional narratives that cross these boundaries. Seas become highways of exchange, as people, publications, commodities, ideas and beliefs move from the western side of Africa to the Americas and back. The Eurasian Steppe is no longer a barrier but criss-crossed with Silk Roads between the Eastern Mediterranean and East China Sea. Globalization is not a late-twentieth-century reality. Indeed the Christian faith has been a global phenomenon from the beginning; it depends whether one follows the story only westwards from Jerusalem, or eastwards and southwards as well.

Intercontinental connections

Some of these intercontinental connections are so well documented that they have become commonplace. Agents of the European and North American missionary movement described on page 15 reappear in most other chapters as authors recount the introduction of Christianity into their particular region. This missionary movement was a smaller part of an extensive migration of Europeans to every other continent, starting in the sixteenth century and tailing off by the middle of the twentieth century. Missionaries were but one category of exported European, alongside government and military officials, traders, settlers, convicts, refugees, explorers and adventurers. However, as the regional histories repeatedly demonstrate, these European and North American missionary agents were not the sole actors in the propagation of Christianity, nor was their understanding of

Christianity accepted by converts in its entirety. Furthermore, the frequent entanglement of these agents with Euro-American political, military and/ or economic power generated complex, contrasting and confusing legacies for the churches in other regions. These themes will be considered in more detail below.

Less well known is the movement of non-European Christian agents who similarly transmitted the faith between continents. Unlike their European counterparts, missionary intent was seldom the primary motive for moving. However, intent does not guarantee missionary effectiveness, nor was it a luxury available to these agents. This was most obviously the case for the enforced removal of 10 to 12 million Africans to the Americas, with the high-water mark of this ravaging falling within our time period. Some of those enslaved came from the well-established Christian communities of the Kingdom of Kongo in what is now Angola, while others received limited instruction and baptism to satisfy papal injunctions in Portuguese slaving centres such as São Tomé, Cape Verde and Luanda. On both sides of the Atlantic, African catechists were key in translating European catechetical instruction into the relevant central African language, including identifying African linguistic equivalents for important theological words, above all the name for God. In South America, they reproduced Christian associations that they had known in the Kingdom of Kongo. These associations not only sustained their faith but also resisted slavery by purchasing the release of their members, supporting them in their initial steps of freedom and by appealing to Iberian monarchs against injustices. The roots of the earliest Christian communities in the Caribbean and North America stretch across the ocean to Kongo (p. 153). The military backbone of the mid-eighteenth-century slave revolt in Stono, South Carolina, was provided by Kongolese Christian soldiers familiar with the use of firearms. As these communities grew, they developed their own distinctive appropriations of Christianity, combining both liberative readings of biblical texts to sustain resistance to slavery and predominantly oral, expressive forms of Christianity within their own congregations beyond the plantation's control (p. 154). African Christian communities in the Americas then sent missionary and political impulses back to the African continent: the founding of Sierra Leone (pp. 27–8); the ministries of Jamaican Christians in Akropong (p. 30); Brazilians led by Pa Antonio in Lagos (p. 31); and Thomas Freeman on the Gold Coast (p. 30). The African renewal movements of Ethiopianism and Zionism (pp. 55–9) developed in conversation with Christian communities of African descent in North America. This included ideological underpinnings in the development of black consciousness on both sides of the Atlantic, ecclesiastical connections, the inspirational role of African-American educational institutions that emphasized practical training (pp. 51–2), as well as the exchange of personnel. In this first regard, Edward Wilmot Blyden (1832–1912), from the Caribbean and resident in West Africa since the 1850s, produced a series of highly influential publications on both sides of the Atlantic that expounded the dignity of African peoples against European racism.

Some have seen the origins of American Pentecostalism in the spiritual-ity of these African communities in the Americas (p. 227, a movement that transformed world Christianity during the twentieth century (Chapter 11), while also acknowledging that some Pentecostal expressions of Christianity across the world have diverse roots unconnected with Azusa Street. Christians of African descent, either directly from the continent (pp. 63–4) or via the Caribbean (pp. 157–8), had by the end of the twentieth century moved to Europe in significant numbers with a missionary vision for what has for them become 'the Dark Continent'. In doing so, they are following in the footsteps of their nineteenth-century ancestors such as the Sierra Leonean merchant James Wilhelm (d. *c.* 1863), who had a profound impact on Henry Venn, leading him to formulate the three-selfs strategy (pp. 15, 29); or the Calabar-born John Jea (b. 1773) who, after childhood enslavement and teenage emancipation, became a travelling preacher not just along America's eastern seaboard but also in England and Ireland, before settling in south-ern England's seafaring city of Portsmouth, where he continued his ministry. It was the increased volume rather than the actual movement of African Christians to Europe that was noteworthy by the end of the twentieth century.

Even less well known are connections between the east coast of Africa and the Asian subcontinent. Some of the first Protestant churches on the East African coast were planted by 'Bombay Africans' (pp. 39–40): Africans from the interior who were enslaved, rescued off slaving dhows and settled in communities in India, from where they returned to Africa to pioneer early Protestant settlements outside Mombasa. It was 'Bombay Africans' such as William Jones, Ismael Semler and David George who provided the continu-ity of pastoral oversight for these communities. In contrast, the ministries of their European counterparts were more fragmented due to sickness, home leave and moral failure. These men were the first East Africans to be ordained into the Anglican Church in 1885. The growing British imperial presence in East Africa built on millennia-old connections between these two continents as personnel were moved within a single imperial system. Indian Muslim soldiers brought in to put down the 1897 rebellion in Uganda against the incoming British were intrigued by the Ganda soldiers they camped along-side, who each night gathered around camp fires to read the Scriptures and to pray. On their return to Quetta, these men from the Bombay Infantry Regiments asked for their own copies of the Bible to read.

From the 1870s Goan Catholics migrated from the west coast of India to East Africa, seeking new opportunities by starting businesses, becom-ing clerks for the incoming British colonial administration and continuing their long-standing roles as sailors and cooks. The Roman Catholic church of Christ the King in the centre of Kampala was built originally to meet their needs. The first benefactors who helped to pay for the plot of land and support the ministry of the priest bore the names Norman Godinho

(1886–1952), Francis Almeida and Eugene Pinto (*fl.* 1920s–1930s), pointing back to the encounter between Portuguese missionaries and Goans in the sixteenth century. The *gomesi*, the national dress for Ugandan women, was created by the Goan tailor Anton Gomes (d. 1928), fusing elements of the Ganda *suuka*, Indian *sari* and British women's fashions for use at the first Anglican high school for girls in Uganda.

Connections between East Africa and India were also forged through publications that represented Christians in one continent to another, just as publications circulated Blyden's ideas widely on both sides of the Atlantic. When the Anglican Christians of Tinnevelly in South India heard about the martyrdom of Baganda Christians in 1886 (pp. 41–2), their clergyman Jesudasen John (d. 1899) sent a letter to the Ganda church. He compared the 125-year history of his own church with that of the 'infant church' in Buganda:

> But as we look back on the past, our Church lacks the bright crown which so justly belongs to your Church as martyrs for the faith in a loving Saviour, whose gospel reached you only a short time ago, and whom, having not seen, you have loved even unto death. We wish you, dear Christian brethren, to feel assured of our sympathy with you in your severe trails for 'when one member suffers all members suffer with it.' We gladly send you our little assistance through the Committee of the Church Missionary Society, to help you as they think best.
>
> (*Church Missionary Intelligencer* (April 1887), p. 254)

The 'little assistance' was a collection of £80, equivalent to £4,000 in today's money, which the Baganda Christians determined to repay. Collections for the Ganda Christians were also taken up in Norfolk Island in the Pacific and Shantou in China. The spiritual experiences of the Indian evangelist V. D. David (1853–1923), presented in pamphlet form and read by a British missionary in Uganda, lit the fires of revival that sent out Ganda evangelists across what became Uganda and launched one of the great African mass movements into the Christian faith (pp. 42–3). Yet this movement of Ganda evangelists was driven as much by political and social factors as by the impulse to share this new-found Christian faith; indeed the 'secular' and 'sacred' are indivisible in such a context.

We are only starting to see the profound interconnections of people, publications, ideas and institutions that occurred not just between Europe–North America and other continents but between and within all continents whose histories feature within this volume. Time and space does not allow us to tell of Indian Christians ministering in nineteenth-century Guyana or of the ministry of the Korean Church to the Korean diaspora in northeast Asia and North America at the start of the twentieth century, which laid the foundations for a missionary movement that today is second only to the United States in sending missionaries overseas. The Christian faith invariably uses pre-existing networks that allow for the exchange of goods, peoples and ideas. If we shift our focus of enquiry away from European and

North American agents, we encounter Christians from every continent willingly or under compulsion, in their person or represented in publications, moving both within and beyond their region, and as they travel, carrying their Christian faith with them.

✳ Intercontinental themes

The attentive reader will also notice that certain themes reoccur across the chapters. While the starting point may be similar across regions, themes unfold in contrasting as well as comparable ways. These chapters, taken together, testify not just to connections across continents by the movement of Christian agents but to shared and contrasting trajectories in both the appropriation and the rejection of the Christian faith. This exercise of discerning broad themes carries with it a real danger of reducing the complex and diverse Christian appropriations on an entire continent to bland summary sentences. Yet without this attempt, we struggle to see the interconnections and so the richness of the tapestry which is greater than nine discrete regional narratives. I have selected but four themes; other topics for consideration could be ecumenism, gender and sexuality, inter-religious encounter, migration, persecution or social justice. Attentive readers will discover other themes within the chapters and continue to mine their own histories for what is significant for them.

1 The centrality of indigenous agents

At every turn in the expansion of Christianity beyond its nineteenth-century heartlands of Europe and North America, indigenous agents have been at the forefront. In some instances, indigenous Christians preceded Western missionary agents: Korea is a notable example (pp. 84–5), but also Sierra Leone (pp. 27–8) and Myanmar among the Karen (p. 119). In other instances, the latter were playing catch-up to the former, such as in Uganda (pp. 41–3). Pentecostalism, all too easily depicted as rippling out from a single Azusa Street centre, actually possessed multiple centres in different regions and periods (pp. 219–20), and so is one of the most profound examples of indigenous agency and appropriation in this period. Missionaries were too few in number, too scattered, too hampered by illness, cultural and linguistic alienation, and colonial entanglements to occupy the centre stage alone, despite that position been given to them by a tsunami of missionary society publications and subsequent histories. The statistics in Table 2 are eloquent testimony to this: contrasting categories of Anglican personnel in one African country on the eve of British colonialism at the high-water mark of the Western missionary movement.

Again the sole missionary translator of the Bible is a myth: the former was deeply dependent on indigenous agents (such as Liang Fa and Wang Tao in

Table 2 CMS European missionaries and African Christians in Uganda 1877–1907

Year	European missionaries	African clergy	African lay teachers	African Christians	Communicants	Scholars
1877	9	–	–	–	–	–
1882	14	–	–	7	–	81
1887	3	–	–	300	50	–
1892	13	–	36	3,400	120	400
1897	43	10	521	14,457	3,343	742
1902	82	27	2,199	38,844	11,145	12,861
1907	104	30	2,036	65,433	18,078	32,393

Source: Figures taken from statistical returns in *CMS Annual Proceedings*

China (p. 69)), first to learn the language and second to translate. The chapters above have given space to naming these agents and documenting their contribution, including, as well as men, notable women such as Gaudencia Aoko (p. 58), Chun Sam-deok (p. 87), Cecilia Nalube (p. 54) and Pandita Ramabai (p. 101).

Some of these agents were employed by Western missionary societies, and upon their shoulders rested the bulk of evangelistic advance and pastoral nurture under missionary supervision. Most Africans heard of Christ from other Africans: Rebecca Nkwebe Alibatafudde (*fl.* 1880s) saw a European missionary for the first time when she went to seek baptism in 1886. Her entire instruction in literacy, and in Christian faith and practice (including silent prayer), and indeed her supply of precious Christian literature, came from other Baganda Christians. Others, often on the fringes of missionary Christianity, in response to a divine call and authorization, charted an independent course. This then gave them the freedom to explore the frontier between the Christian faith and pre-existing belief systems (see below). The results were sometimes spectacular. Numbered among them are individuals such as William Wadé Harris (p. 57), Gil Seon-ju (p. 88), Felix Manalo (p. 126), Ni Tosheng (p. 74), Kawai Shinsui (p. 81) and Te Whiti (p. 213). Much of indigenous Pentecostalism has followed in their footsteps, although often not always acknowledging this debt, seeking similar outcomes by different means. However, the most shadowy group of indigenous agents consists of those who moved for reasons other than their faith: to trade, to seek a better life, to find employment opportunities – and even those who were moved against their will through enslavement. As they went, they either took their Christian faith with them and shared it in a new land or encountered this new faith there and carried it elsewhere. Perhaps it was only at the end of the twentieth century, as we recognized the significance of migrating missionaries (pp. 63–4, 157–8), that we became more attuned to their presence in other periods (pp. 162–3, 234–6) and therefore able to grasp that the 'professional', fully funded missionary is the product of a particular period of Christian history. Tragically, in the Middle East, such migrations have led to the emptying of the region's Christian populations as believers have fled systematic persecution and chronic instability (p. 187).

2 The significance of pre-existing religious systems in Christianity's reception

Conversion to Christianity is more revising or reordering, less replacing, the maps by which we navigate our way through both seen and unseen worlds. In the prelude to conversion, significant features on the map may no longer work in practice: we are becoming functionally agnostic as the old gods are weighed on the scales and found wanting. Drought cannot be turned aside by time-honoured specialists, cycles of witchcraft accusations have decimated social cohesion, the slaughtered cattle did not rise. New powers and new opportunities have emerged on our horizon, sometimes associated with incoming Christian agents: literacy, guns and political power (Buganda, p. 41), employment (China, p. 72), liberation from oppressive politico-religious systems (India, pp. 96–8). Pursuit of these new opportunities and this new faith together is completely reasonable if a major function of religious systems is to bring this-worldly blessing and protection. Such perspectives suggest that conversion to Christianity rarely erases the prior belief system, despite the best efforts of some of its missionaries. Instead maps are revised and reordered, often in ways that only become clearer in subsequent generations, leading to distinct and diverse appropriations of the Christian faith across the regions under consideration in this volume. At its most basic, there never was and certainly is not now a 'one-size-fits-all' approach to the Christian faith. At the same time, these diverse appropriations share Christian elements common to all; maps do not remain completely unchanged by conversion. However, the extent of change is often generational, as the significance of Christianity to the pre-existing elements becomes more defined through the forging of Christian responses to specific, local concerns.

During the period of these chapters, indigenous religions have proved the most fertile ground for appropriating Christianity (different words have been used to describe these religions, including 'ethnic', 'primal' or 'traditional'). In Asia, while Hinduism was revived by its encounter with missionary Christianity (p. 94), 'advasis' (tribal groups) of north-east India offered a spectacular contrast (pp. 99–100). A similar pattern can be traced among the Hmong (p. 122), Isan (pp. 117–18) and Karen (p. 119) in comparison to their uninterested Buddhist neighbours, among Indonesian tribal peoples and in comparison to the majority Islamic population (p. 130). However, this has been most pronounced with practitioners of indigenous religions in sub-Saharan Africa and Oceania. The use of indigenous names for God in translations of the Bible opened up a dialogue between the Christian faith and indigenous religions. In that conversation, the 'high god' component is often expanded, while the mediators between the former and humans are substantially reimagined away from divinities, ancestors, spirits and objects of power towards Jesus and lesser intermediaries such as Mary and the saints – Protestants were at a distinct disadvantage here. Yet the needs petitioners took to these intermediaries did not cease with Christian conversion: fertility, healing from sickness, prosperity, protection from malign spiritual and temporal forces, social harmony. It is little wonder that the rains of Independency and Pentecostalism fell on such fertile soil after the drought of Enlightenment-shaped missionary Christianity, which in comparison offered so few crossing places between the seen and unseen worlds.

A similar trend can be observed where conversion has occurred from one of the other 'world' religions to Christianity. The need to honour one's parents beyond as well as before the grave does not evaporate for Chinese or Korean Christians shaped by their Confucian heritage (pp. 68, 87). The very cultural and ethnic diversity of the Caribbean has produced 'blended' belief systems such as Rastafarianism, Santeria and Voodoo (pp. 153, 156–7). Former samurai took their devotion to their feudal lord, their high ethical ideals and their fraternal solidarity into their Christian bands that spread out to both evangelize and reform Japanese society (pp. 79–80). While some outcomes from Hong Xiuquan's Taipings were disastrous, this was a radical reading of the Christian Scriptures using indigenous categories that Western missionaries overlooked, with equally problematic consequences in the following century (pp. 70–1).

Relating their faith to their rich and millennia-long cultural and religious heritages has become a central concern for Christians across the southern continents, going to the heart of their identities (see below). A similar question now must be faced in the new wastelands of historic European and Australasian Christendom. How and where are shafts of light to be found in the wider non-Christian culture that is indifferent to metaphysical formulations but holds cherished notions of 'belief', for example in relationships of affection? Just as the early converts in the south discerned, all is not pagan darkness and night. To the first Baganda converts, biblical verses sounded strangely familiar, echoing proverbial wisdom taught by their mothers and grandmothers by the fireside at night, down through the generations.

While conversion to Christianity from among the practitioners of indigenous religions has been stratospheric in the period, among other world religions it scarcely got off the ground. The pre-existing religious systems of Buddhism, Hinduism and Islam have largely rejected attempts at Christian conversion. Due to colonial entanglements, Christian missionaries were often in positions of relative power in relation to practitioners of both world and indigenous religions. Indeed these entanglements either revived, protected or provoked these world religions (see below). It also led to converts being labelled 'rice Christians' (induced to convert to Christianity because of openings to power, p. 98). Yet this label overlooked the converts' active choice to leave a religious system which barred them from socio-economic and cultural benefits for one that did, although they faced similar challenges within the Church (pp. 105–6). The period witnessed greater conversion from those of Confucian heritage, with Korea a notable example and to a lesser extent China (Chapter 4).

Even among the indigenous peoples of North America and Australia, whose belief systems have strong parallels to those in Africa and Oceania, Christianity has made little progress (pp. 213–14). In Russia (pp. 169–70) and China (pp. 73–4), Marx, not Christ, emerged as the saviour to lead the masses out of oppression. Further westwards in Europe, intellectual and cultural seeds present in 1800 gradually flourished into widespread indifference to religions (pp. 19–20), with Christianity's prior monopoly singling it out as an obvious target, alongside the perceived 'otherness' of Islam. What were the heartlands of the faith at the start of our period now seem more the new wastelands, yet even here faith-communities stubbornly remain. In short, gains have balanced out losses in the face of global population growth, so that the portion of the world that is Christian in 2000 is about where it was in 1900 (pp. 4–6). As these chapters demonstrate, we prefer to focus on conversion to rather than rejection of the Christian faith.

In other regions, the issue was one of intra- rather than inter-religious dialogue. In 1800 Christian communities in north-east Africa, Europe, the Middle East and Asia could trace their origins back into the first millennium. During the next 200 years, they encountered incoming Christian communities who practised the faith in very different ways from them. Of these, Pentecostal Christians comprised perhaps the single largest and most widespread group (ch. 11 and sections of all other chapters), although Pentecostalism can also be understood as the latest Christian chapter in the primordial human religious quest to leverage unseen powers for temporal transformation. Sometimes these interactions were characterized by hostility, even persecution, particularly if the host community was in the majority and/or could use state resources against the incomers (pp. 138, 166–7, 169, 171, 189); sometimes ancient communities embraced reform and revitalization in the face of defections to incoming groups (pp. 27, 167, 196). By the end of the twentieth century, the world was in the midst of a profound period of intra-Christian encounter as Christians from the burgeoning churches of the southern continents migrated northwards to cooler geographic, spiritual and ecclesiastical climates (pp. 63–4).

3 The relationship between Christianity and state power

At the start of our period, the prevalent mode for church–state relations was Christendom: the understanding that a territory and its people are Christian, with the state supporting and being supported in this settlement, although its precise nature varied from country to country, often as a result of the Reformation. This Christian territory stretched from the Atlantic to the Bering Strait, with a precursor in Ethiopia and its final manifestation in Latin America and the Philippines. While the United States was created consciously rejecting the command economy of the European established churches for free-market volunteerism (p. 14), it still retained the underlying Christian territorial identity and a comparable sense of 'manifest destiny' (the belief that white Americans were ordained by God to extend their control across North America). The same could be said of Australasia (p. 211). At the end of our period, Christendom had not been replicated in the faith's new southern heartlands, nor sustained in the old heartlands of the north.

Unlike in Latin America, European powers were unable to pursue the Christendom option as they moved eastwards. Here, their relatively small numbers were dwarfed by the scale of the continents and populations that were home to a diversity of cultures and religions more ancient than theirs. The presence of zealous missionaries evangelizing local populations was bad for commerce and for colonial rule, particularly of the indirect kind. Therefore European trading organizations such as the Dutch and British East India companies initially kept missionaries out of the areas where they operated (pp. 92, 130), as did plantation owners on their estates in the Caribbean (p. 154). Christian preaching either sparked religious tensions or encouraged liberative aspirations. Paradoxically, European commercial and political ventures in Africa, Asia and the Caribbean separated Christianity from Christendom, much to the frustration of missionary enthusiasts both on the ground and back home. The East India Company's practice of taxing religious sites in its territory for their security and upkeep led it to be labelled 'the church-warden of Juggernaut' and the 'dry-nurse of Vishnu', essentially an accusation of company-sponsored Hinduism (John W. Kaye, *Christianity in India* (London: Smith, Elder & Co., 1859), pp. 381, 385). Britain actively kept Christian missionaries out of northern Nigeria (p. 32) and in northern Sudan both supported Islamic institutions and forbade Christian missionaries from evangelizing Muslims.

After the break-up of the Ottoman Empire in 1920 the Dutch ruled over the largest Muslim empire in the world. Only occasionally did anything approaching Christendom emerge, such as the Wesleyan Church in Tonga (p. 209) or the Anglican Church in Buganda (p. 43), while the enduring Christendom of Ethiopia predates that of Europe (pp. 26ff., 47ff.). In most instances the plurality of faiths and identities, particularly within states whose only unity lay in the minds of their colonial creators, rendered the Christendom option unworkable in practice. The Philippines and Latin America are the great exceptions, although even here the state-supporting/ed Catholic Church has seen significant competitors emerge, particularly of the Pentecostal kind (Chapters 6 and 7).

In regions where missionaries were seen more as a help than a hindrance, the relationship between colonial and ecclesiastical authorities was far from straightforward. While missionary societies benefited from colonial subsidies for their social service provision, and colonial governments got healthcare and education for indigenous populations on the cheap (p. 50ff.), the former persistently complained the provision was not enough and resented the latter's introduction of a parallel secularized system, often as a result of the inadequacies of missionary provision (pp. 51–2). Colonial authorities were frequently irritated by missionary special pleading for causes close to their heart, such as Christian marriage legislation that failed to embrace local realities, alongside their vocal support for indigenous populations in the face of oppressive colonial policies. The marriage between European colonial governments and Western missionaries was one that failed to live up to expectations on both sides.

Yet from an indigenous perspective, it was so close a union that it was hard to discern where colonial power ended and missionary influence started. Missionary access to the interior of China rode on the coattails of the country's enforced opening up through Western political and military violence (p. 69). The early, promising movement of the Māori to Christianity was soured by the land wars that received support from some missionaries in the name of civilizing mission (pp. 212–13). Most Japanese churches supported their government's imperial ambitions and so introduced Japanese expressions of Christianity in Japanese imperial territories (p. 82), making indigenous expressions of Christianity tantamount to resistance (e.g. in Korea, p. 88). As a result, in China (p. 73), India (pp. 102–3) and Indonesia (p. 130), while Christians actively participated in political independence movements, the historic ties between their faith and Western colonialism led some nationalists to question Christians' commitment to the national project (pp. 73–4, 109, 130). Ironically, colonial-sponsored mission schools became incubators for nationalist leaders (p. 60). Mission-sponsored modernizing was enthusiastically taken up by Chinese (p. 73) and Indian nationalists (pp. 95–6), while leaving Jesus behind. As indigenous Christians encountered overbearing European rule within their churches, they voted with their feet, using independency (pp. 55ff., 74, 80–1, 126, 213) as an instrument to fashion churches for themselves. Reuben Spartas Mukasa (1899–1982), founder of a Ugandan independent church, summed up the aspirations of such movements: 'a church established for all right-thinking Africans, men who wish to be free in their own house, not always being thought of as boys' (quoted in F. W. Welbourn, *East African Rebels* (London: SCM Press, 1961), p. 81). Here, Christian believers experienced the freedom to forge identities free from European colonization of consciousness.

Western missionary entanglements with European colonial power bequeathed a damaging legacy to Christians in Africa, Asia, the Caribbean, the Middle East and Oceania. Despite this legacy, Christians emerged into a new era of relating to their fellow citizens in post-independence governments. Where Christian communities formed a sizeable section of the population, for example in Africa, parts of Asia and Oceania, church leaders and members have pursued a range of different options. In some instances the churches have *cooperated* with governments in a narrative of national development, providing social services, educating the citizenry in their voting rights and monitoring elections. In this narrative, church and state occupy separate spheres – the spiritual and the political – and one is not to stray beyond one's allotted space. Presidents do not say the baptismal formula; church leaders don't lecture presidents on policy. Others leaned towards *co-option*: financial support for a high-status church building project at a national level, the church roof at a constituency level, a vehicle donated at consecration at a diocesan level. In settings where needs are multiple, resources limited and bounty from a millennium-long state-church support non-existent, this option is understandable, yet it limits independence of voice and action. Finally, some *confront*, speaking truth and reconciliation to their sacrificed societies with conviction that costs life, or offering the only alternative civil structure in the midst of state collapse. Christians in such settings have hammered out operational political theologies while the Western churches in comparison have little to offer and much to learn.

In parts of Asia, in the Islamic regions of Africa and above all in the Middle East, these minority Christian communities have walked a tightrope between accepting or avoiding state-sponsored spaces, while their regimes have oscillated between outright persecution, harassment, indifference, legal protection and co-option. Some launched robust apologies not only for their presence but also for their contribution to the common good, for example the record of Japanese Christians in social welfare and in literary creativity (pp. 83–4). The Christian communities of the Middle East, whose situation at the start of the period was imperilled, by the end find it to be precarious in the extreme. Here ancient communities with roots back to Jesus' time are now hanging on by their fingertips (p. 187).

While Christendom was not replicated in the southern continents, it was also severely eroded in the historic heartlands of the faith during our period. This process was sometimes sudden and violent, as in Russia and Eastern Europe. Here the Orthodox Church's call for state liberative reform was too little, too late (pp. 169–70). The struggle for liberation was left to secular communists, who had little time for an institution closely aligned with an oppressive state. Through these cycles of twentieth-century political change, the churches of Eastern Europe and Russia were entangled in a web of political and ethnic loyalties: sometimes a site of resistance to state oppression (Poland, Ukraine, pp. 19, 164, 174–5), sometimes a site of collusion (Baltic states, pp. 172–5), sometimes moving from one to the other (Georgia, pp. 175–6, and Romania, pp. 166–7), compounded by inter- and intra-denominational divisions. At the start of the twenty-first century the Russian Orthodox Church again found itself closely aligned with the post-communist state. In doing so, it became the target of radical protesters who had no illusions that Putin (and the political system he represented) had taken up residence in Christ the Saviour Cathedral.

In Europe, the erosion of Christendom was gradual. This allowed time along the way for the churches to both baptize and resist such monstrosities as slavery (pp. 14–15, 153), colonialism (p. 15) and national socialism (pp. 17, 18). The difference between the two groups was never one of neat opposites: anti-slavery commitment resulted in encouraging European governments to pursue actions that paved the way for European colonialism. At the period's close, the corrosive acids of cultural secularism relegated Christians in Australasia, Canada and Europe to the political and social margins (pp. 19–20, 216). Occasional forays into the public square were still permitted: to exhibit European Christian heritage on state occasions; to issue episcopal pronouncements that are reported but have negligible impact; or to plug with its own diminishing resource base the gaps left by a retreating welfare state. Consequently, they have much to learn from long-standing historic minorities in the Middle East, Asia and Islamic Africa, such as the communion of the saints and the communion of the few (p. 179).

It is perhaps only in North and South America that the notion of Christian territory is still operational, although increasingly contested. The extent to which North America is following the European secularizing trajectory is debated. For example, both African-American Christians and conservative white Evangelicals had a significant impact in the public square during the second half of the twentieth century (pp. 20–1) in ways that would be unimaginable in many European countries. In South America, the churches' close association with Iberian colonial political power left them wrong-footed with the rise of republicanism in the nineteenth century (p. 136ff.), yet the allure of the centre proved too great when it came to the military governments of the twentieth century (p. 143). Prominent church figures pivoted away from political power towards the powerless, often at considerable personal cost in the face of brutal regimes (p. 145ff.). Their populations in turn pivoted away towards secularism and Pentecostalism, the latter with its offer of empowerment within the brutalizing daily life created by these same brutal regimes (pp. 144–5), while some of its leaders pivoted towards politics (p. 150). Perhaps in every era the Church is like a moth, drawn to the lamp of political power, performing a fluttering dance of attendance, only to fall out of the lamplight with burnt wings. The period is characterized by both surprising and anticipated linkages and breakages between church and state.

4 Trajectories in regional theologizing

The starting point for African and Asian theologians was an openness to what God was doing within their religious traditions and history, alongside a rejection of Europeanized Christianity (pp. 70–1, 80–1, 103–4). Both address the key issue of identity: how is my identity as an African or Asian enhanced rather than undermined by my Christian faith? Christians in the Pacific Islands similarly negotiated ways beyond Europeanized Christianity. Where the faith was appropriated within indigenous categories and using indigenous languages, this produced a pronounced fusing of Christian and indigenous identities through successive generations (pp. 209–10). In the Caribbean, identity was again a central theological concern, alongside race, culture and socio-economic oppression (pp. 154–5). This issue has become increasingly acute for Indian Christians as the country's ruling political party advocates an exclusive link between Indian identity and Hinduism (pp. 109–10). While never having anything like the dominant position of Hindu nationalists, African scholars such as the Ugandan Okot p'Bitek (1931–82) were deeply suspicious of African theologians' Christianizing of the African religious past: 'The African deities of books, clothed with the attributes of the Christian God, are, in the main, creations of the students of African religions. They are all beyond recognition to the ordinary Africans in the countryside' (*Decolonising African Religions: A short history of African religions in Western scholarship* (New York, NY: Africa Diasporic Press, 2011), p. 42).

The numerical dominance of Christianity south of the Sahara allowed African Christian intellectuals more room to manoeuvre in comparison to their more hedged-in South Asian counterparts. It may also explain why South Asian Christians have reacted against the virus of Western-imported denominations with church union movements (p. 104), while these have made less headway in African countries. Such division caused by European Christian intrusion was another of p'Bitek's criticisms. These regional theological impulses often take a 'top-down' approach, with educated thinkers (often graduates of mission schools) probing the interrelationship between Christianity and Caribbean, Confucian, Hindu, indigenous African or Pacific religious heritage. In contrast, the theologians of Latin America and South Africa focused less on the faith's engagement with culture and more on political, social and economic systems of oppression (pp. 145–9), although Indian Dalit (pp. 105–6) and Korean minjung theologies also pursued this trajectory. Caribbean theology blended both perspectives (pp. 154–5). At a grassroots level, believers across the southern continents flocked to initiatives that gave Christian expression to the perennial human quest in this world to ward off misfortune and secure blessing, above all Pentecostalism (see relevant sections in all chapters plus ch. 11, esp. pp. 226–8). In this sense, the Christianity of Euro-America, with its contested and limited crossing places between the seen and unseen worlds (a necessary adaptation to surrounding secularism), was something of a global oddity by the end of the twentieth century (pp. 19–21).

Addendum: Researching and writing world Christian history

Attentive readers will notice that the bulk of the resources in the 'Further reading' section below are specialist titles only available via Global North publishing platforms which are all too frequently beyond the readers of

International Study Guides: students in theological institutions in the Global South. While this injustice is to be lamented, it is not an excuse for inaction. The discussion questions are a call for students, inspired by this publication, to use the histories of their own Christian communities to document intercontinental links and themes for themselves. There are rich resources buried away in church archives, in the memories of the elders, in an unpublished memoir at the back of a desk drawer or in a tin trunk banished to the attic, an unpublished thesis by a faculty member. As a diligent student, you will locate these through patient enquiry, perseverance and prayer, and from these sources fashion the narratives and themes that are vital to your community. The future of world Christian history is yours.

❓ DISCUSSION QUESTIONS

While the Global North may have the research libraries and the missionary society archives, the Global South has the church archives and the people. Therefore you have more access than you may expect to the history of Christianity in your region and its intercontinental links and themes.

Intercontinental links

Who else from beyond your community apart from European or North American missionaries brought Christianity to your region? What stories can you discover of Christians moving to other regions? Does your church have branches in other regions? If so, how did these branches come into existence?

Don't only think about 'missionaries': individuals formally sponsored and sent out from one region to another. Individuals migrate for a host of reasons and through a whole range of structures and take their Christian faith with them or discover it on arrival.

The history textbooks in your college library may focus more on 'missionaries', so you may need to talk to the elders about the memories they have, or think about family, friends and church members who have migrated.

Intercontinental themes

Which recurring themes struck you as you read the chapters? Why are these themes important for you and for your community?

Other themes have been suggested, such as ecumenism, gender and sexuality, inter-religious encounter, migration, persecution or social justice. If one of these is important to you, start by finding out more about it in your region and see if you can find similarities and contrasts in the other regions described in the different chapters of this book.

Sharing what you have found

How can you share with a wider audience what you have discovered about how the Christian faith has expanded across continents? College assignments usually require writing essays for a grade. Are there truths you have discovered here that you want to share more widely? How about an article in a church newsletter or secular newspaper? What about a presentation in your church or to your fellow students?

Further reading

Appelman, Jan. *Church of Christ the King, Kampala, 1930–1970: A history of the parish* (1970).

Cabrita, Joel, Maxwell, David, Wild-Wood, Emma. *Relocating World Christianity: Interdisciplinary studies in universal and local expressions of the Christian faith*. Leiden: Brill, 2017.

Day, Abby. *Believing in Belonging: Belief and social identity in the modern world*. Oxford: Oxford University Press, 2011.

Hodges, Graham Russell. *Black Itinerants of the Gospel: The narratives of Joh Jea and George White*. Madison, WI: Madison House, 1993.

Koschorke, Klaus. 'History of Christianity in Africa and Asia in comparative perspective', in Klaus Koschorke and Jens Holger Schjørring (eds), *African Identities and World Christianity in the Twentieth Century* (Wiesbaden: Harrassowitz, 2005), pp. 265–81.

Koschorke, Klaus and Hermann, Adrian (eds). *Polycentric Structures in the History of World Christianity*. Wiesbaden: Harrassowitz, 2014.

P'Bitek, Okot. *Decolonising African Religions: A short history of African religions in Western scholarship*. New York, NY: Africa Diasporic Press, 2011.

'Rebecca Nkwebe Alibatafudde's story', *Dini Na Mila*, vol. 2, nos 2–3 (Dec. 1968), pp. 5–11.

Reed, Colin. *Pastors, Partners, and Paternalists: African church leaders and Western missionaries in the Anglican Church in Kenya, 1850–1900*. Leiden: Brill, 1997.

Sharkey, H. J. 'Jihads and crusades in Sudan from 1881 to the present', in S. H. Hashmi (ed.), *Just Wars, Holy Wars, and Jihads: Christian, Jewish, and Muslim encounters and exchanges* (Oxford: Oxford University Press, 2012), pp. 263–82.

Stanley, Brian. *Christianity in the Twentieth Century: A world history*. Princeton, NJ: Princeton University Press, 2018.

Thornton, John K. 'On the trail of Voodoo: African Christianity in Africa and the Americas', *The Americas*, vol. 44, no. 3 (1988), pp. 261–78.

Walls, Andrew F. 'Christianity in the non-Western world: a study in the serial nature of Christian expansion', in Andrew F. Walls (ed.), *The Cross-Cultural Process in Christian History: Studies in the transmission and appropriation of faith* (Maryknoll, NY: Orbis, 2002), pp. 27–48.

Walls, Andrew F. 'Eusebius tries again: reconceiving the study of Christian history', *International Bulletin of Missionary Research*, vol. 24, no. 3 (2000), pp. 105–11.

Walls, Andrew F. 'Worldviews and Christian conversion', in Andrew F. Walls and Mark Gornik (eds), *Crossing Cultural Frontiers: Studies in the history of world Christianity* (Maryknoll, NY: Orbis, 2017), pp. 35–48.